Contents

Preparation

i	How to use the Journal Pages
ii	How to use the Schedule Planner
iii-v	Schedule Planner

Main Journal Pages

1-105	15 Weeks of Daily Workout Log Sheets

Appendices

A1	Skeletal Muscle Map
A2	Contact Details for Suppliers and Sports Clubs
A3	Fitness Expenses Log
A4	Base calorie Requirements when Sedentary
A5	Calorie Expenditure by Activity
A6	Personal Nutrition Charts
A7	Session Store
A8	Statistics Tracker
Back	General Notes

Journal Date Range

Start:

End:

How to use the Journal Pages ...

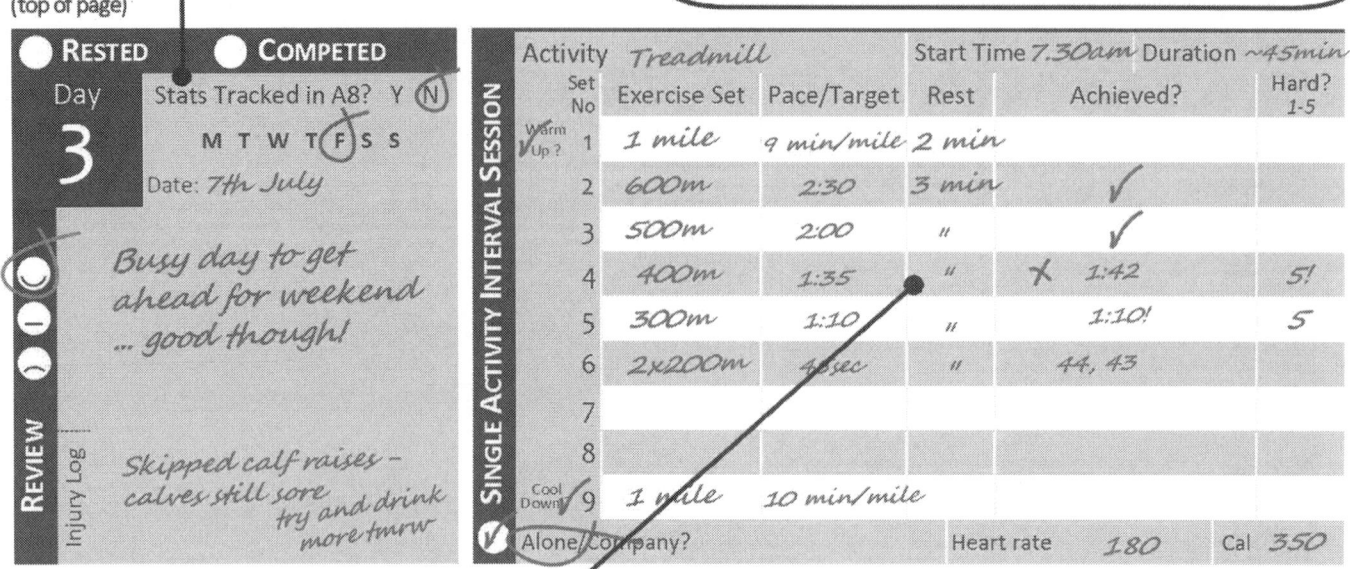

Tick off your 5 portions of fruit & veg each day to make sure you don't miss one.

Table A7, at the back of the book, is your Session Store. There you can write out, just the once, any workouts that you repeat regularly. You can give them a code in A7 too. You only then have to make a note of the code in each daily journal entry.

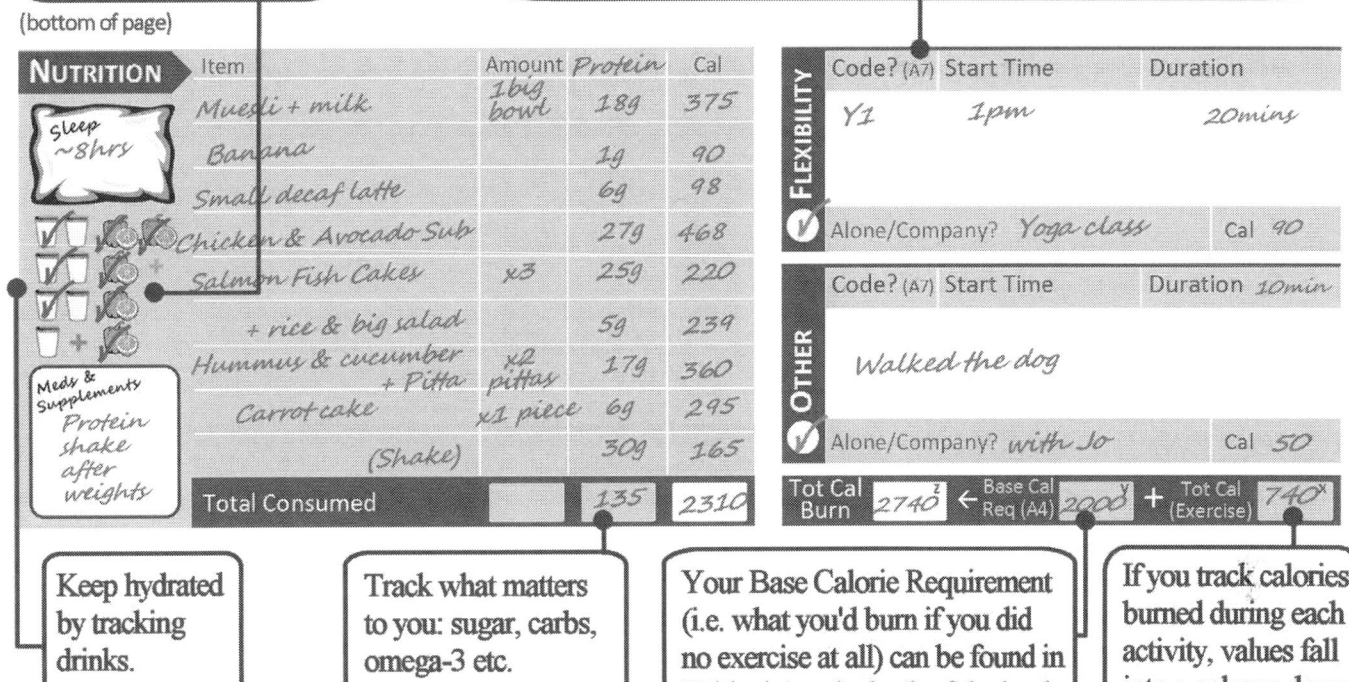

Keep hydrated by tracking drinks.

Track what matters to you: sugar, carbs, omega-3 etc.

Your Base Calorie Requirement (i.e. what you'd burn if you did no exercise at all) can be found in Table A4 at the back of the book.

If you track calories burned during each activity, values fall into a column down the side of the page. You can sum them for the day here.

How to use the Schedule Planner ...

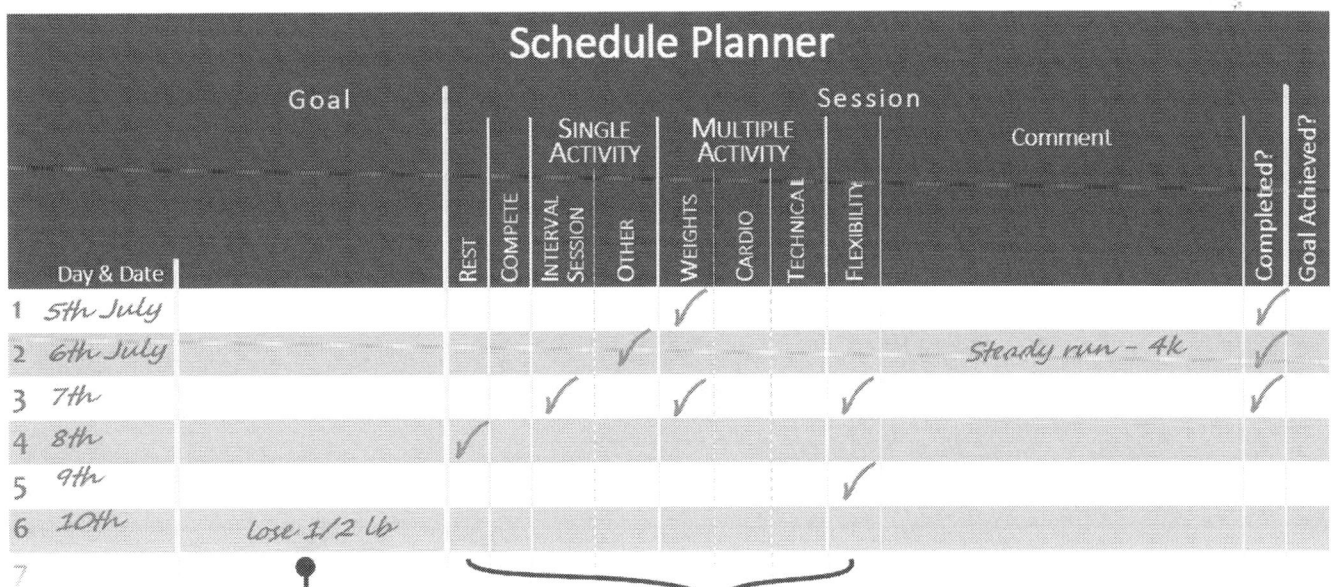

Start by setting your goals. E.g. losing some weight, improving a Personal Best or winning a competition. Try to make them incremental and realistic. Then think about which activities you'll need to do.

Each of the activity types on the daily journal pages is given a column in the Schedule Planner so you can just tick off which sessions you intend to do when.

Schedule Planner

Day & Date	Goal	Session								Comment	Completed?	Goal Achieved?
		Rest	Compete	**Single Activity**		**Multiple Activity**						
				Interval Session	Other	Weights	Cardio	Technical	Flexibility			
1												
2												
3												
4												
5												
6												
7												
8												
9												
10												
11												
12												
13												
14												
15												
16												
17												
18												
19												
20												
21												
22												
23												
24												
25												
26												
27												
28												
29												
30												
31												
32												
33												
34												
35												

Day & Date	Goal	Rest	Compete	Single Activity		Multiple Activity			Flexibility	Comment	Completed?	Goal Achieved?
				Interval Session	Other	Weights	Cardio	Technical				
36												
37												
38												
39												
40												
41												
42												
43												
44												
45												
46												
47												
48												
49												
50												
51												
52												
53												
54												
55												
56												
57												
58												
59												
60												
61												
62												
63												
64												
65												
66												
67												
68												
69												
70												

Day & Date	Goal	Session								Comment	Completed?	Goal Achieved?
		Rest	Compete	Single Activity		Multiple Activity			Flexibility			
				Interval Session	Other	Weights	Cardio	Technical				
71												
72												
73												
74												
75												
76												
77												
78												
79												
80												
81												
82												
83												
84												
85												
86												
87												
88												
89												
90												
91												
92												
93												
94												
95												
96												
97												
98												
99												
100												
101												
102												
103												
104												
105												

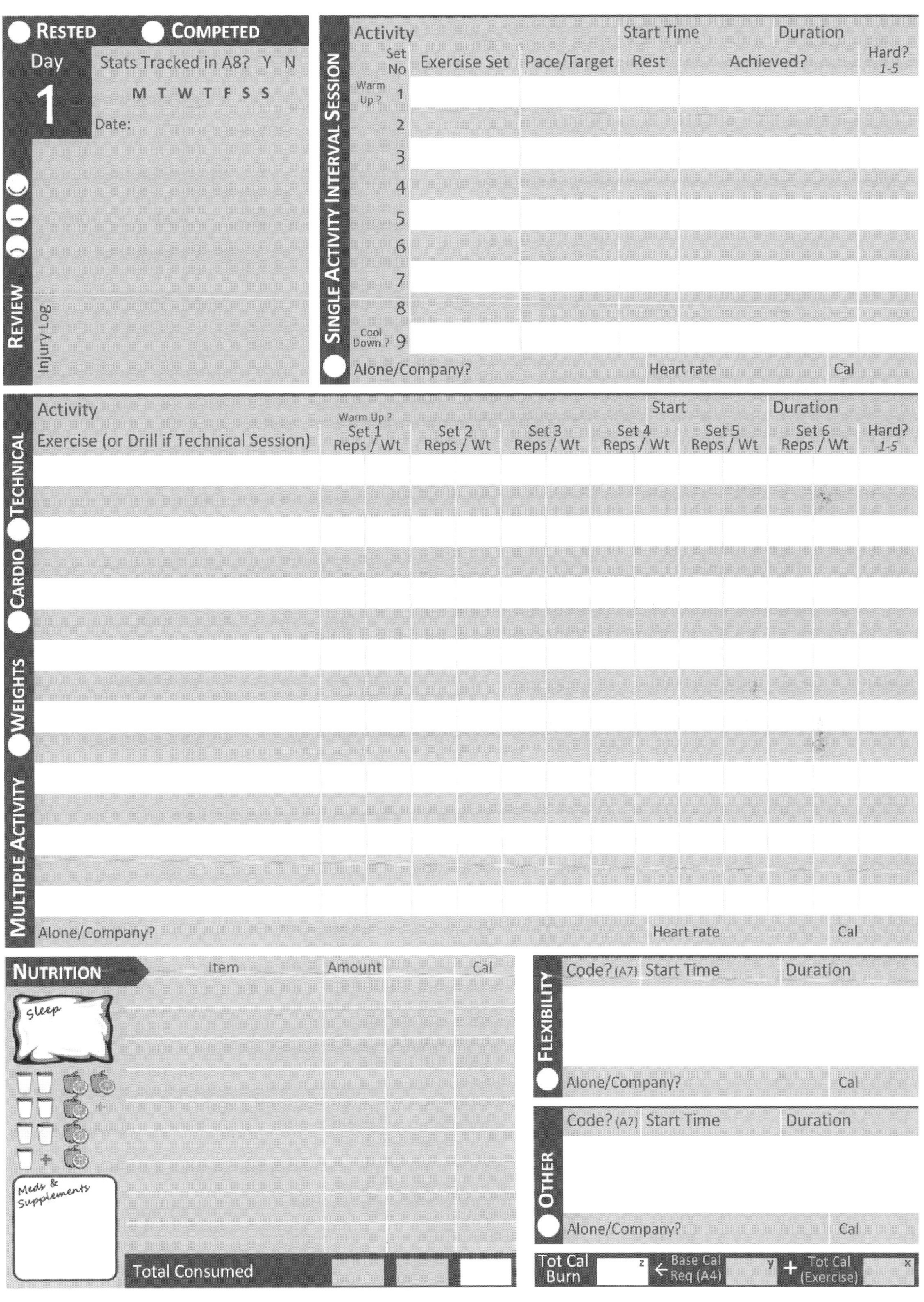

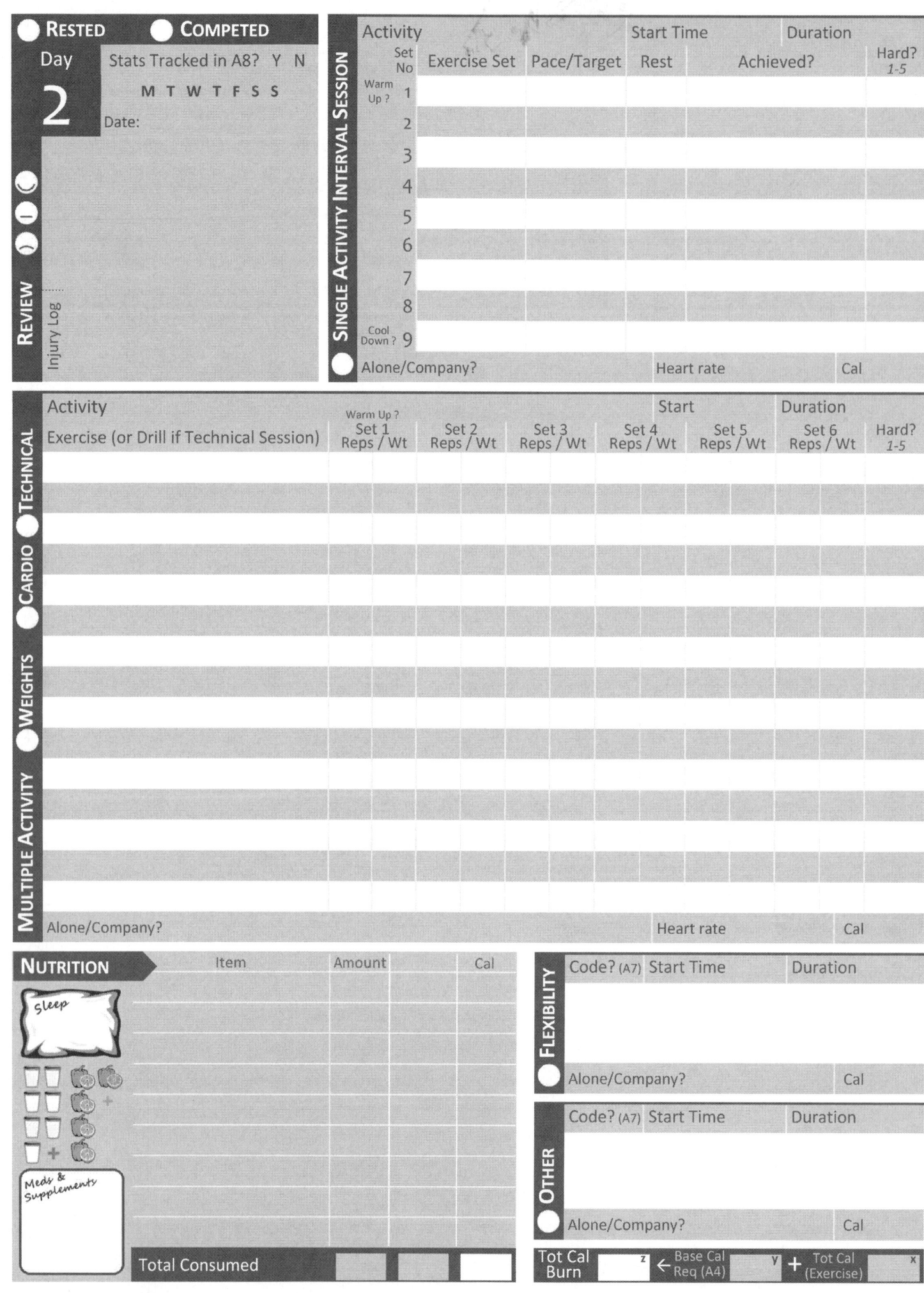

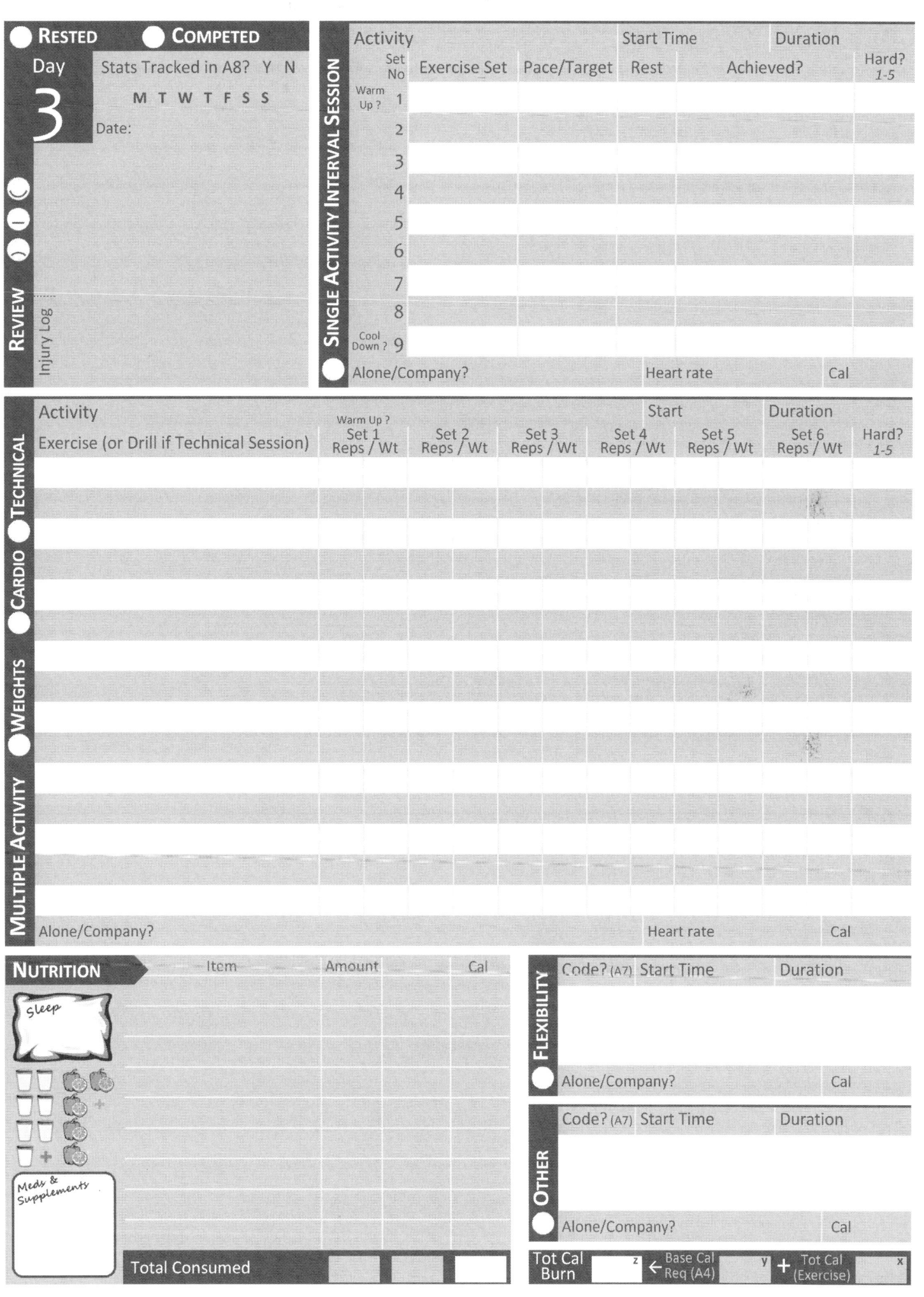

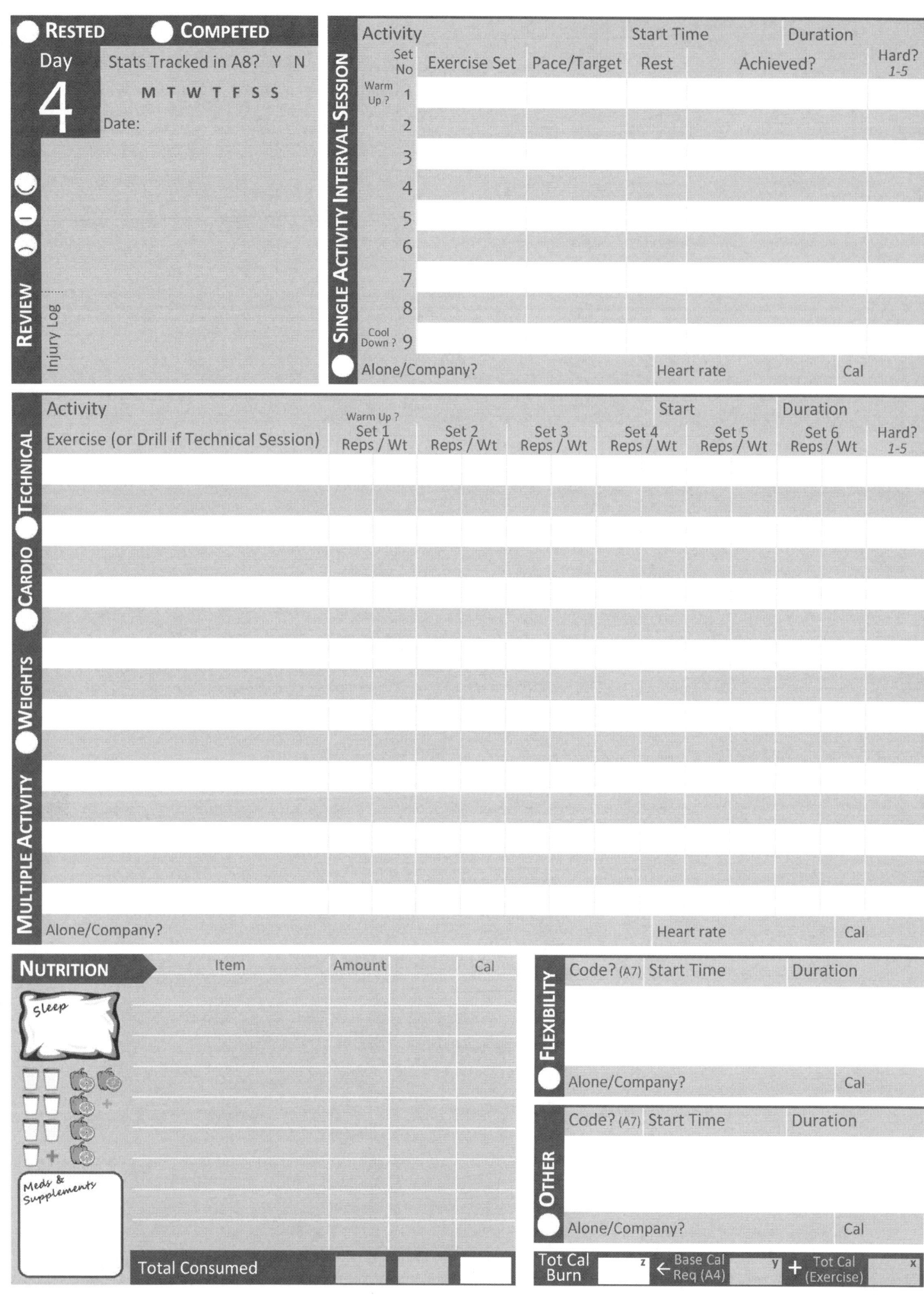

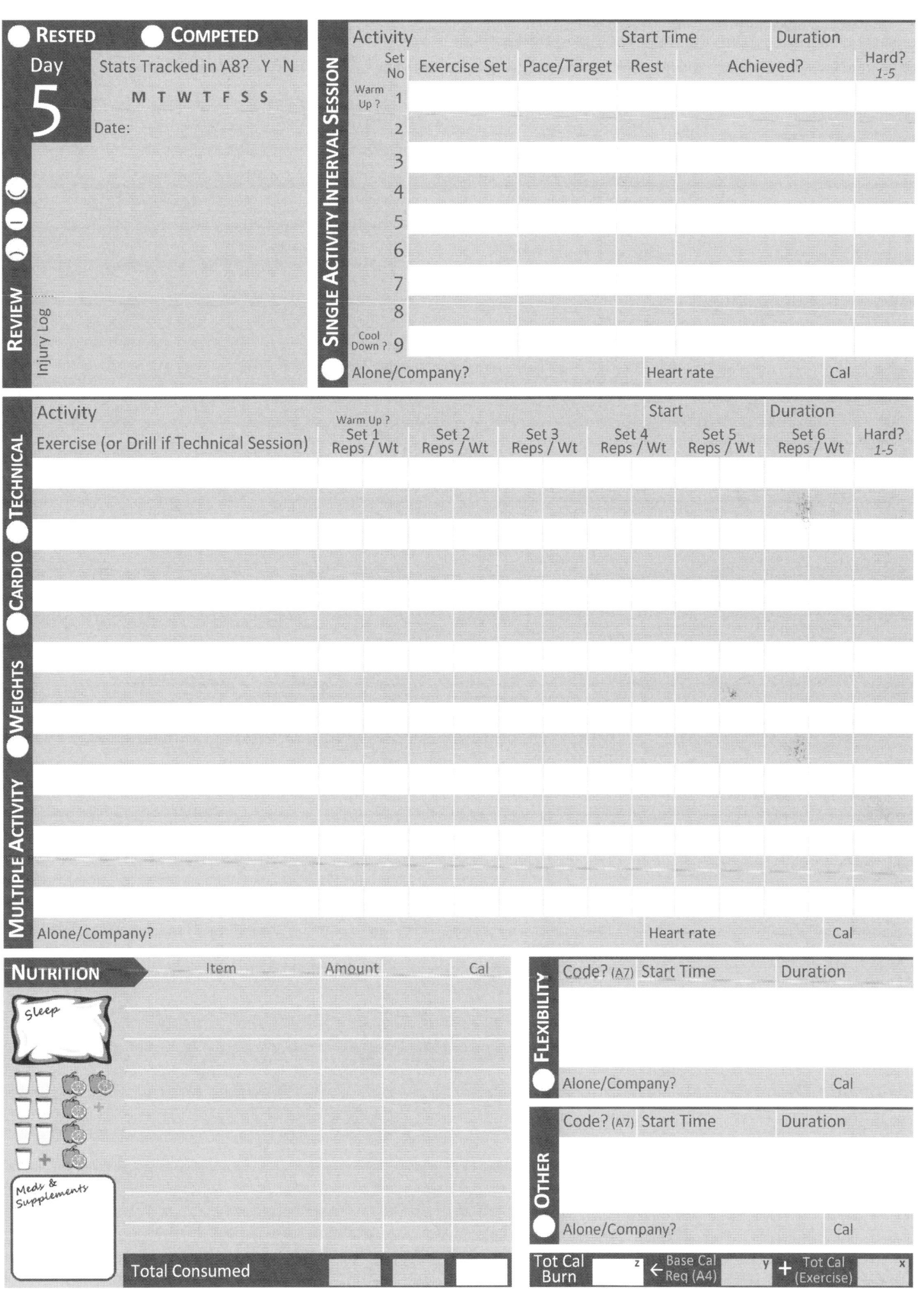

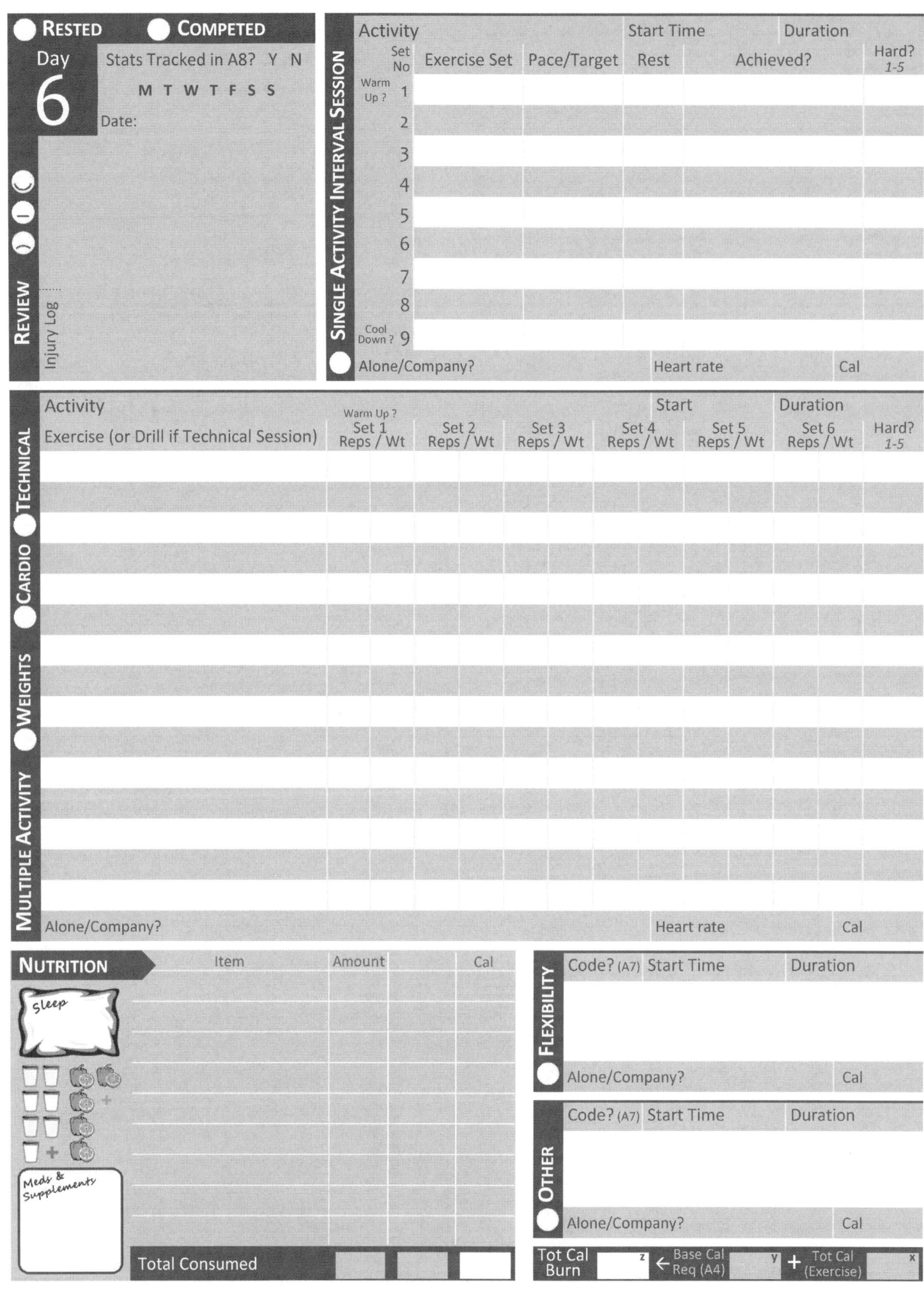

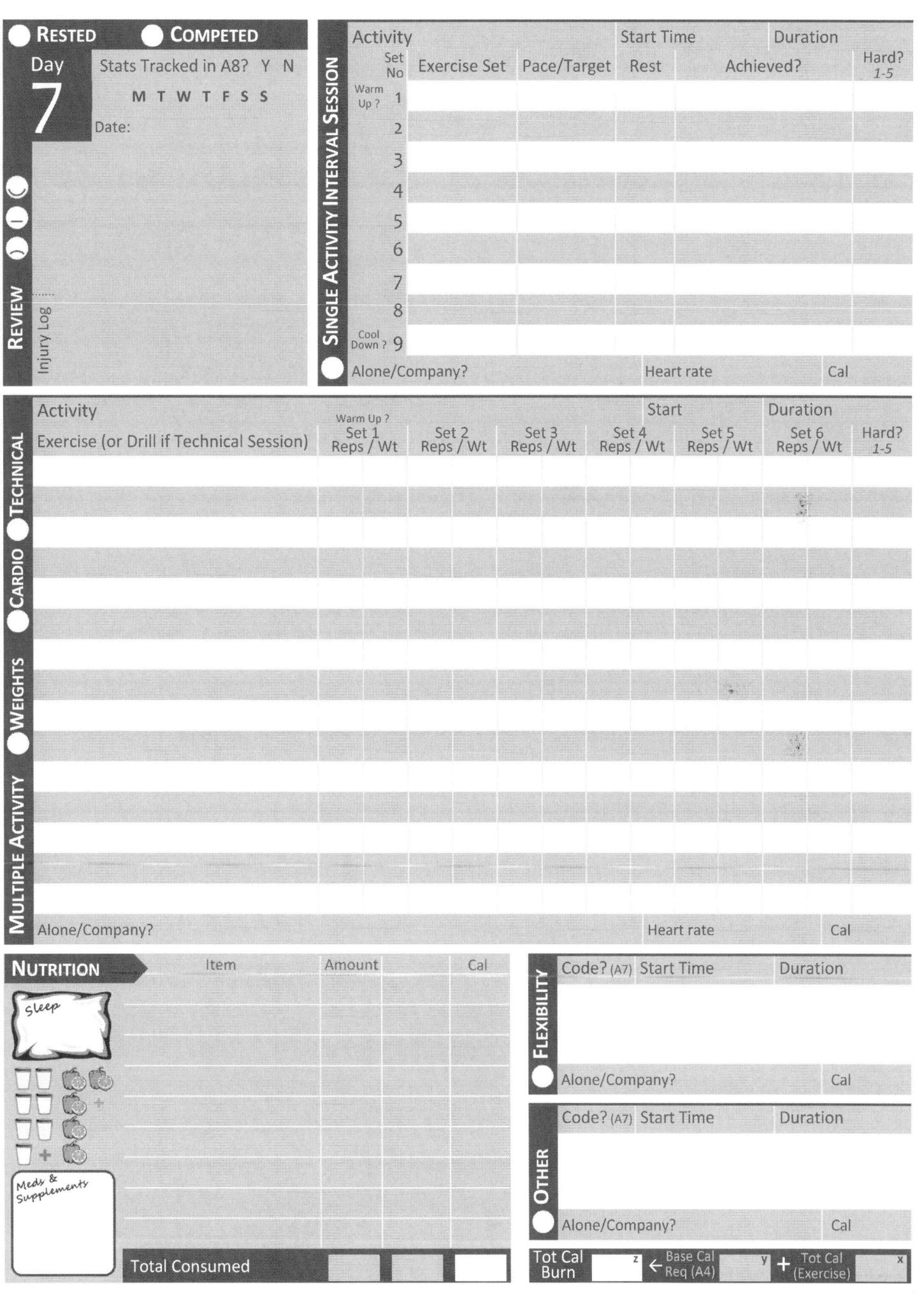

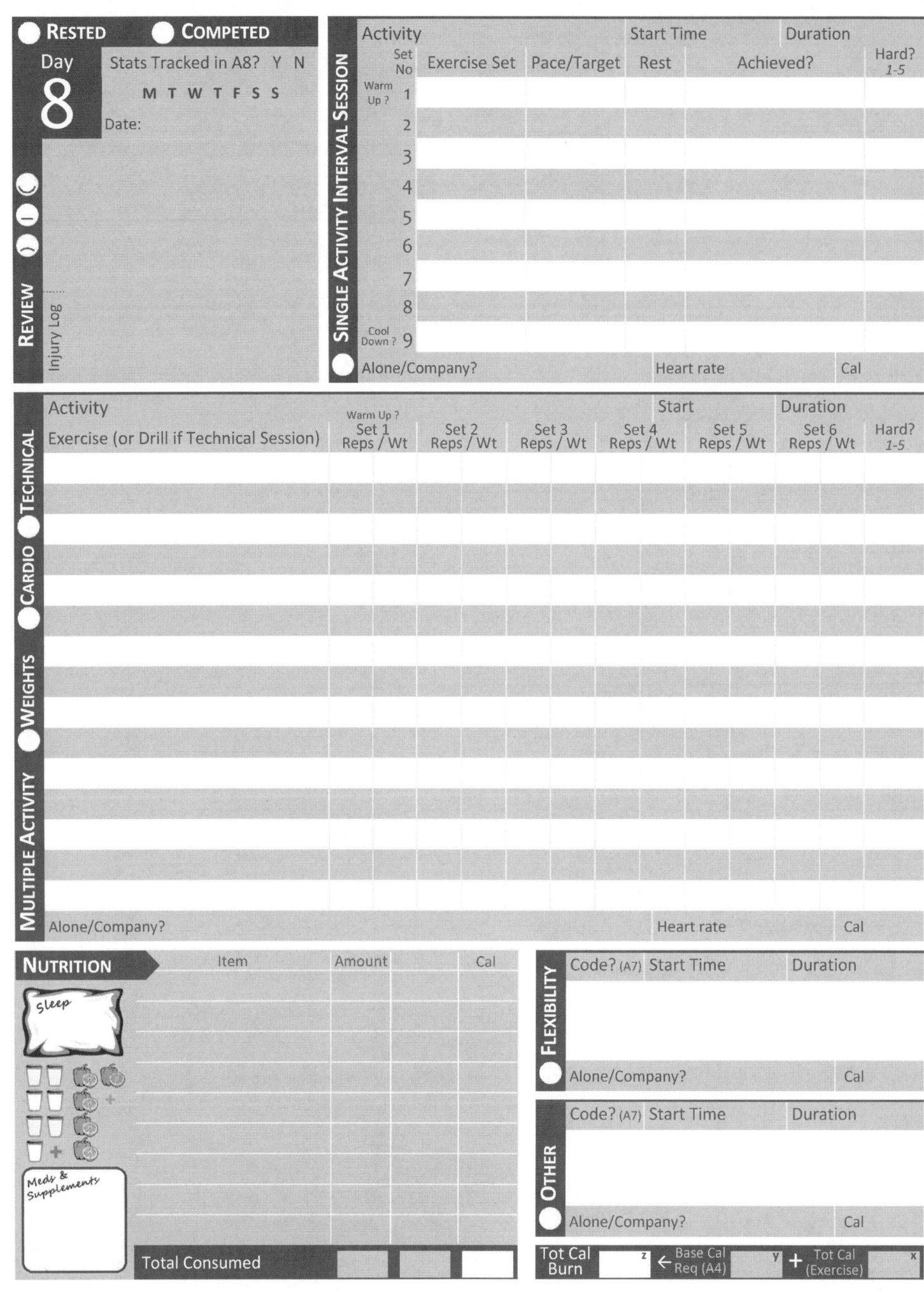

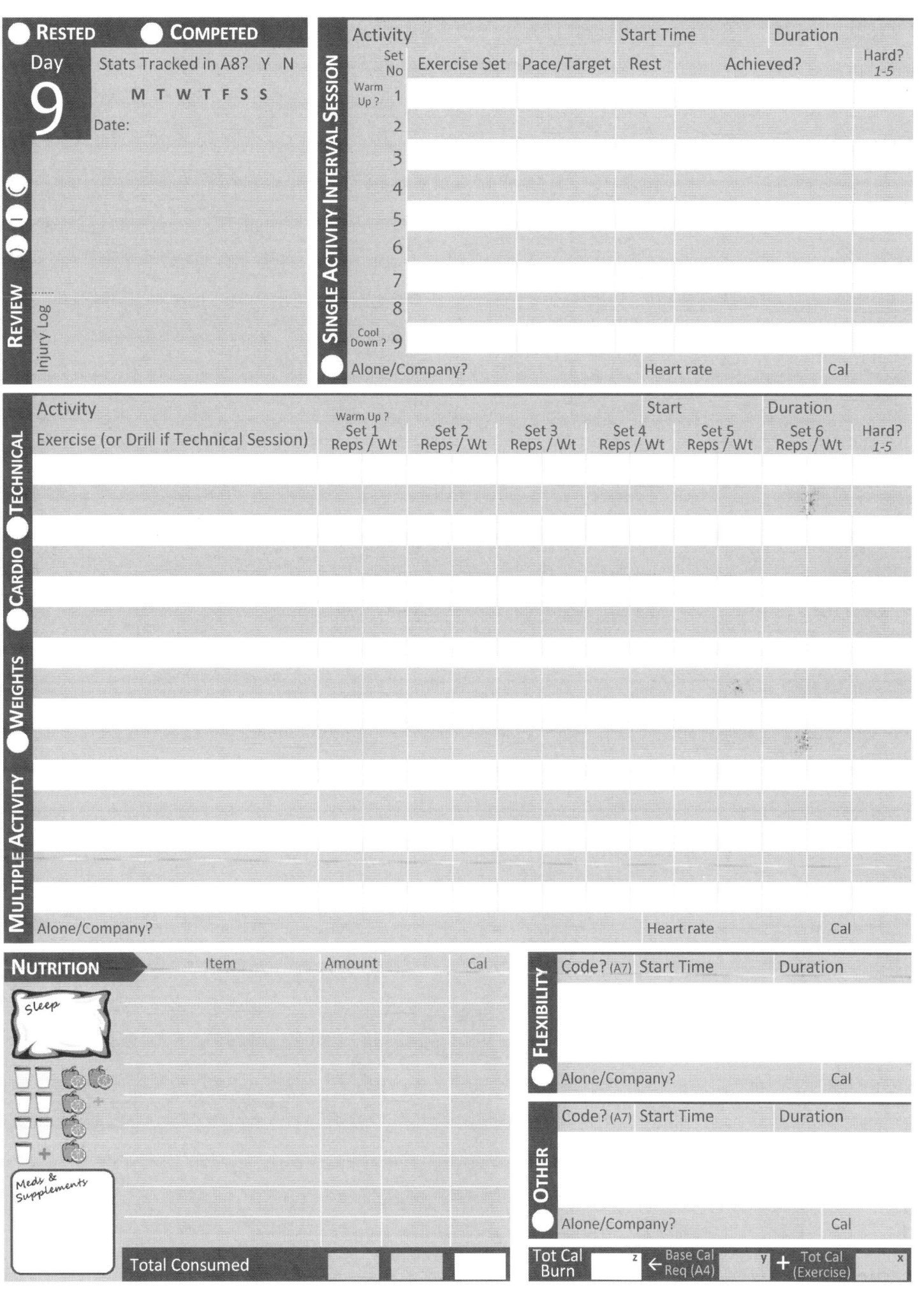

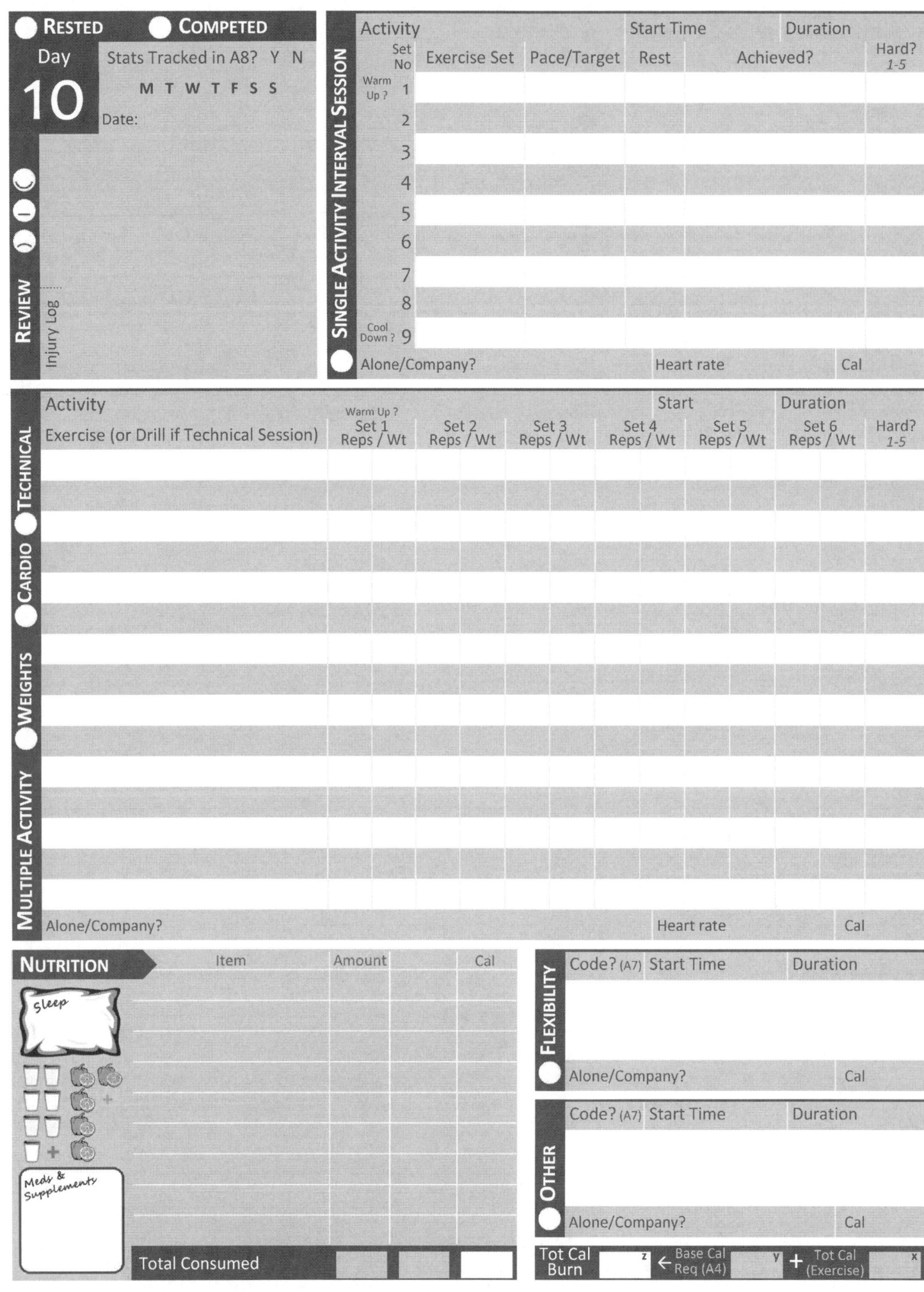

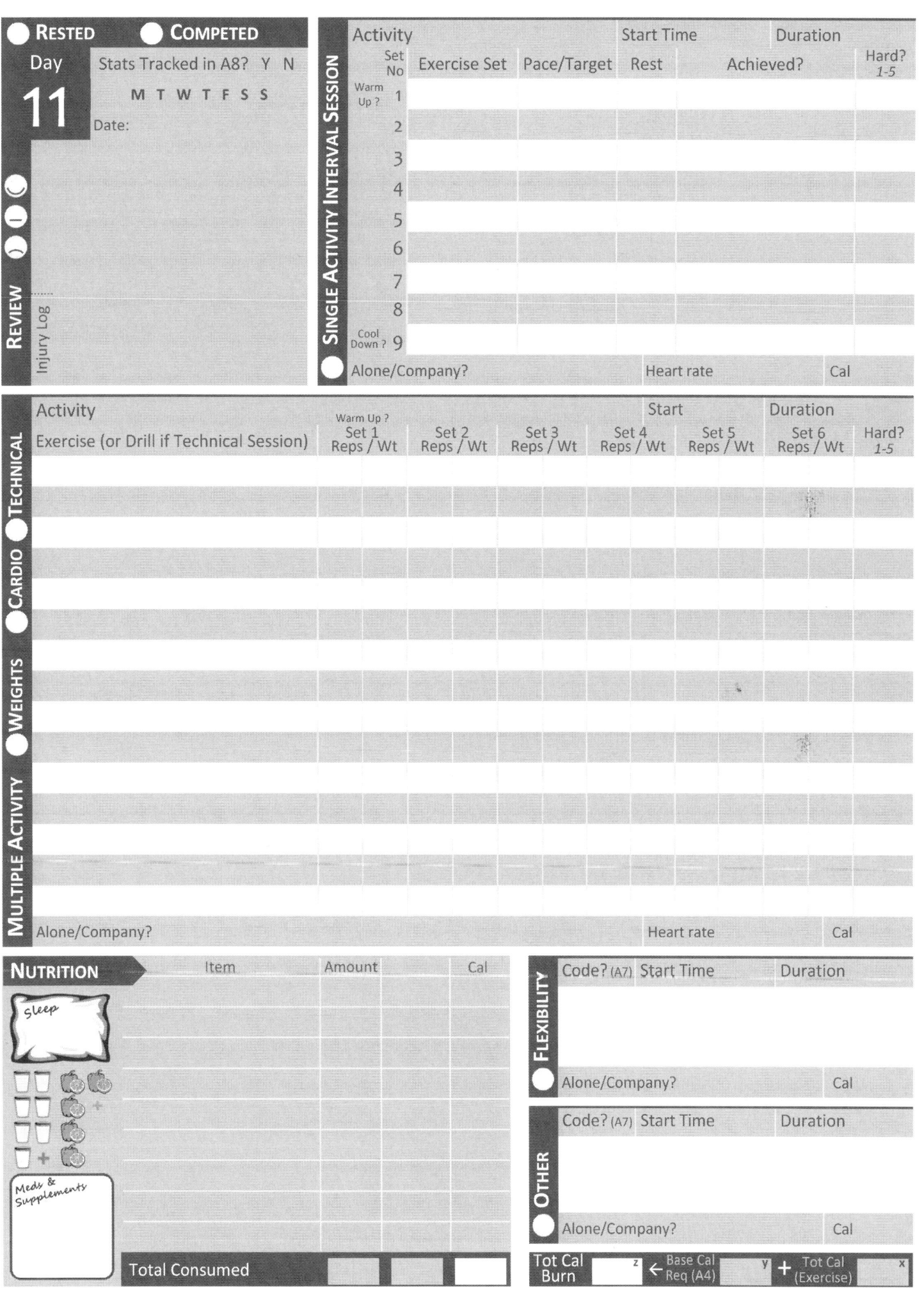

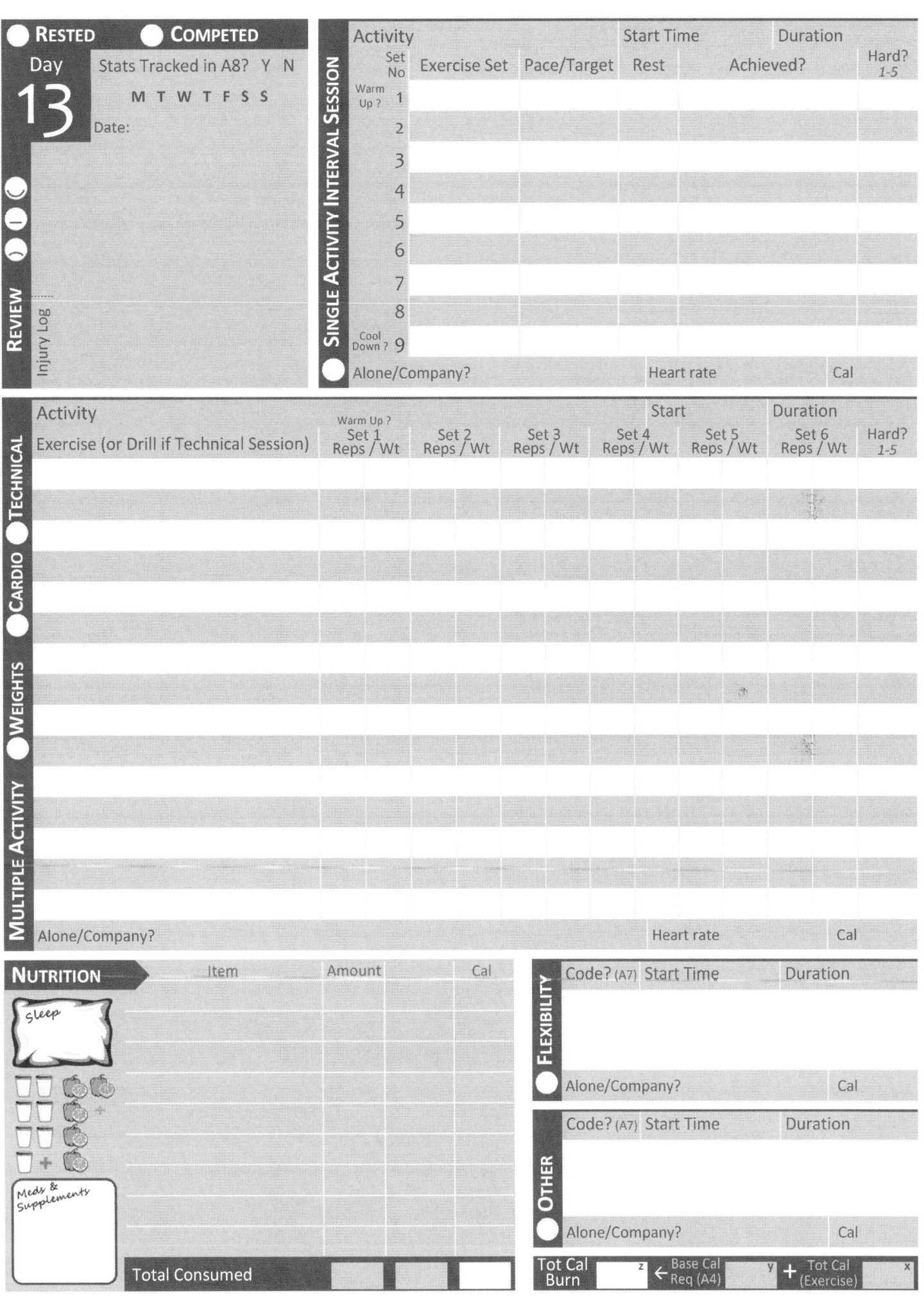

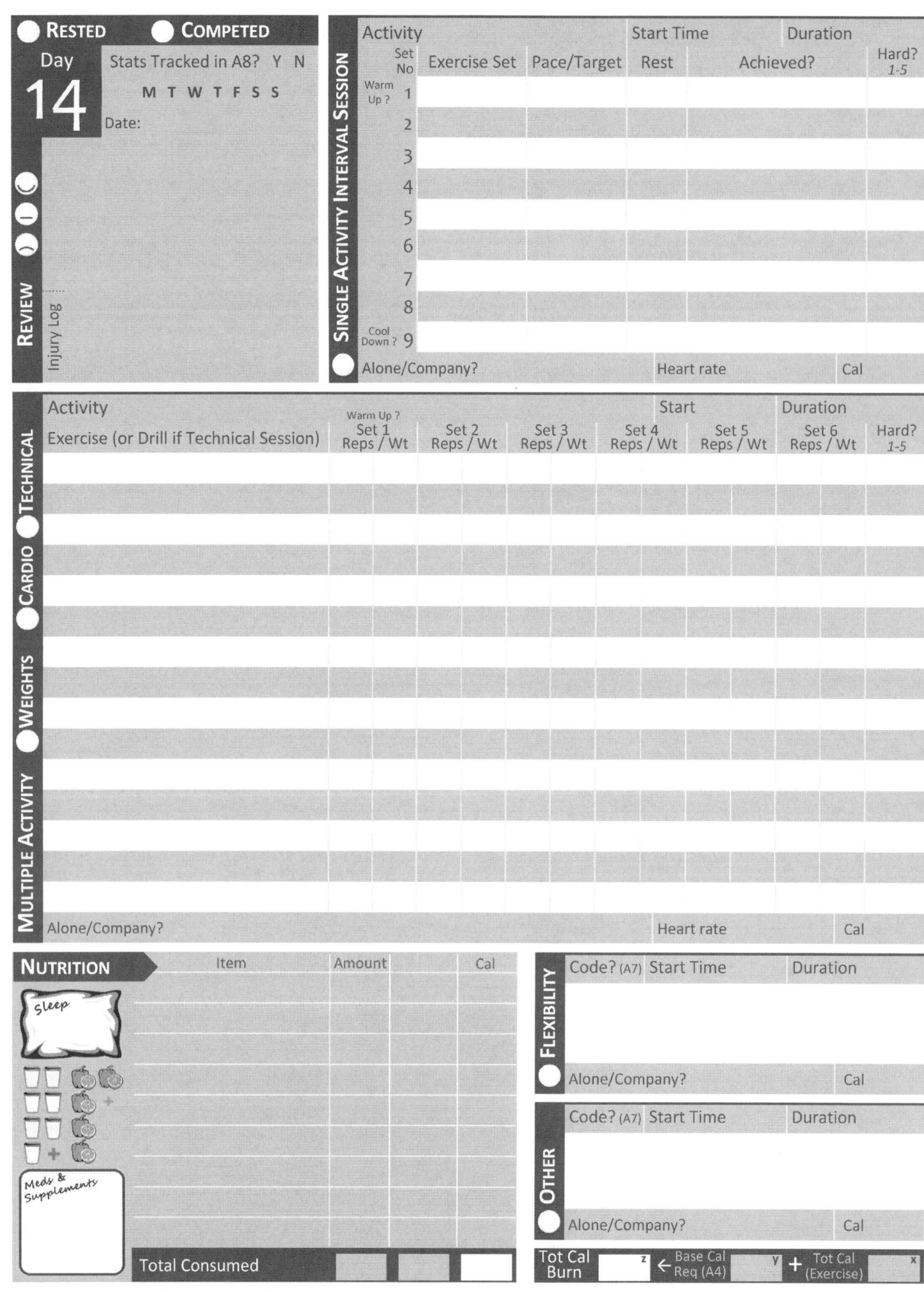

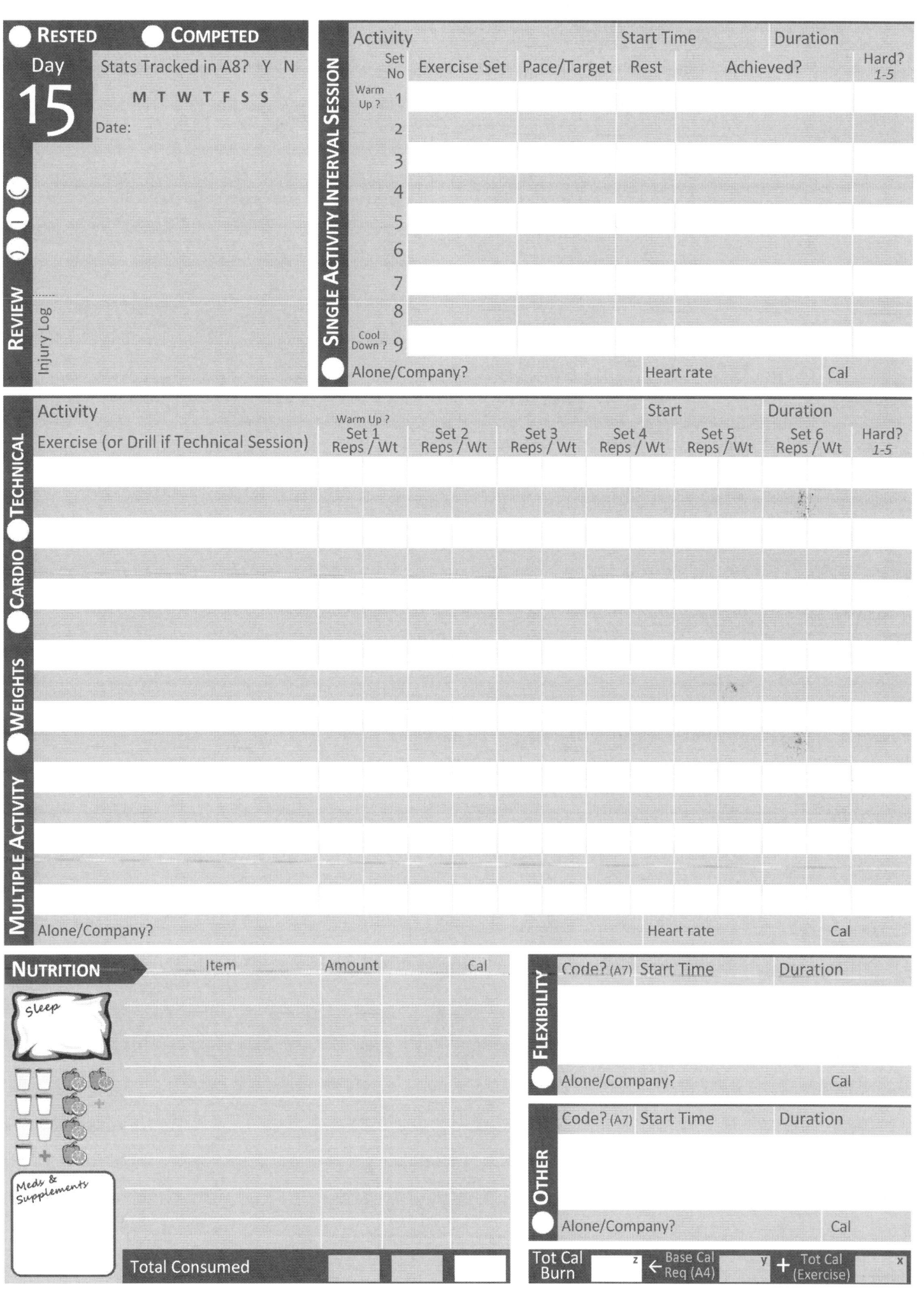

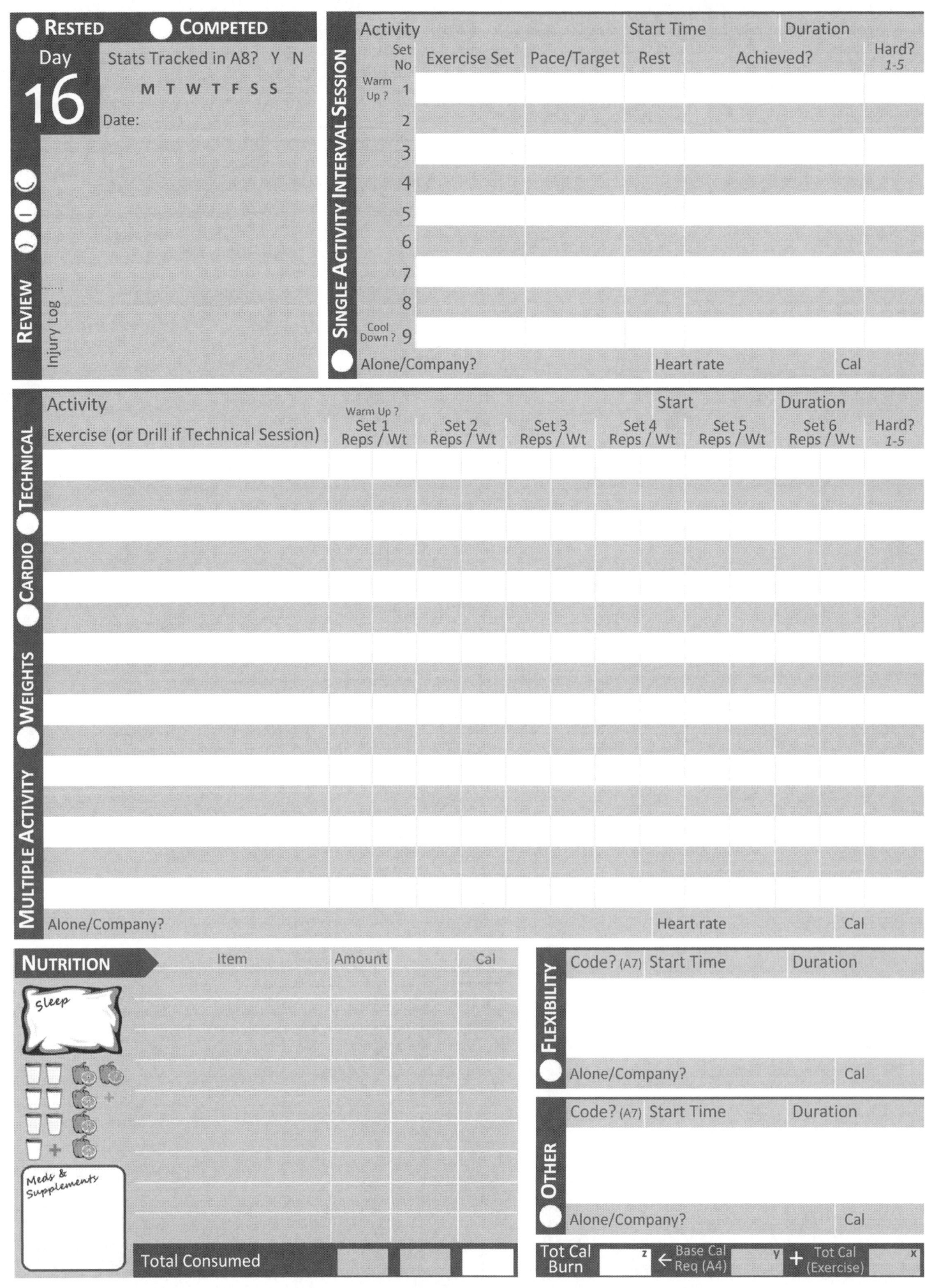

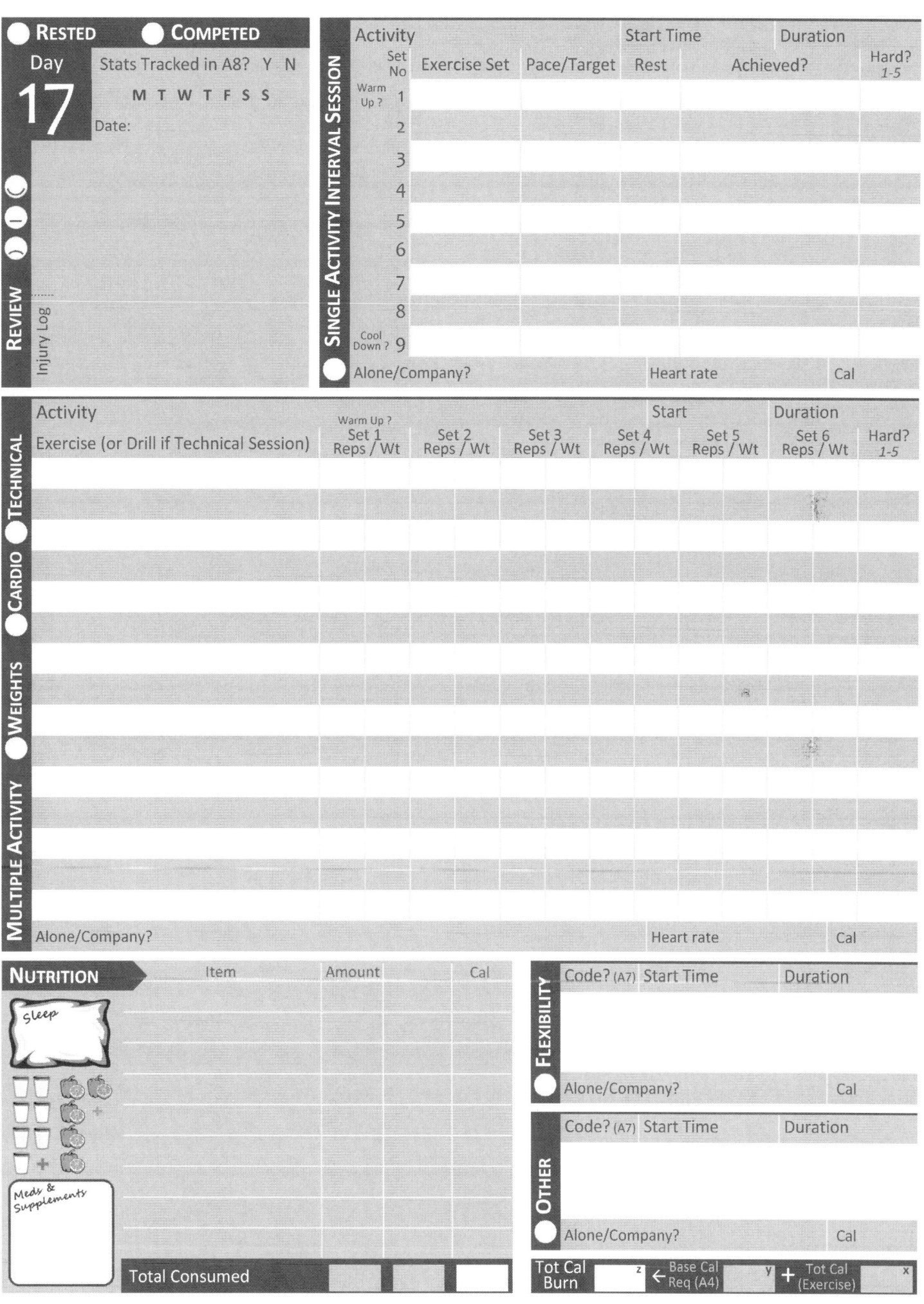

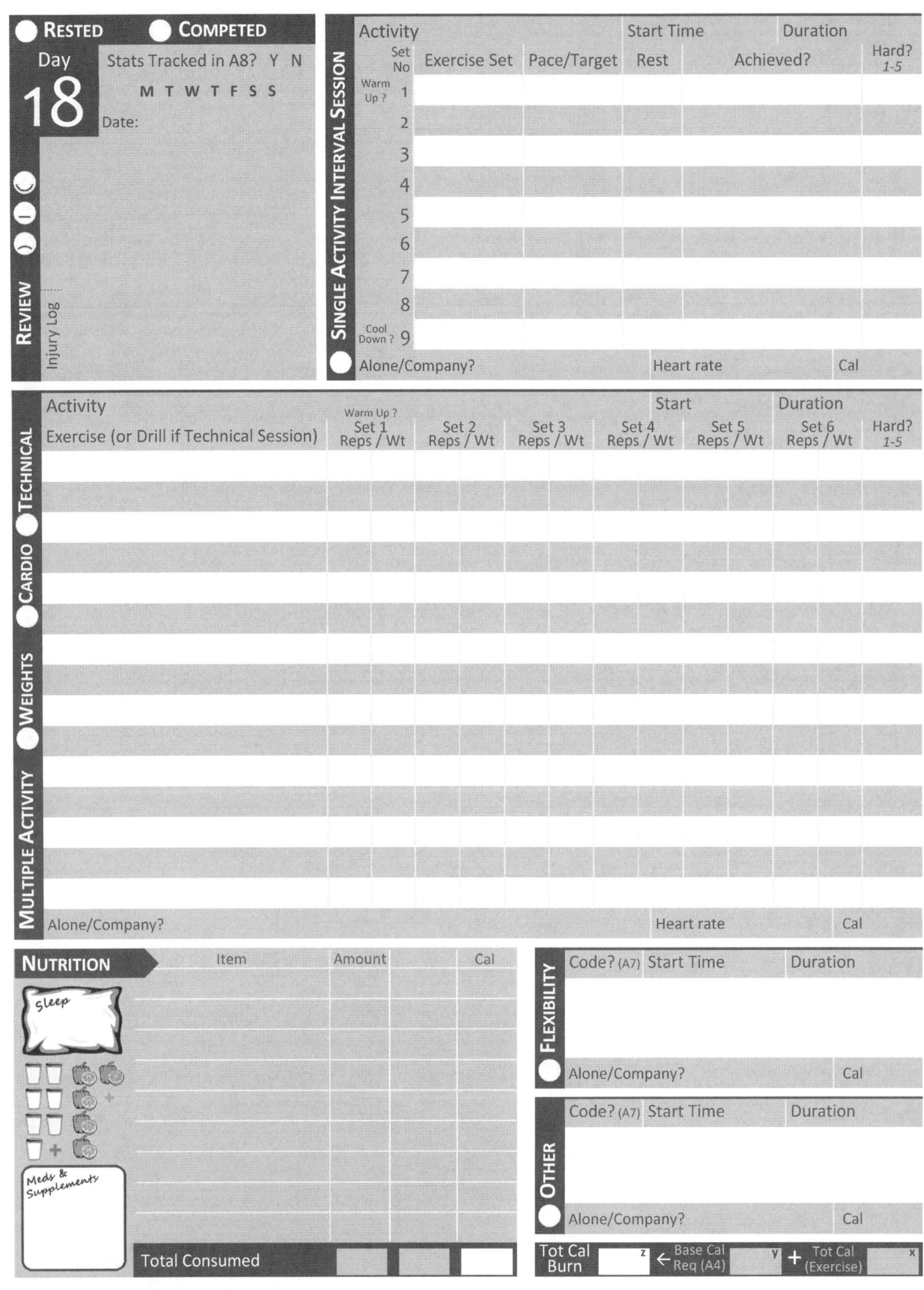

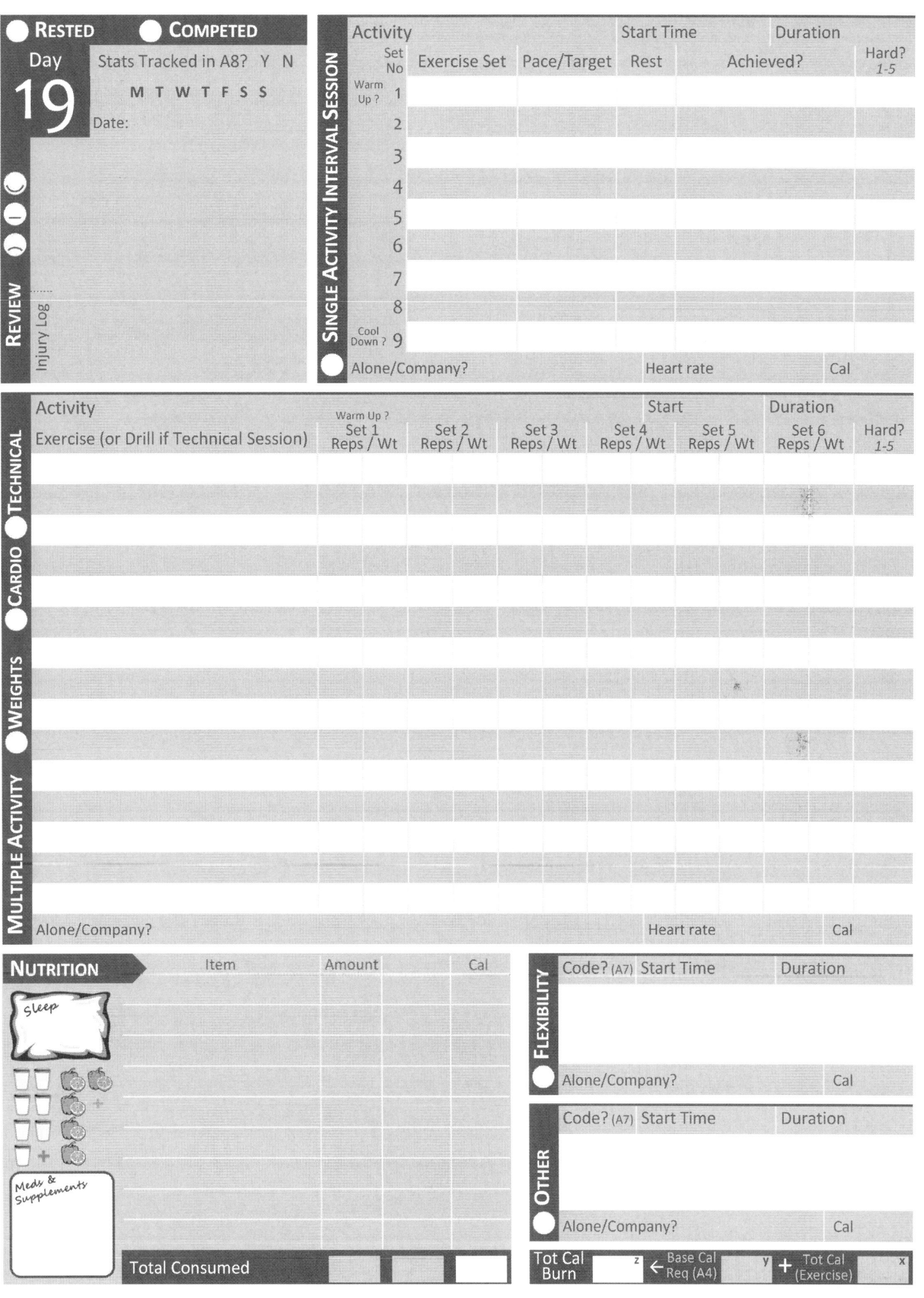

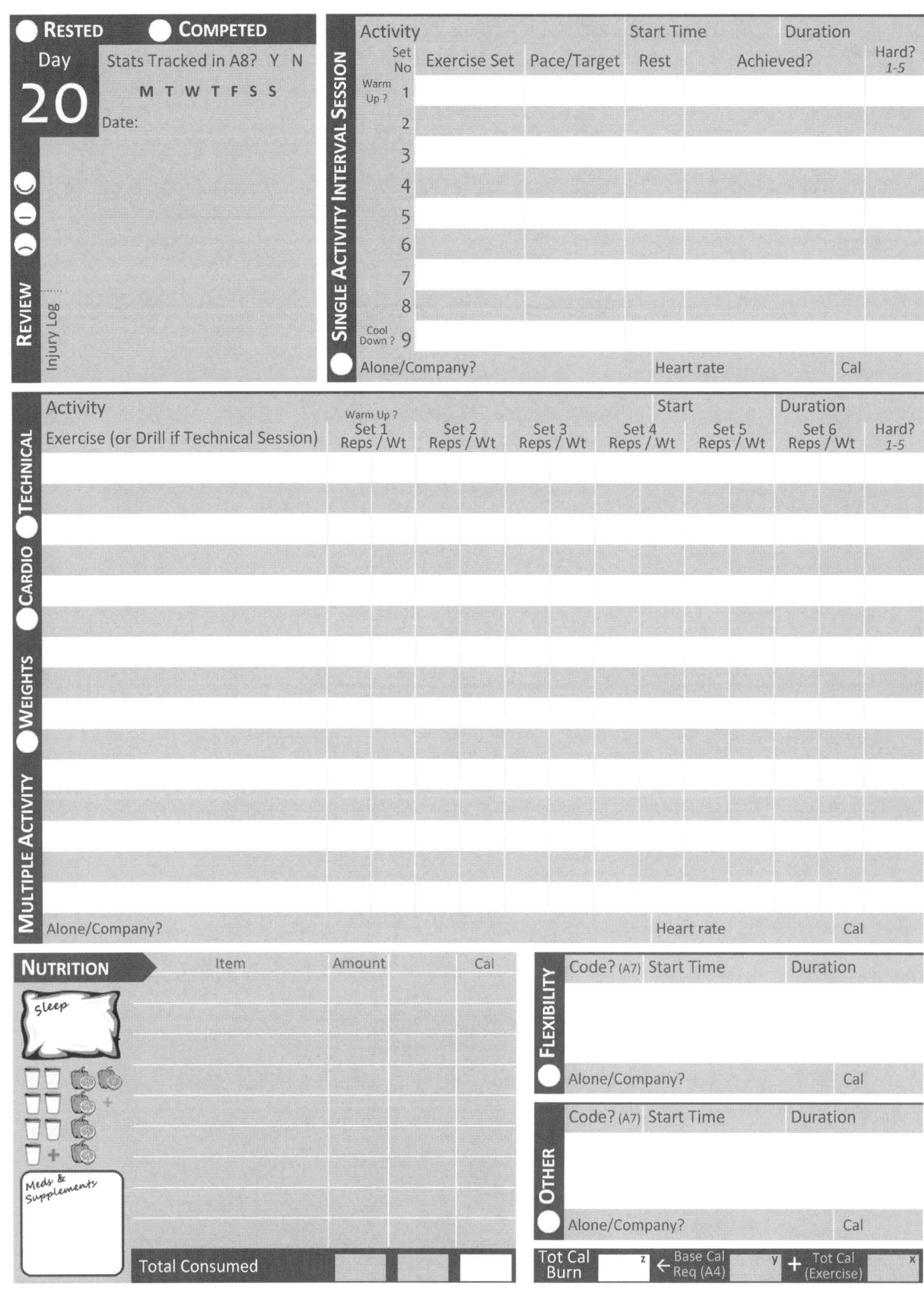

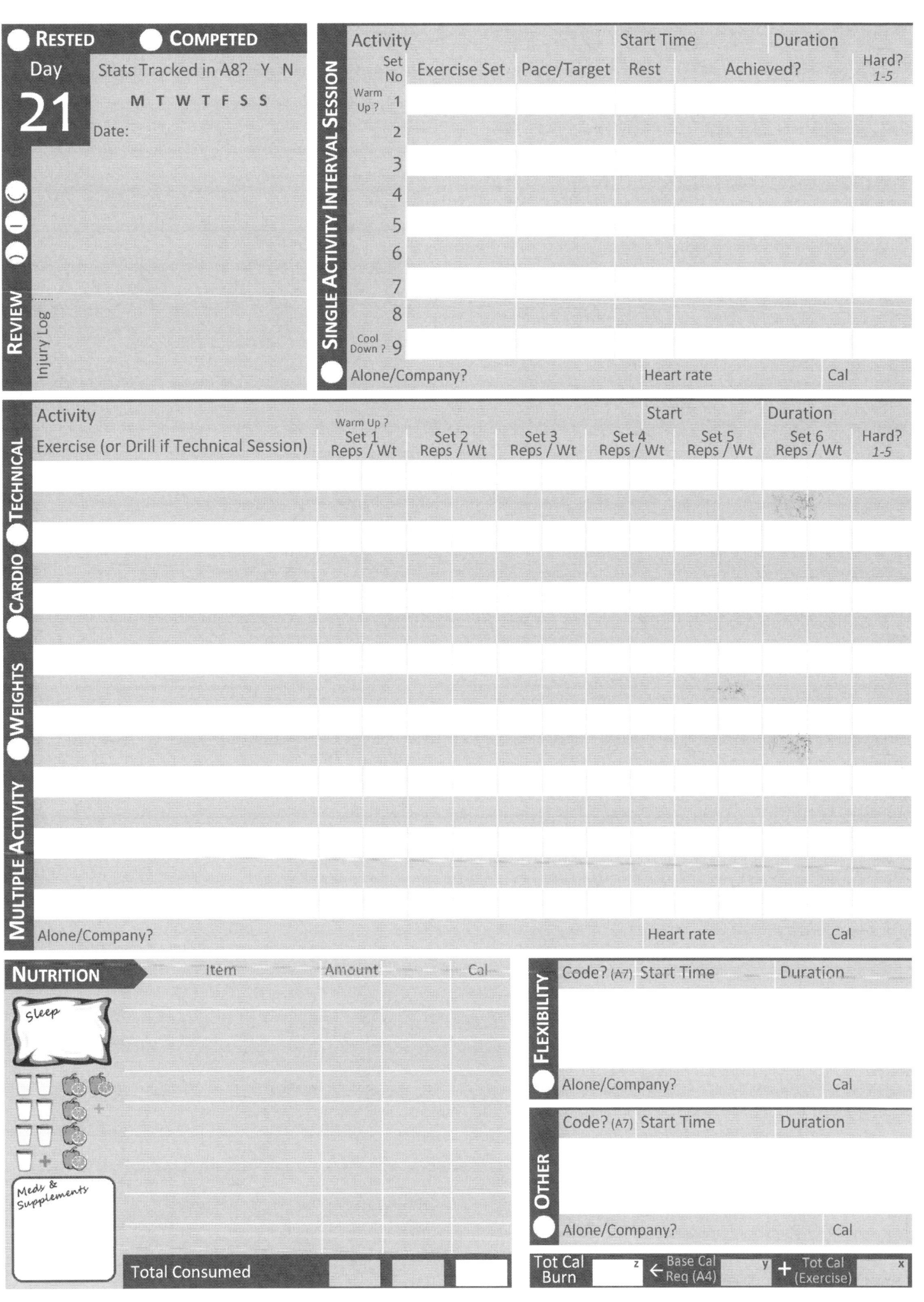

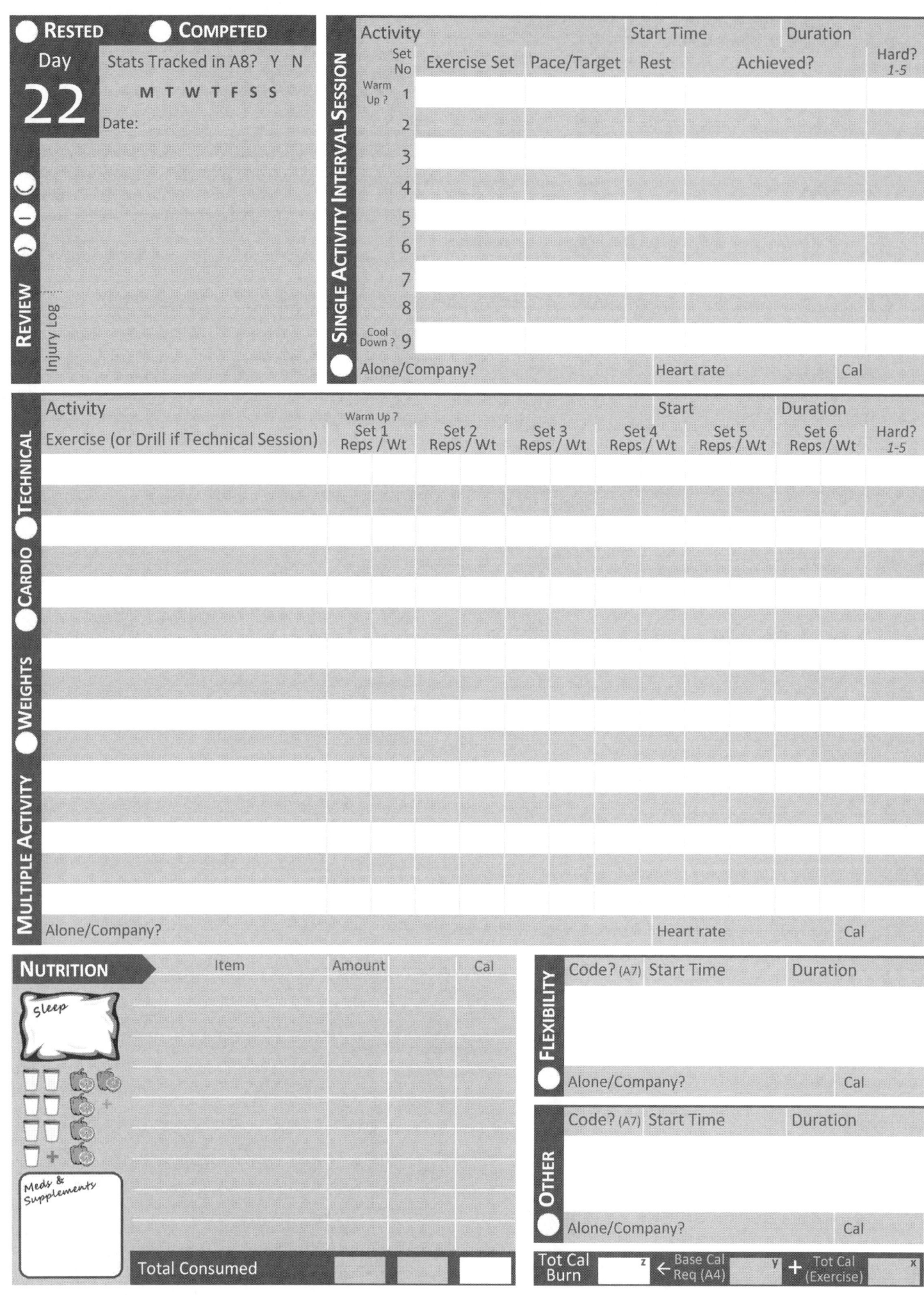

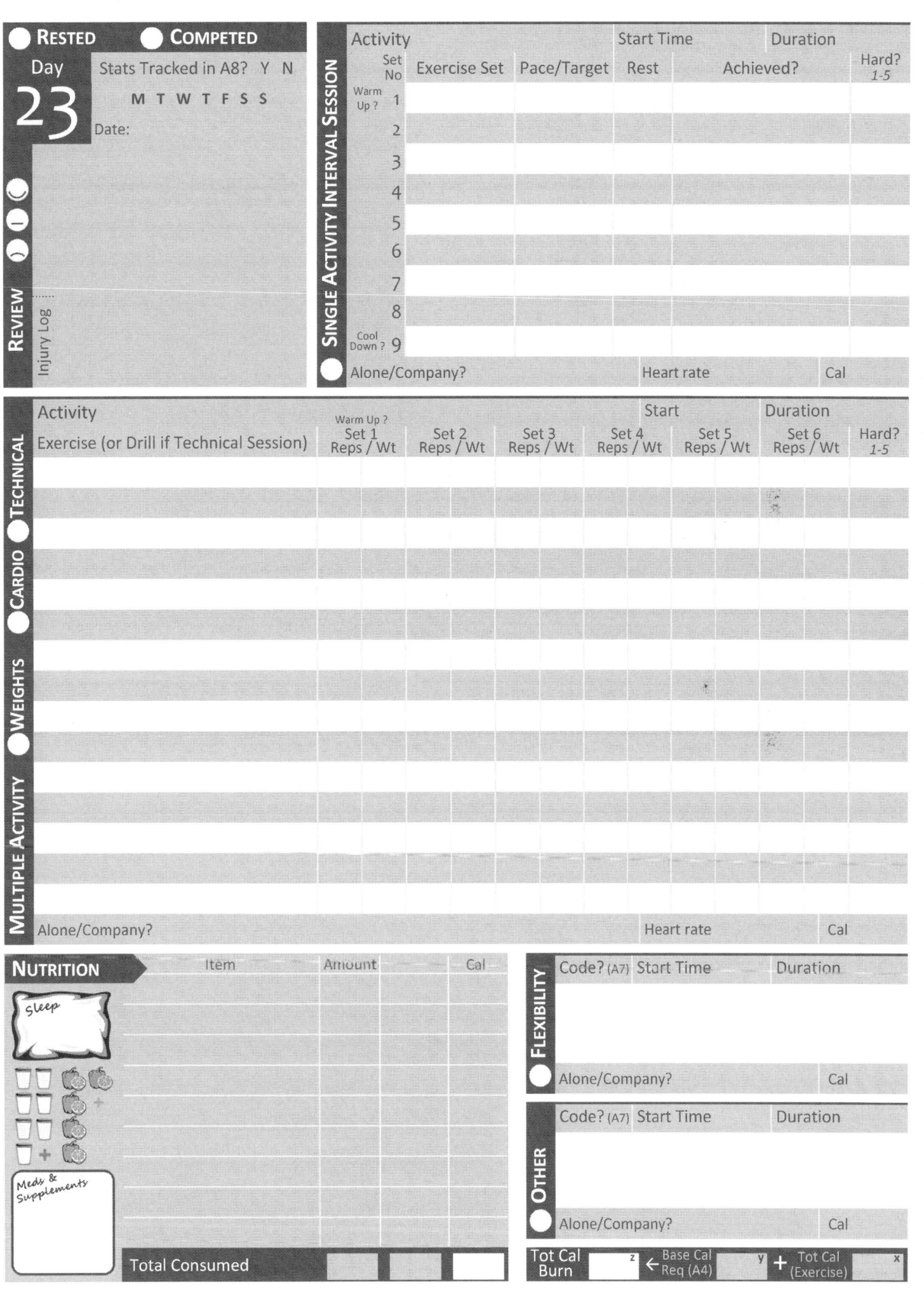

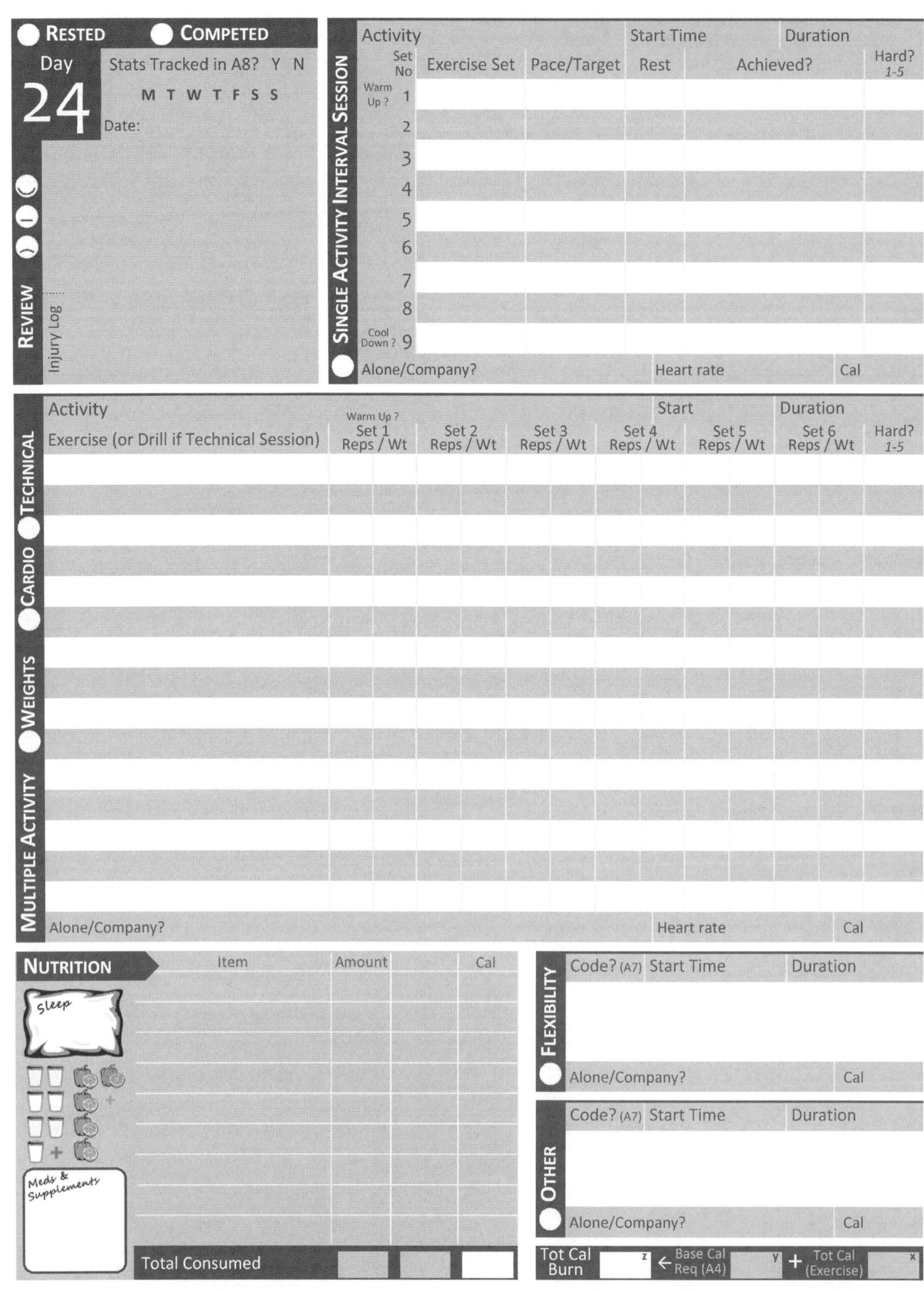

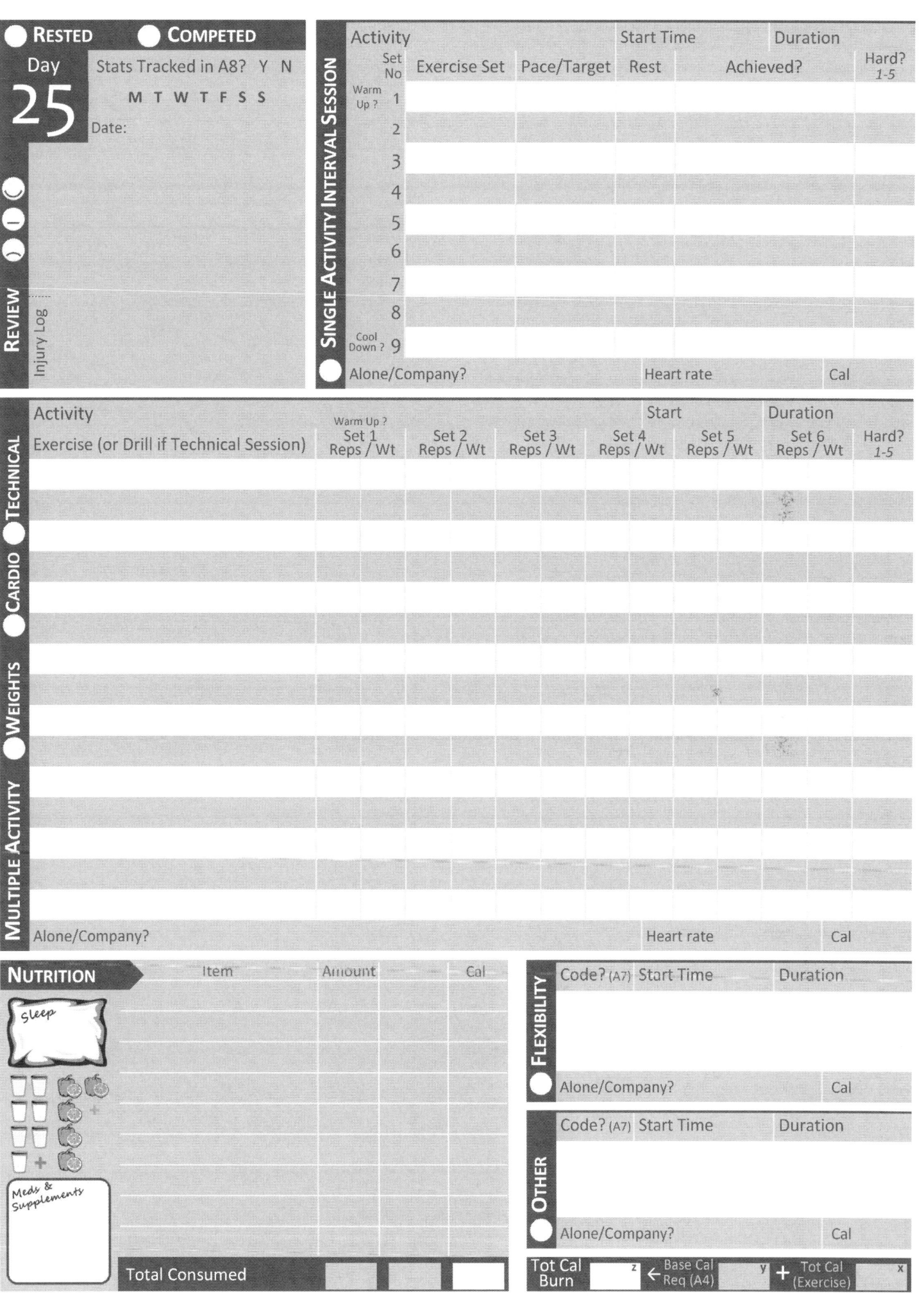

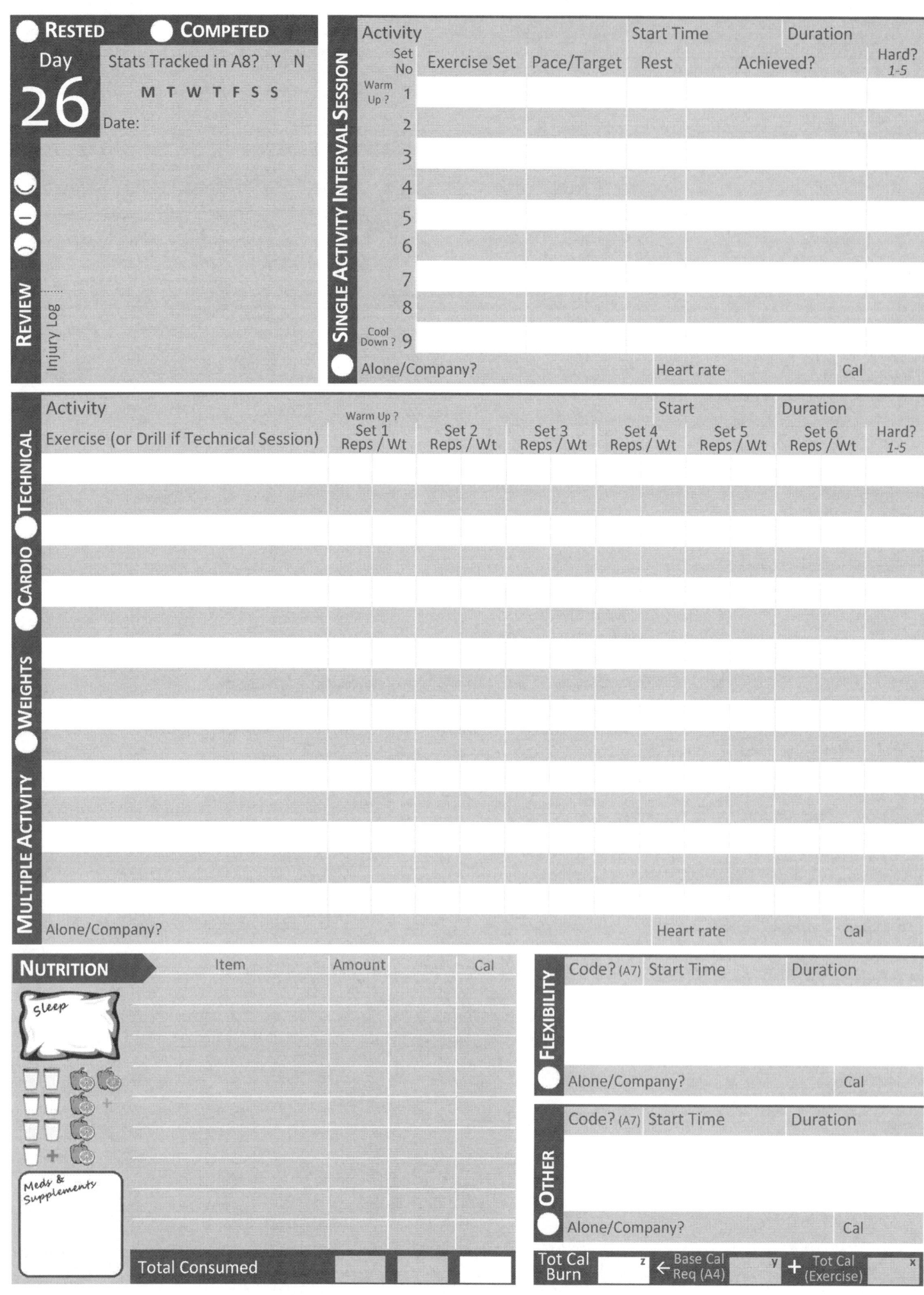

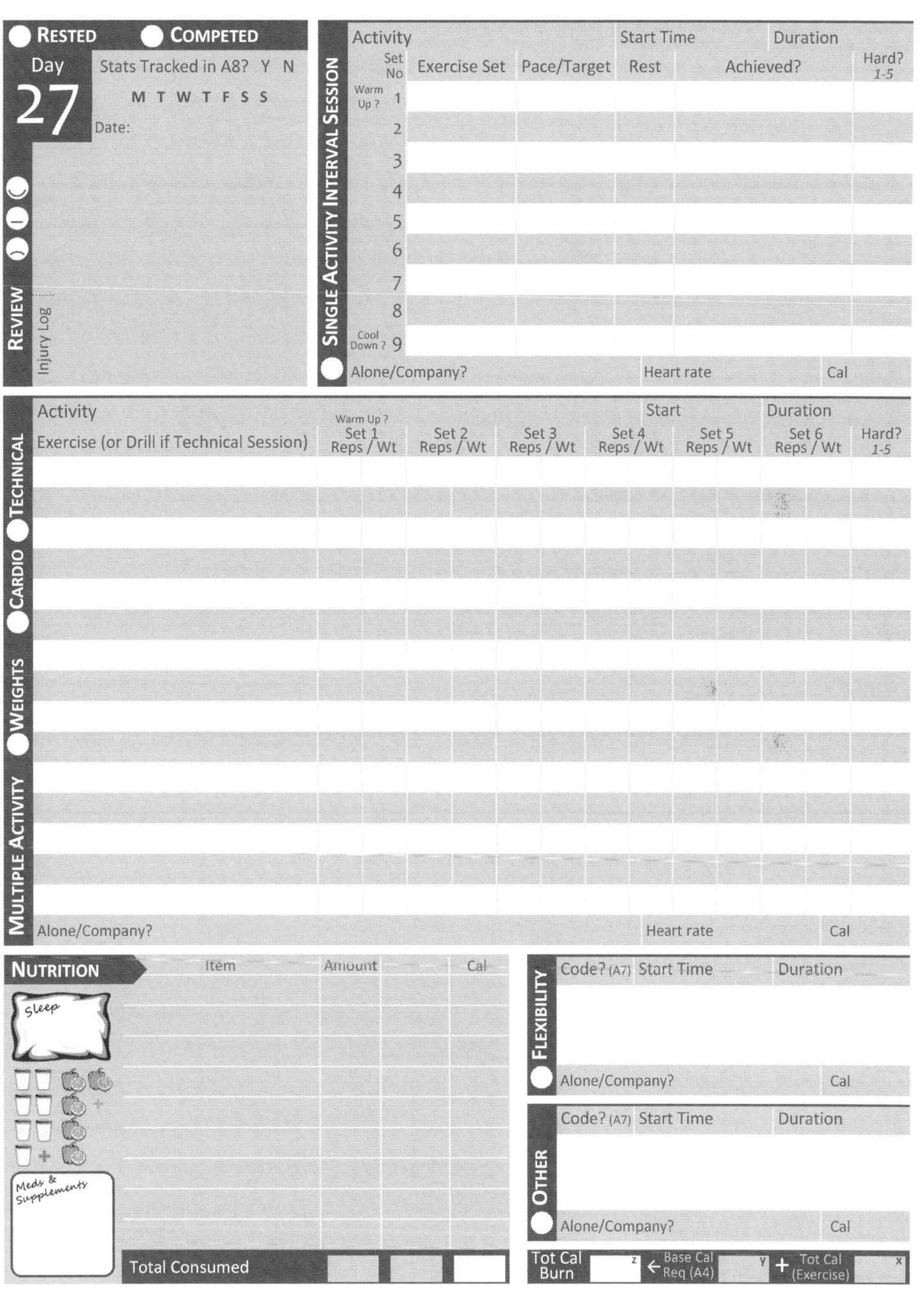

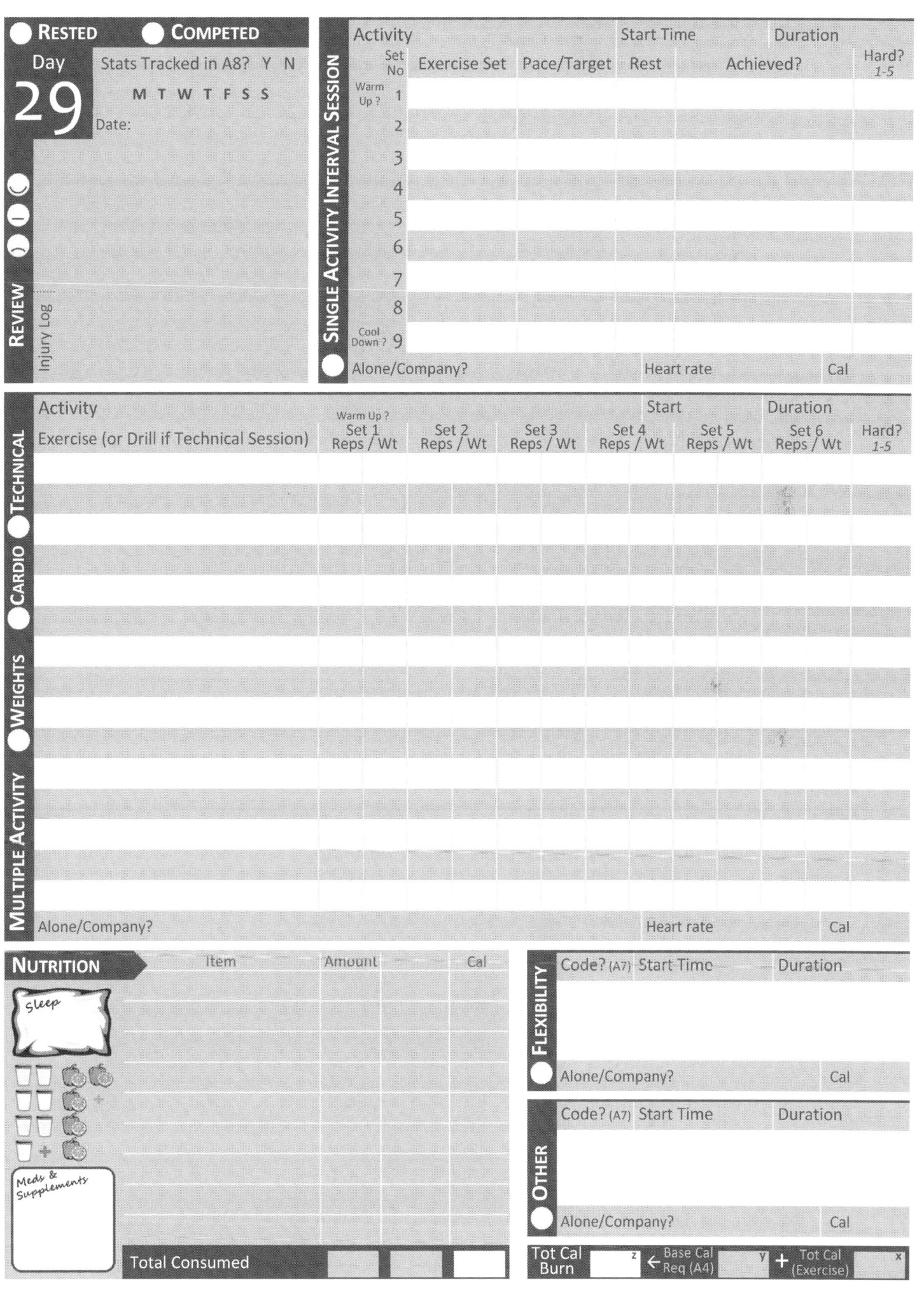

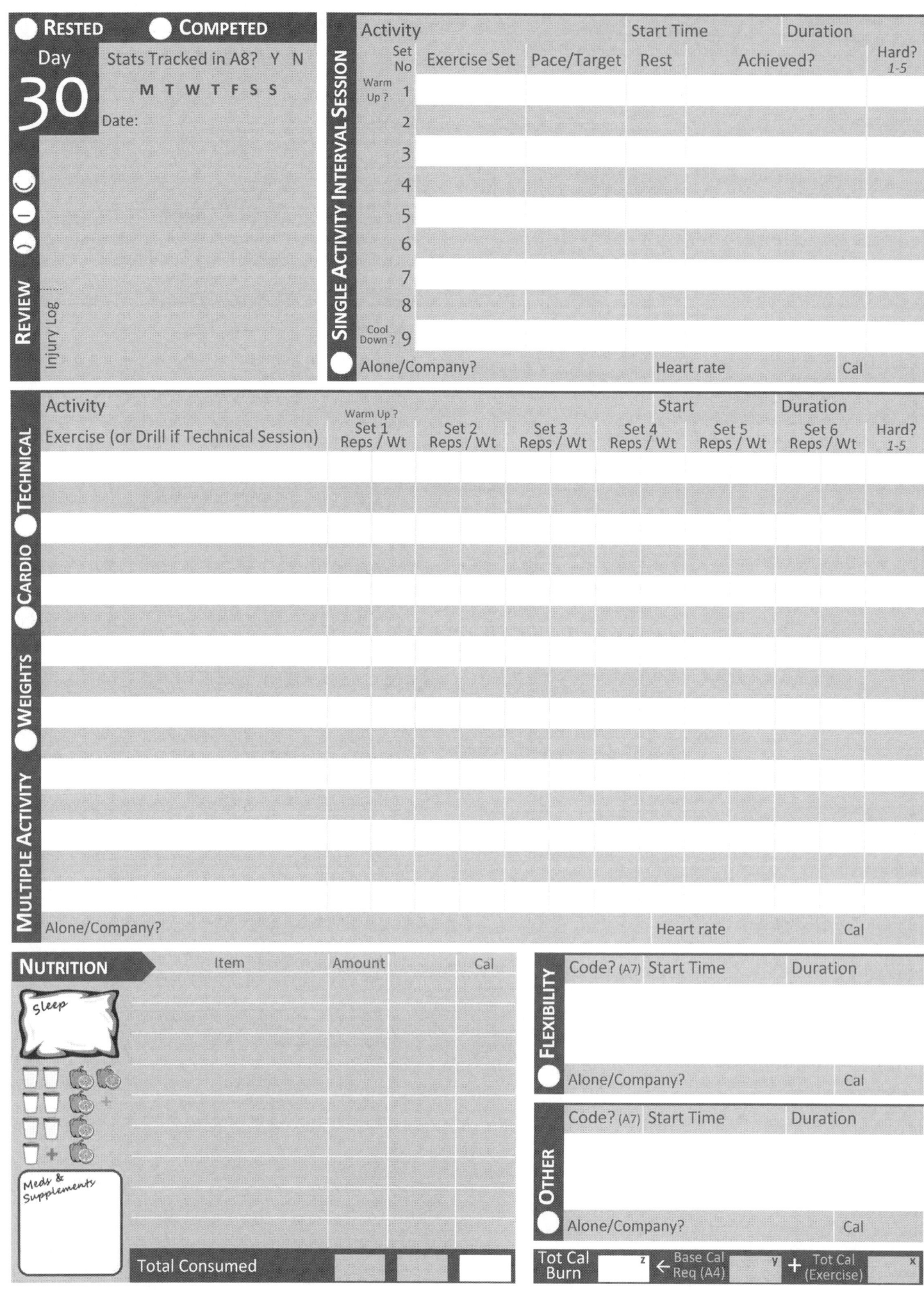

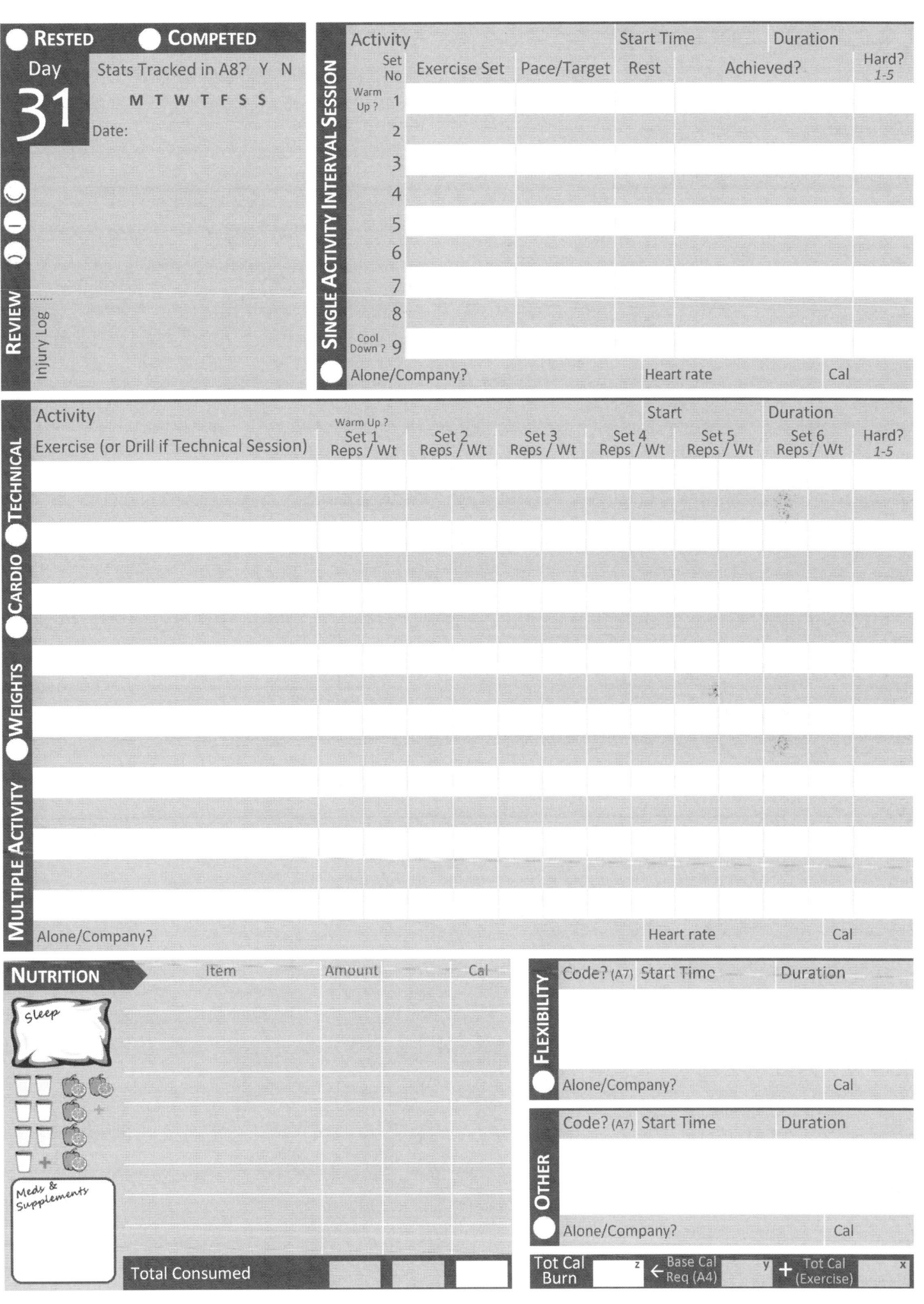

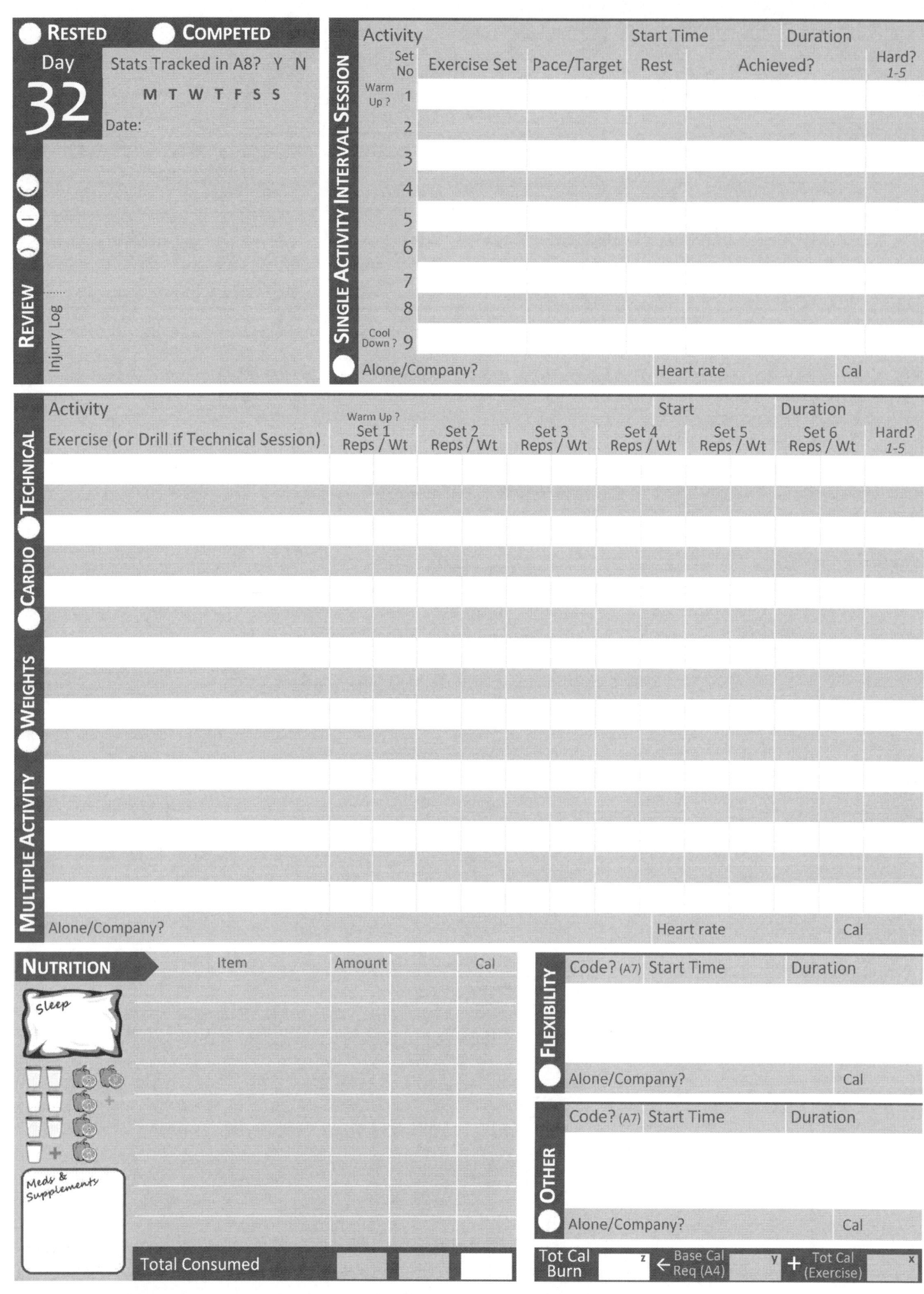

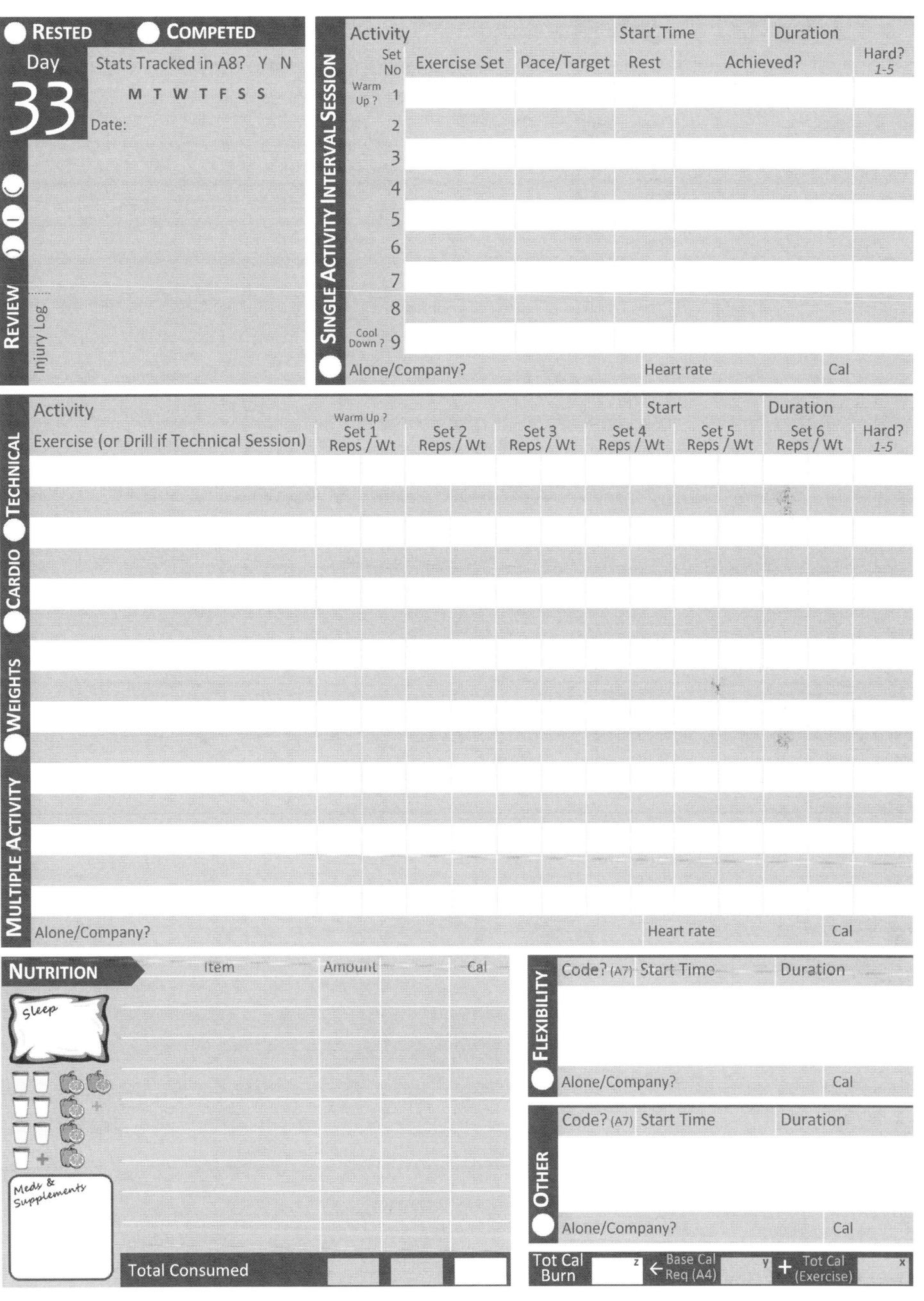

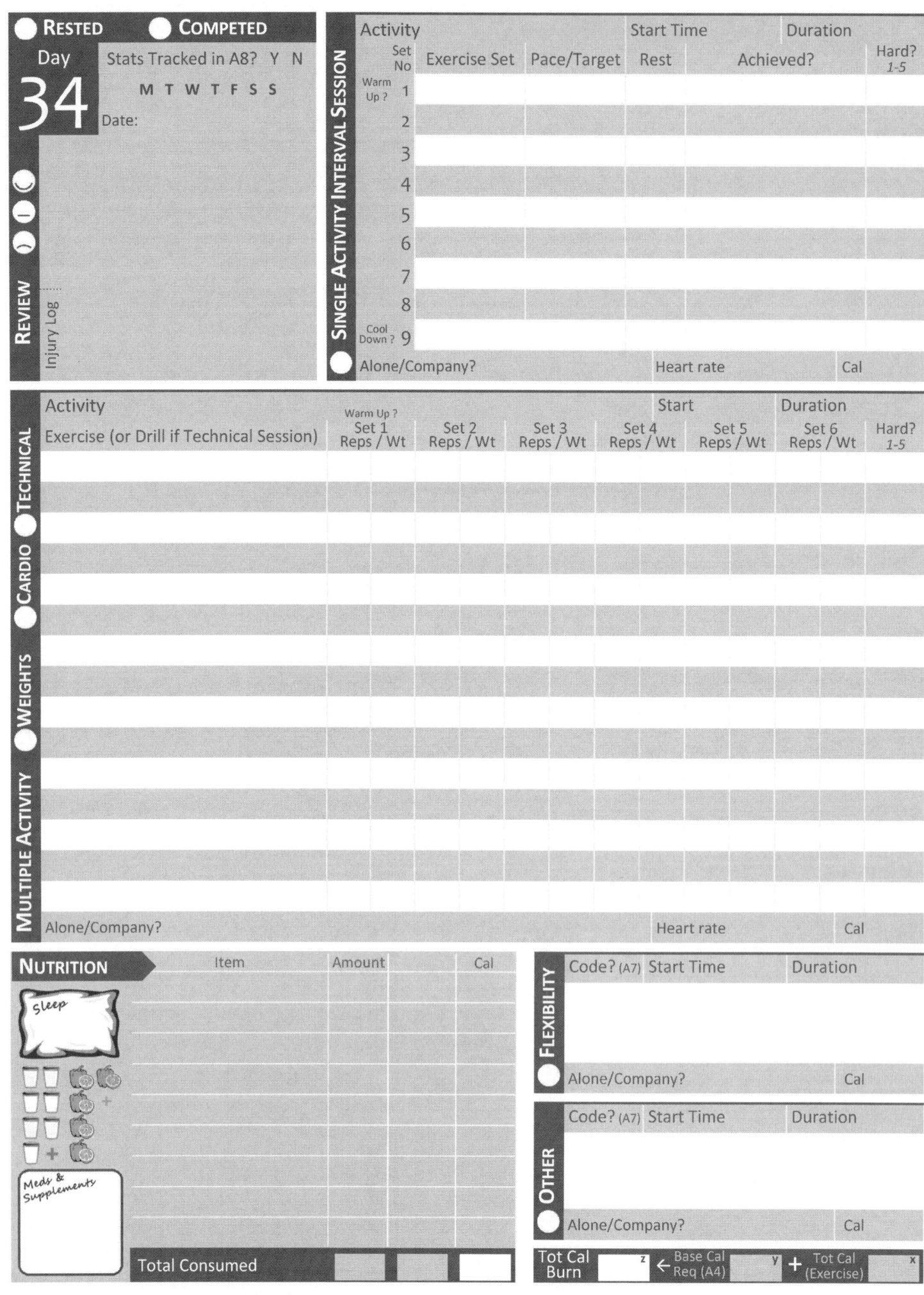

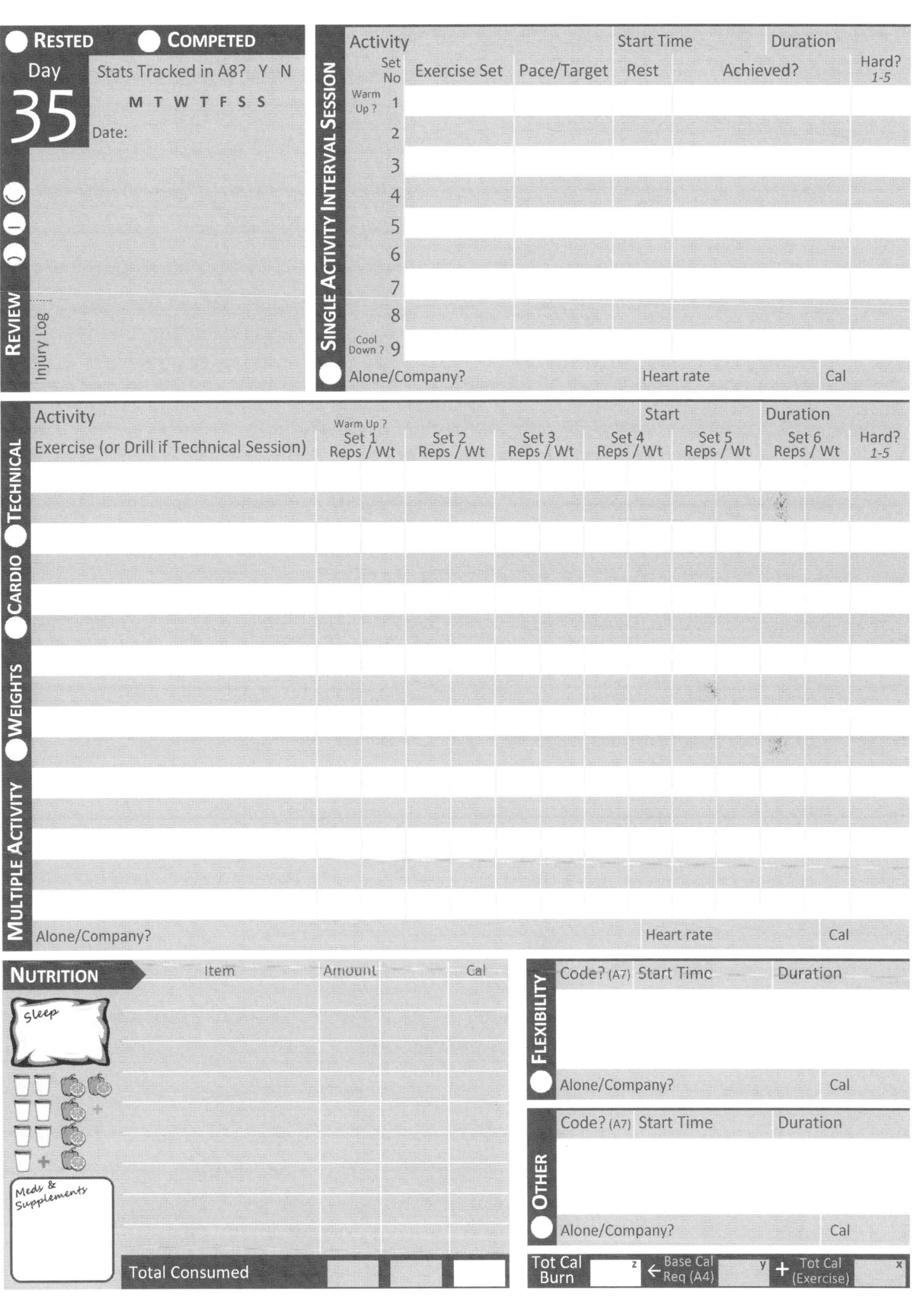

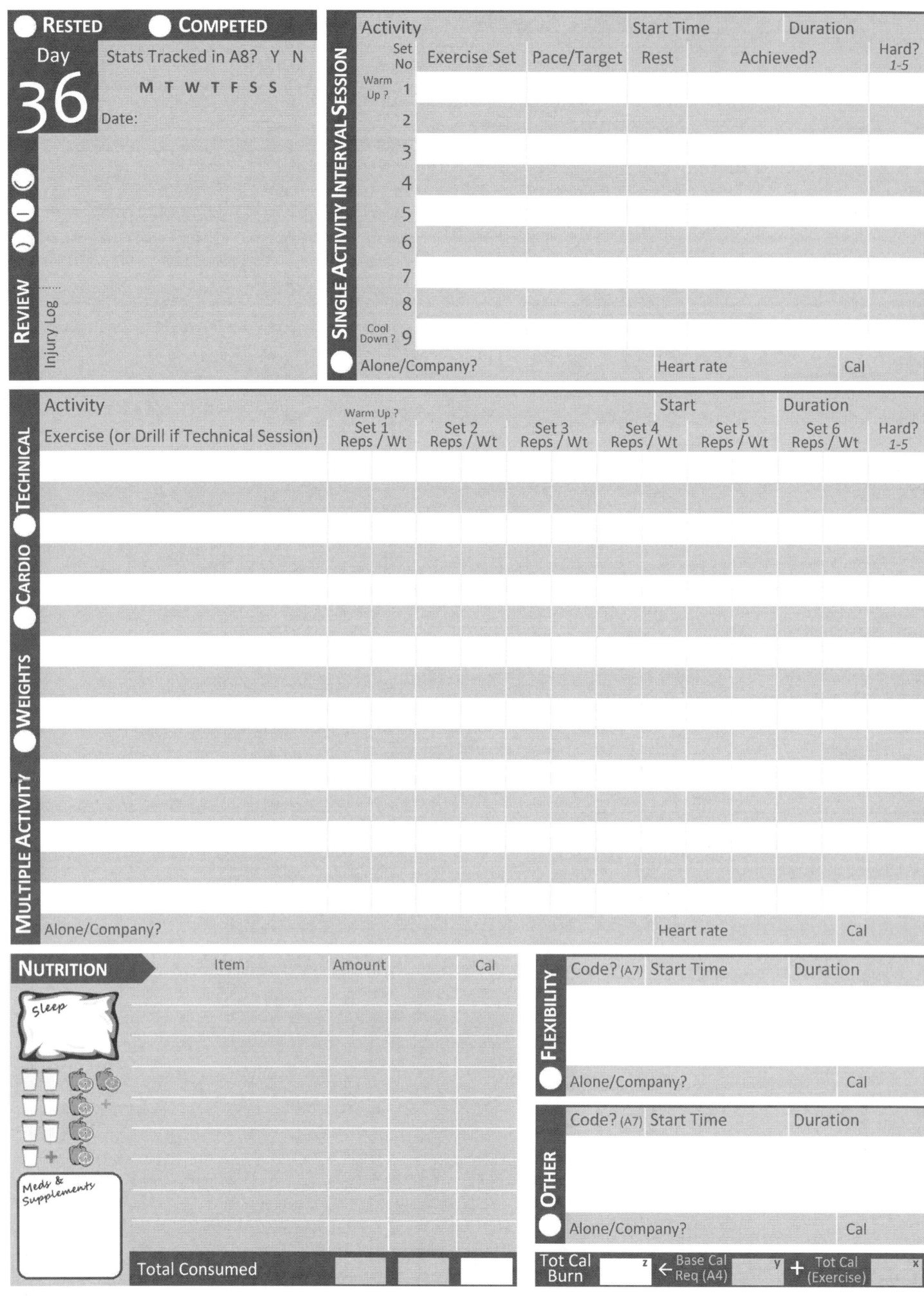

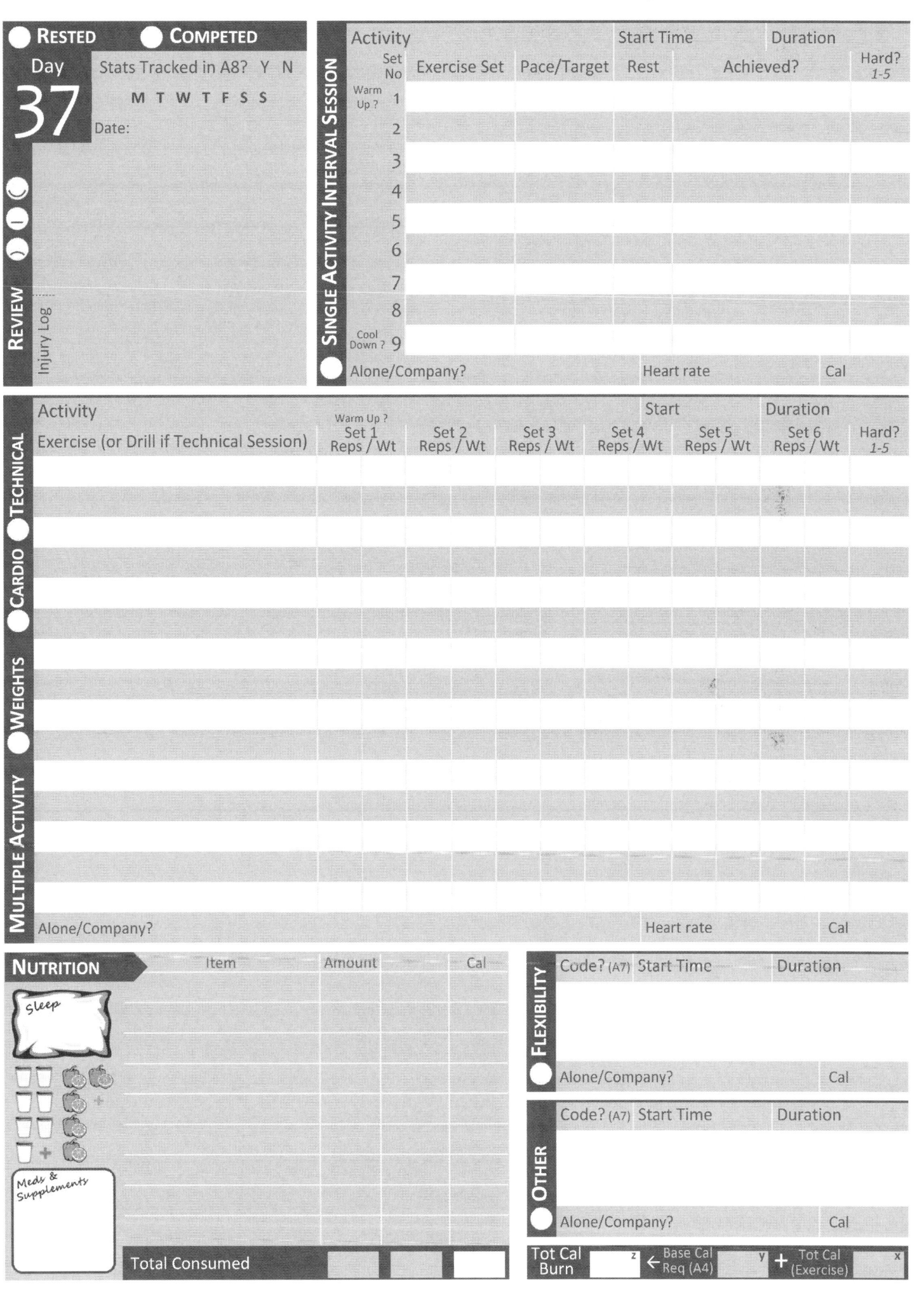

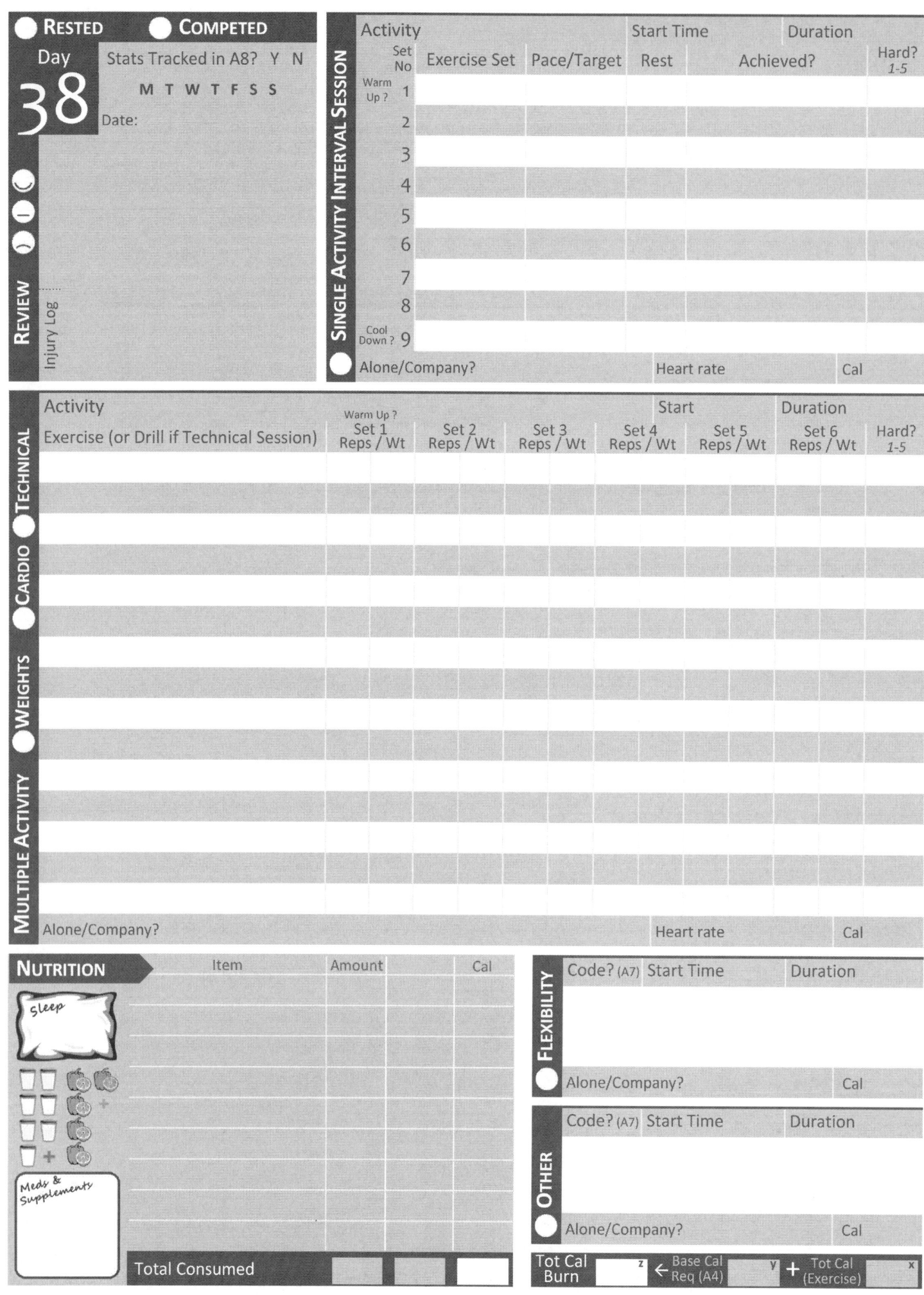

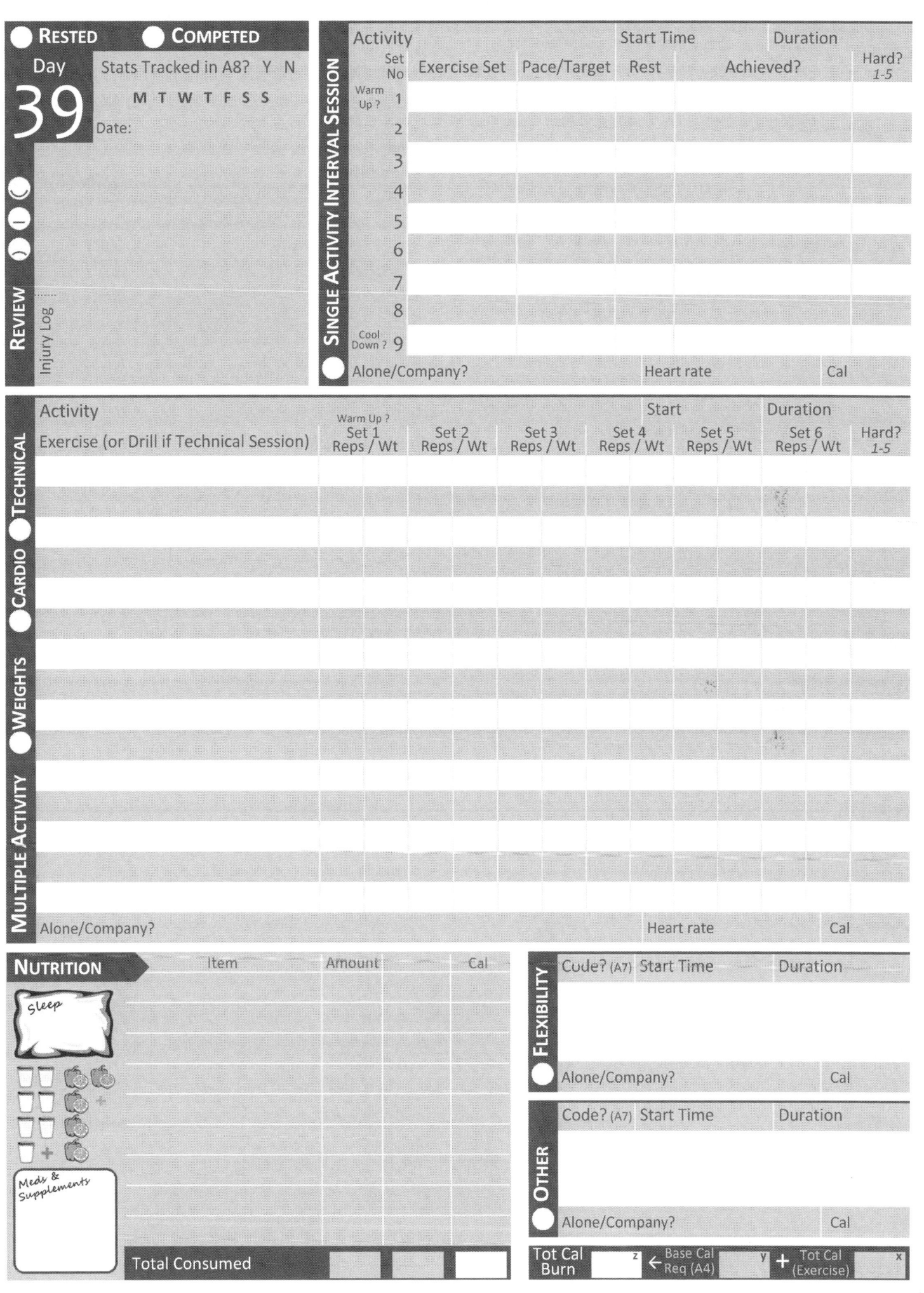

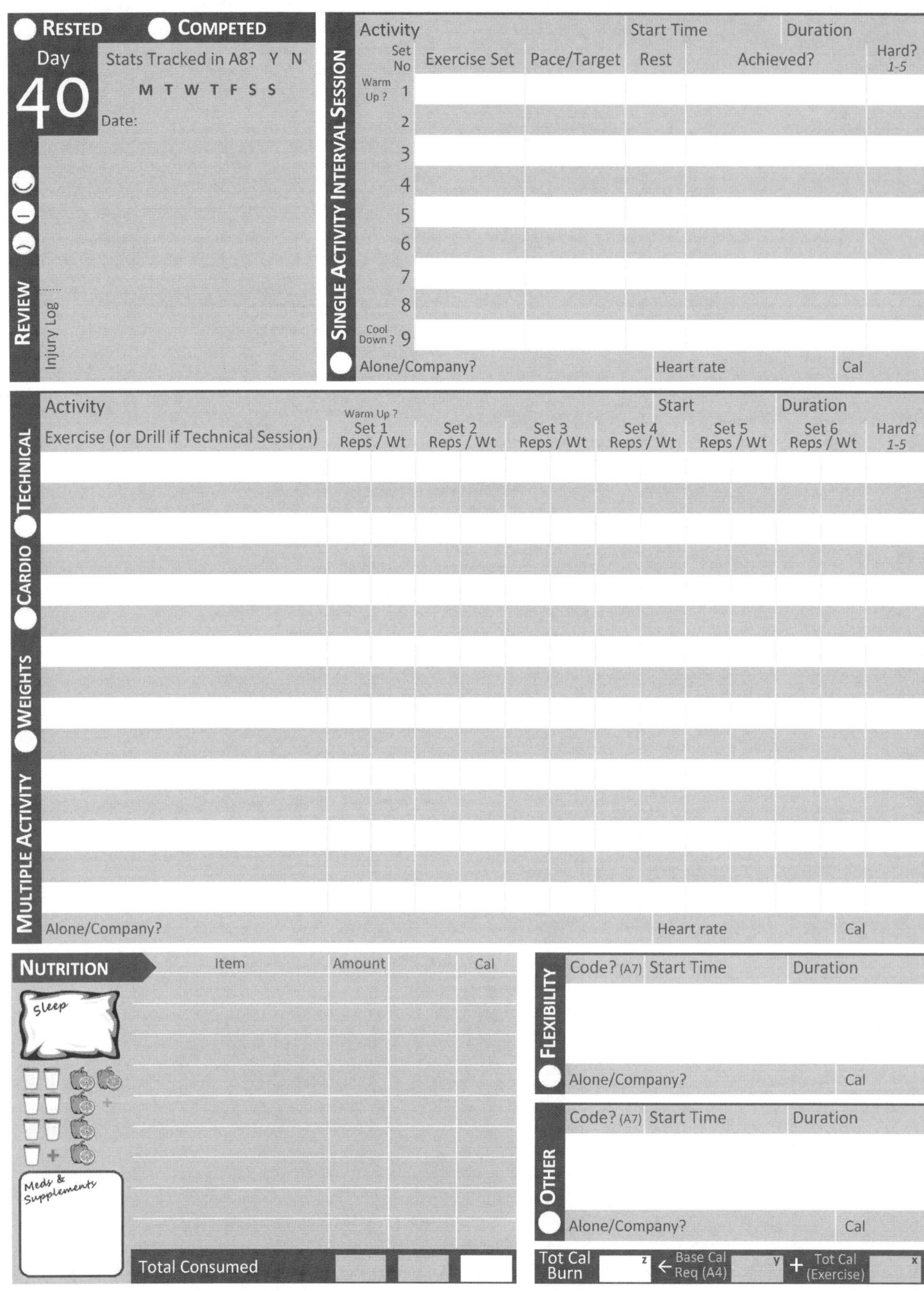

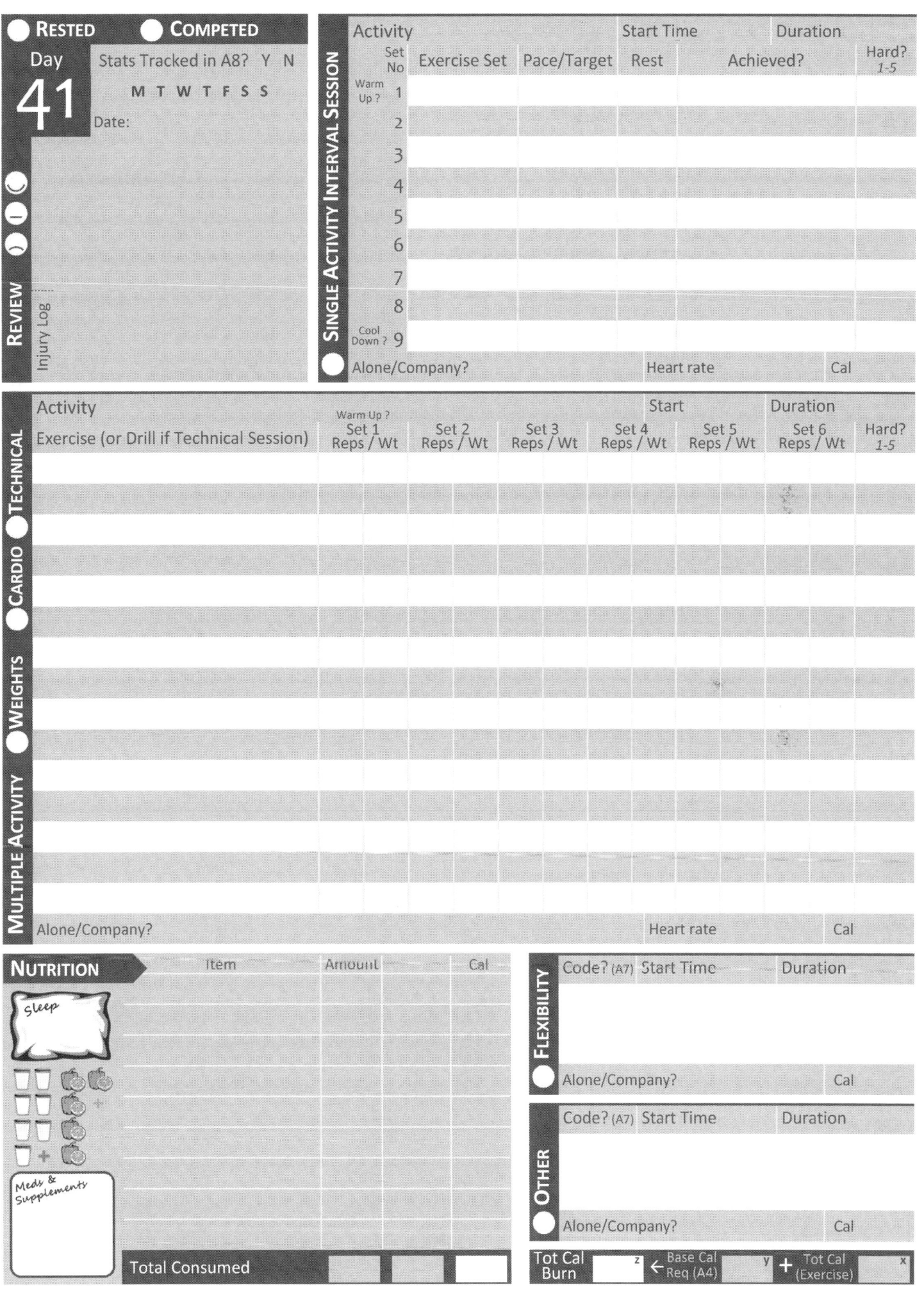

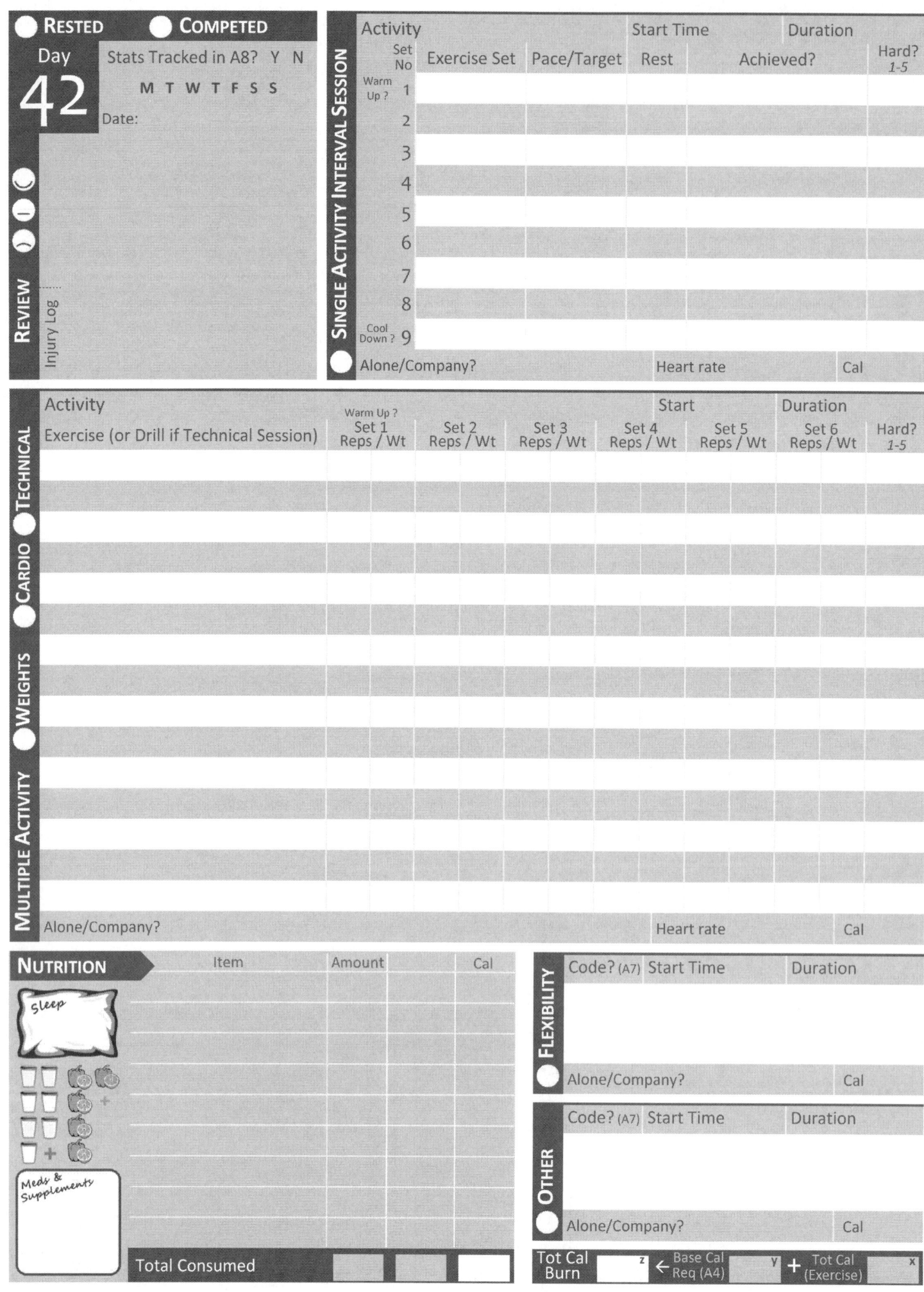

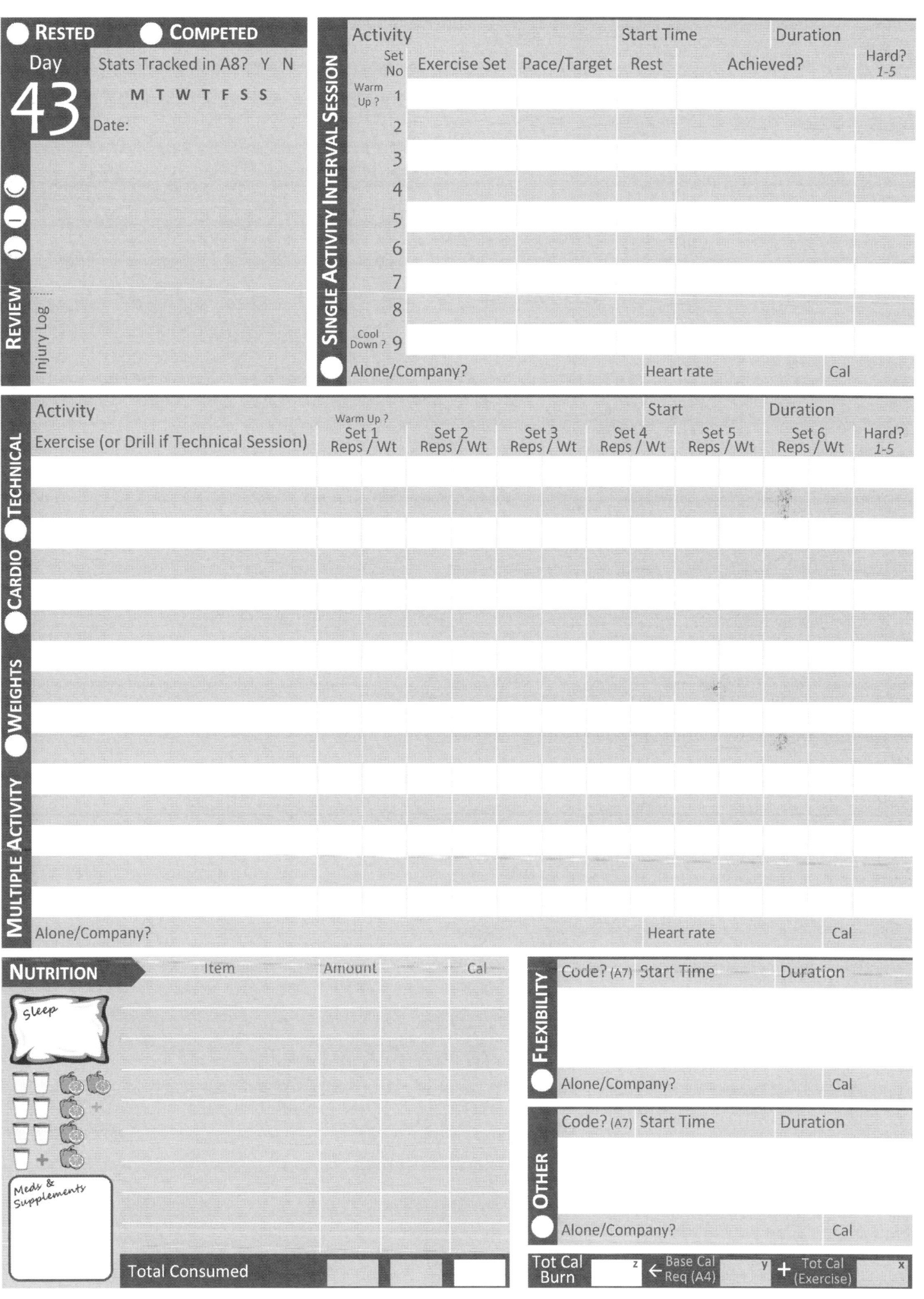

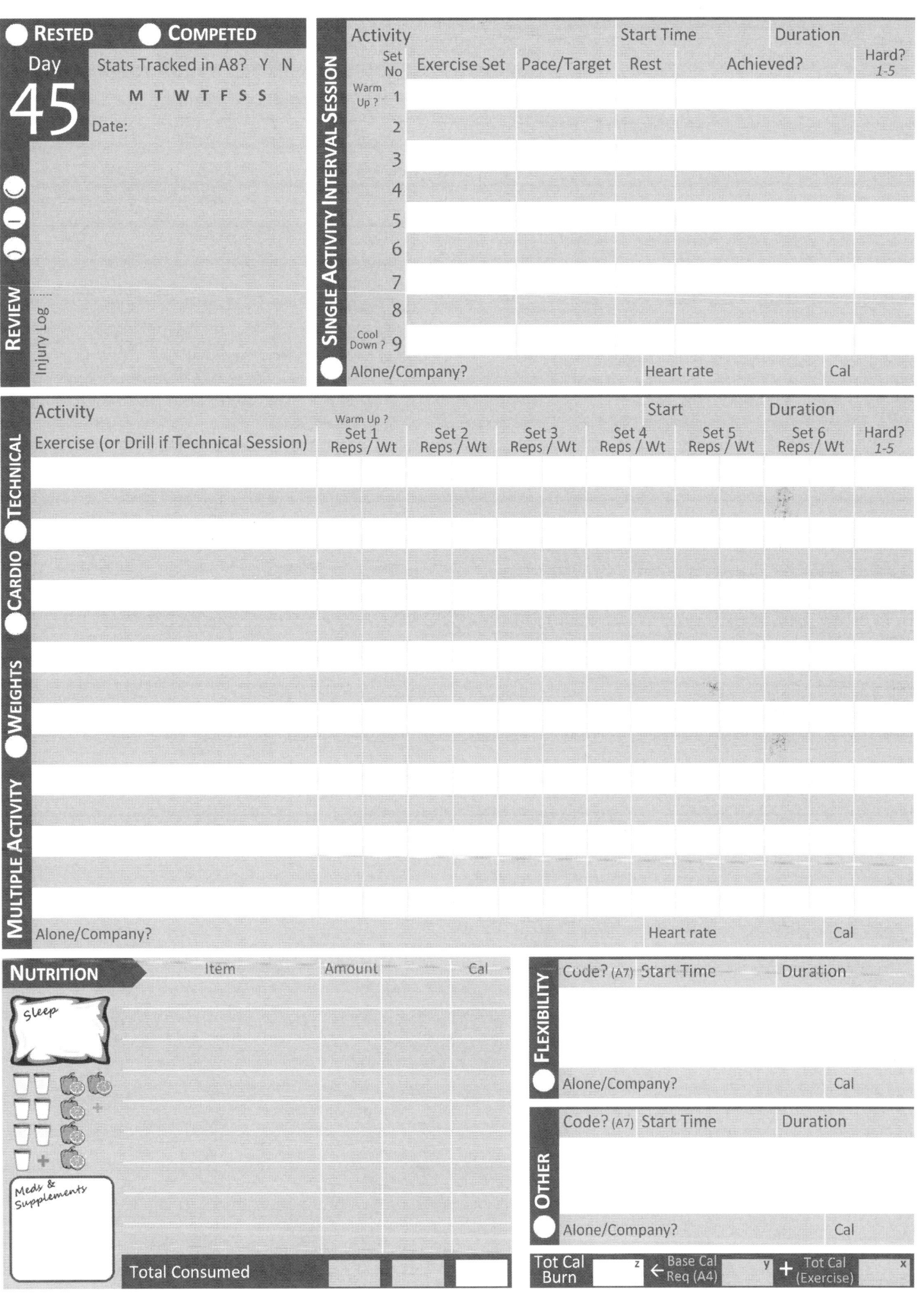

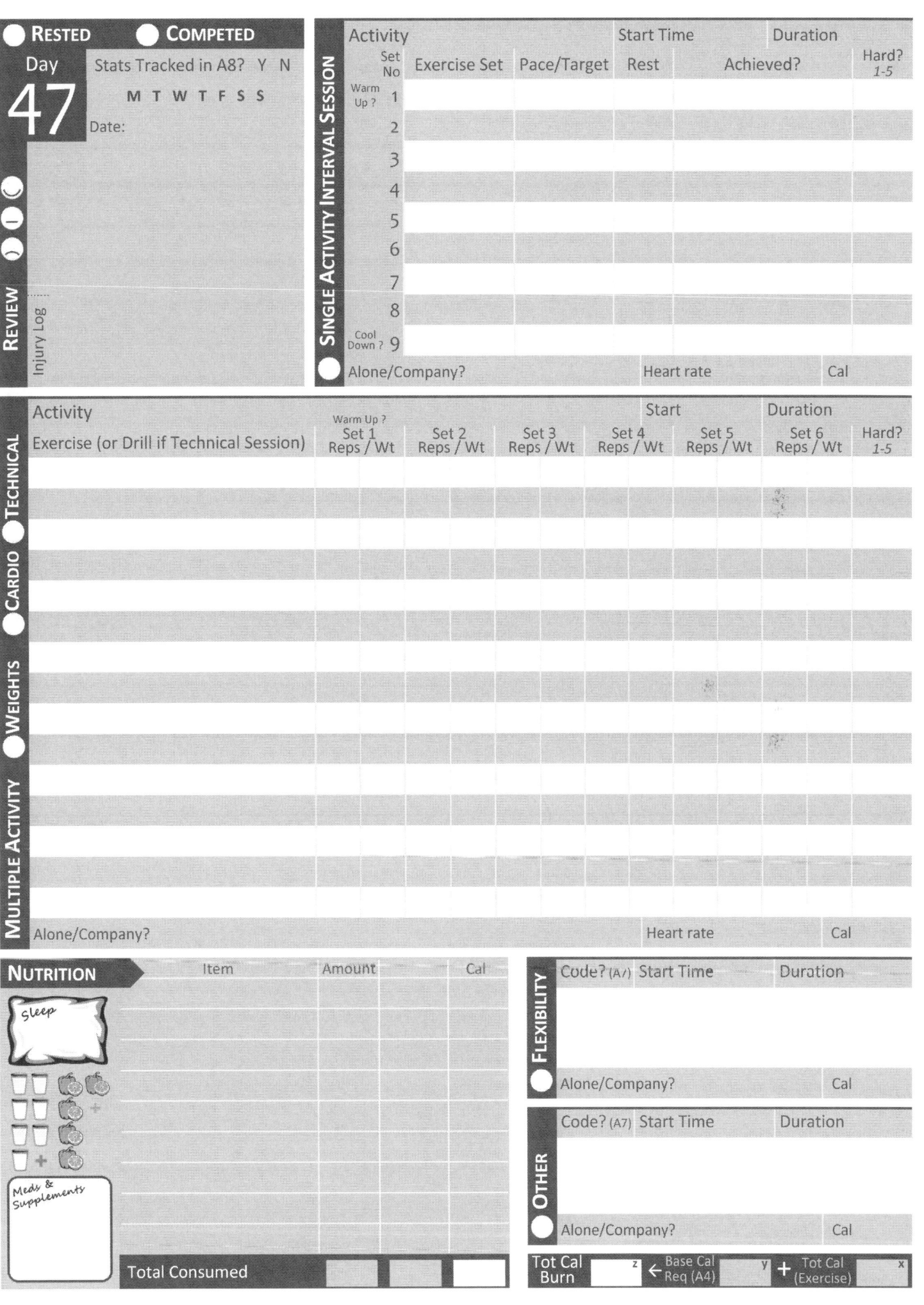

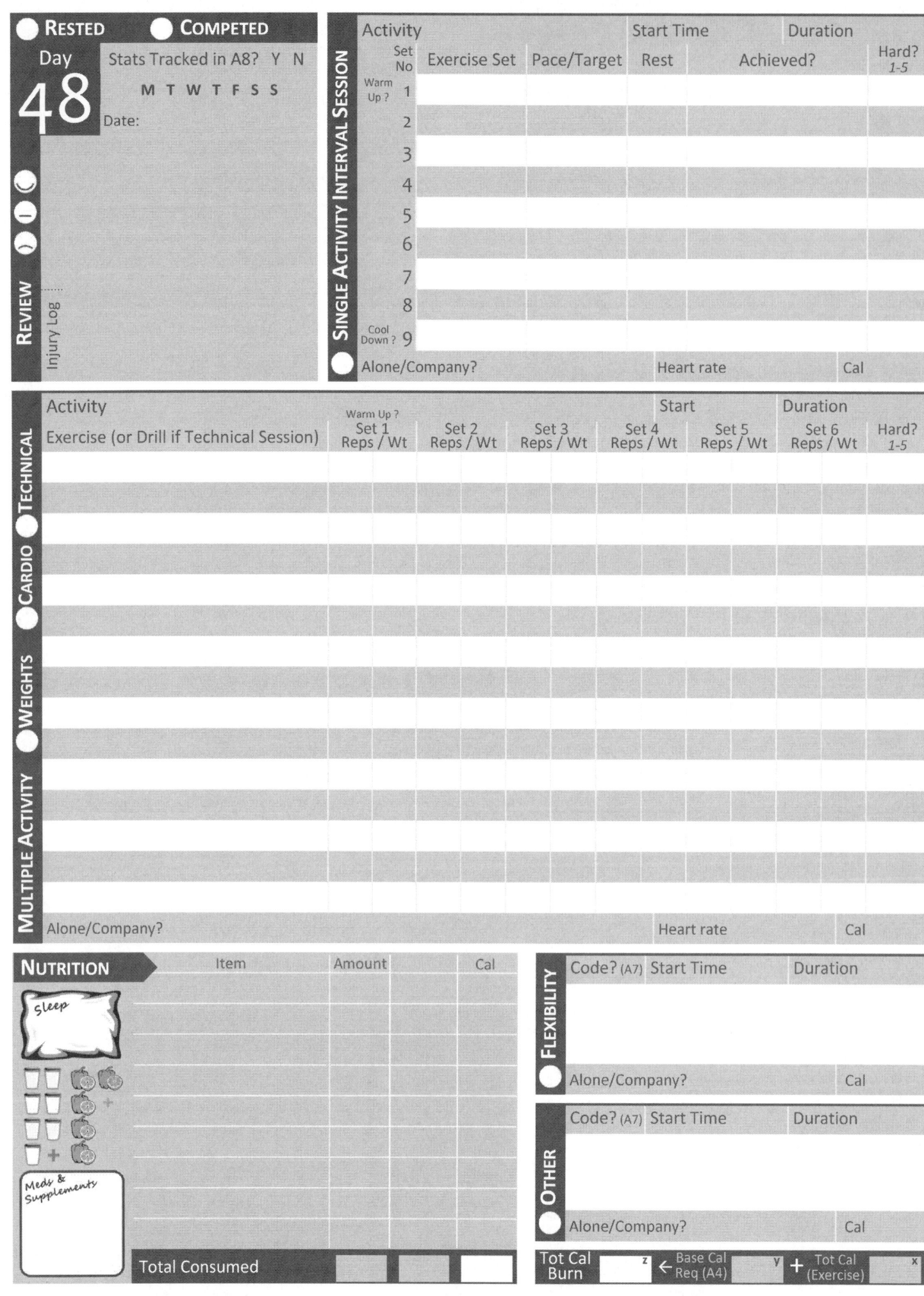

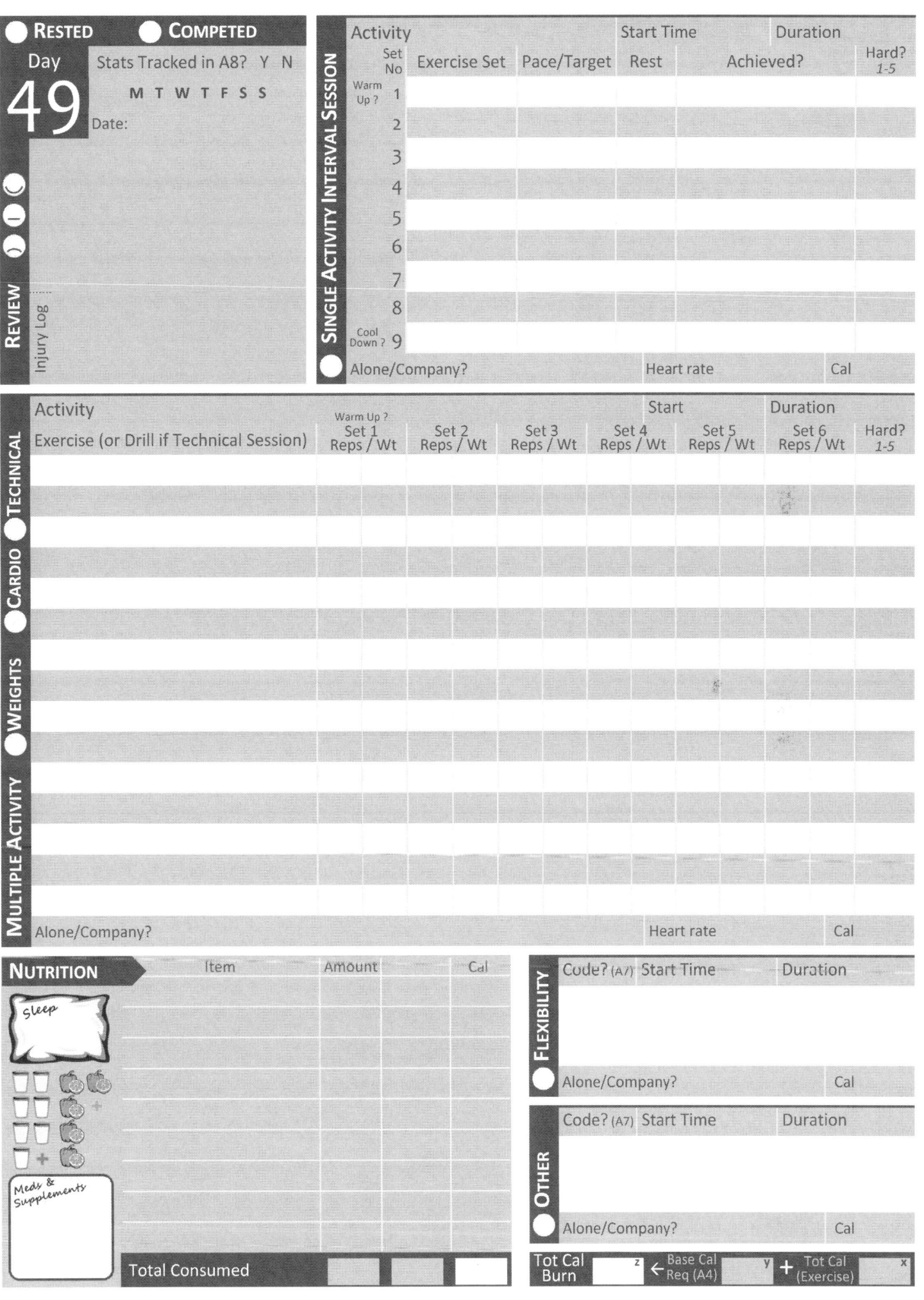

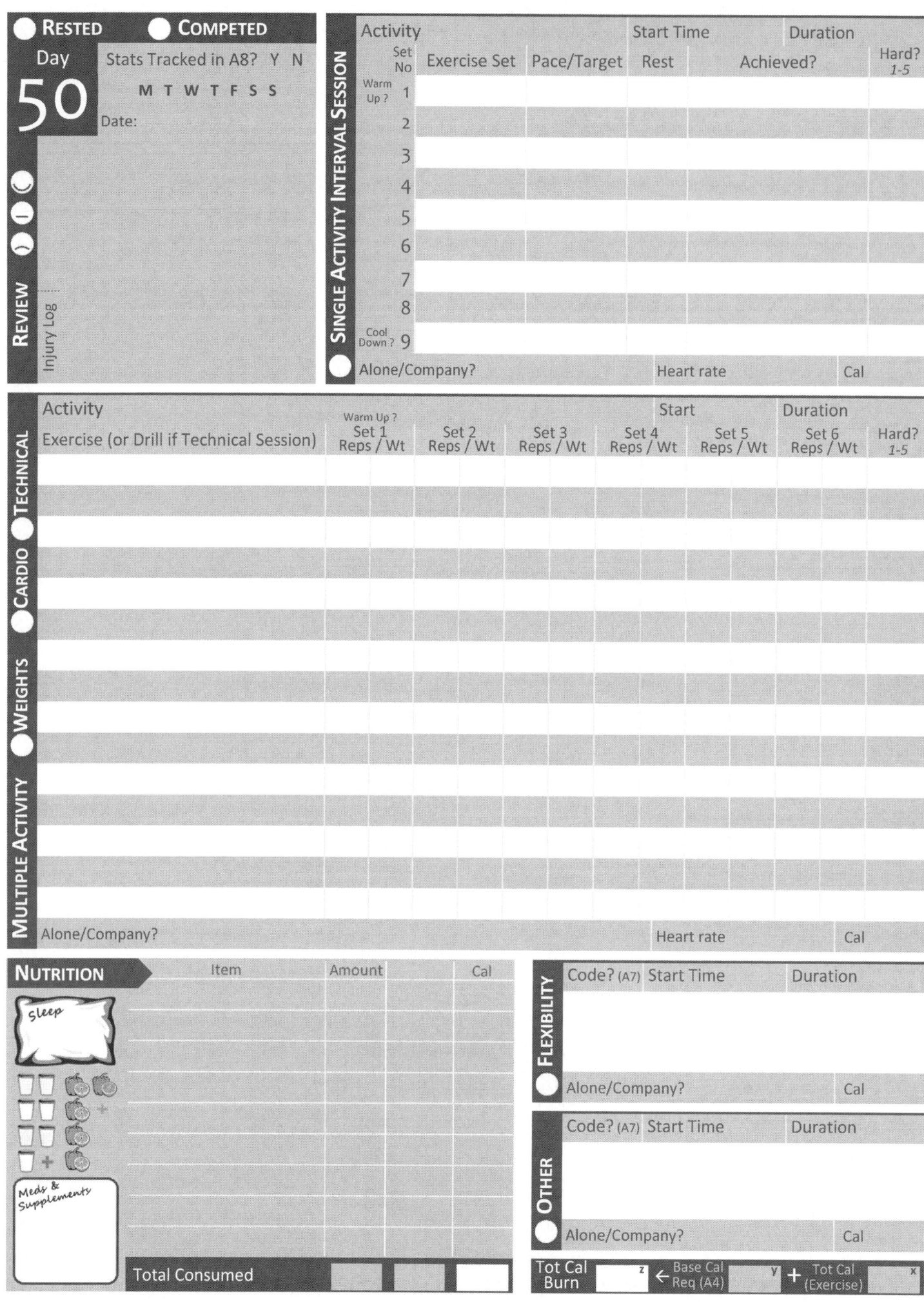

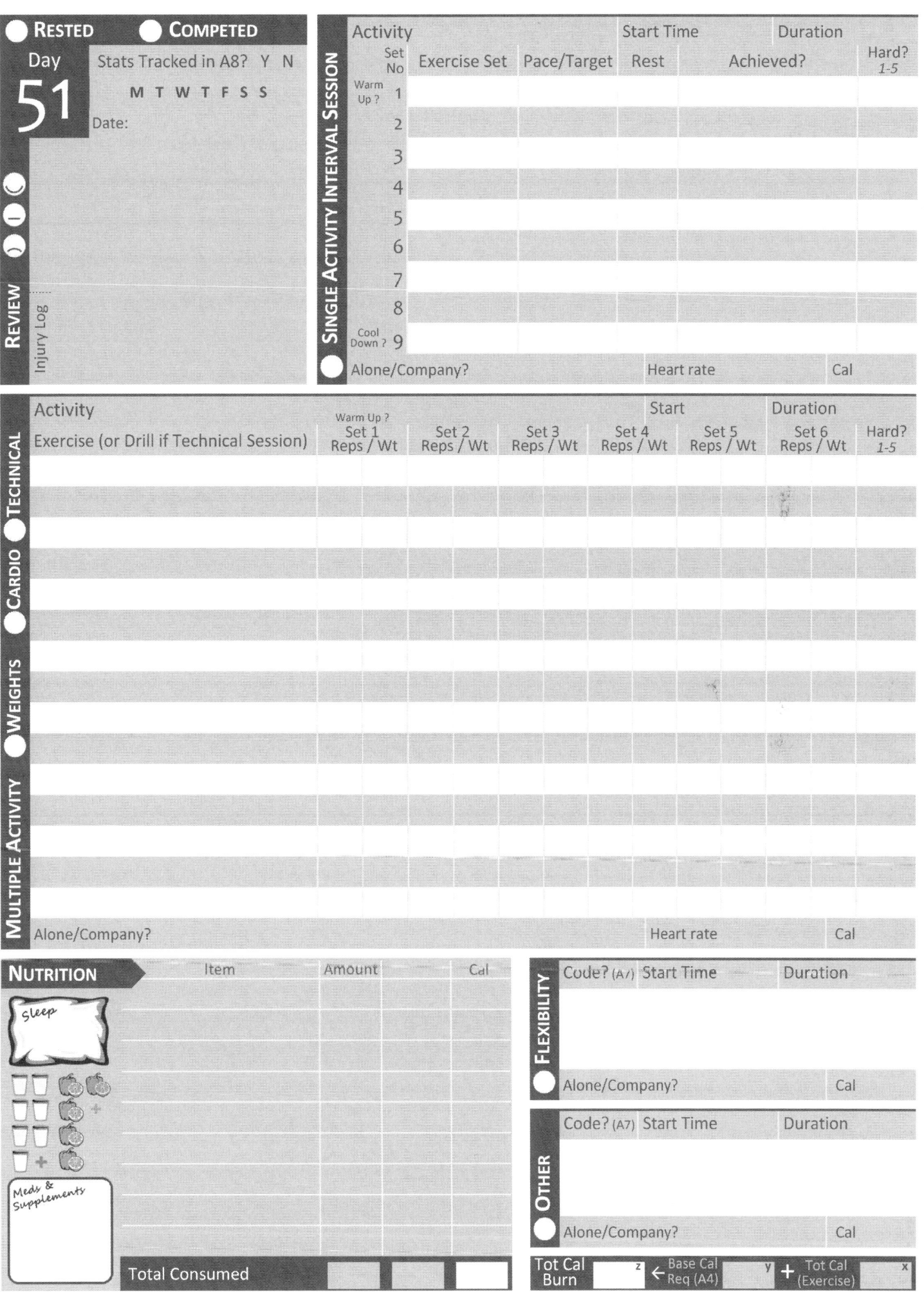

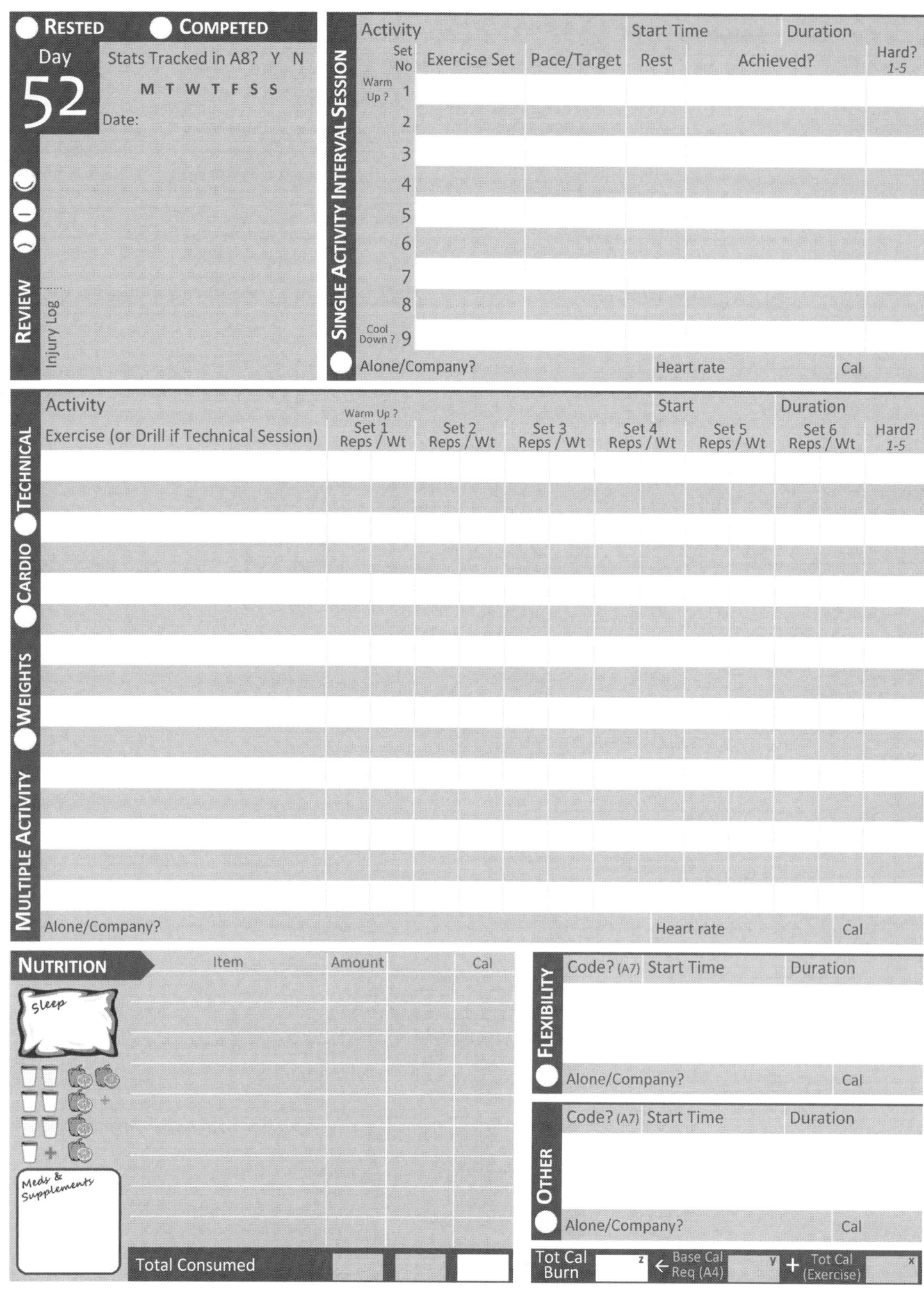

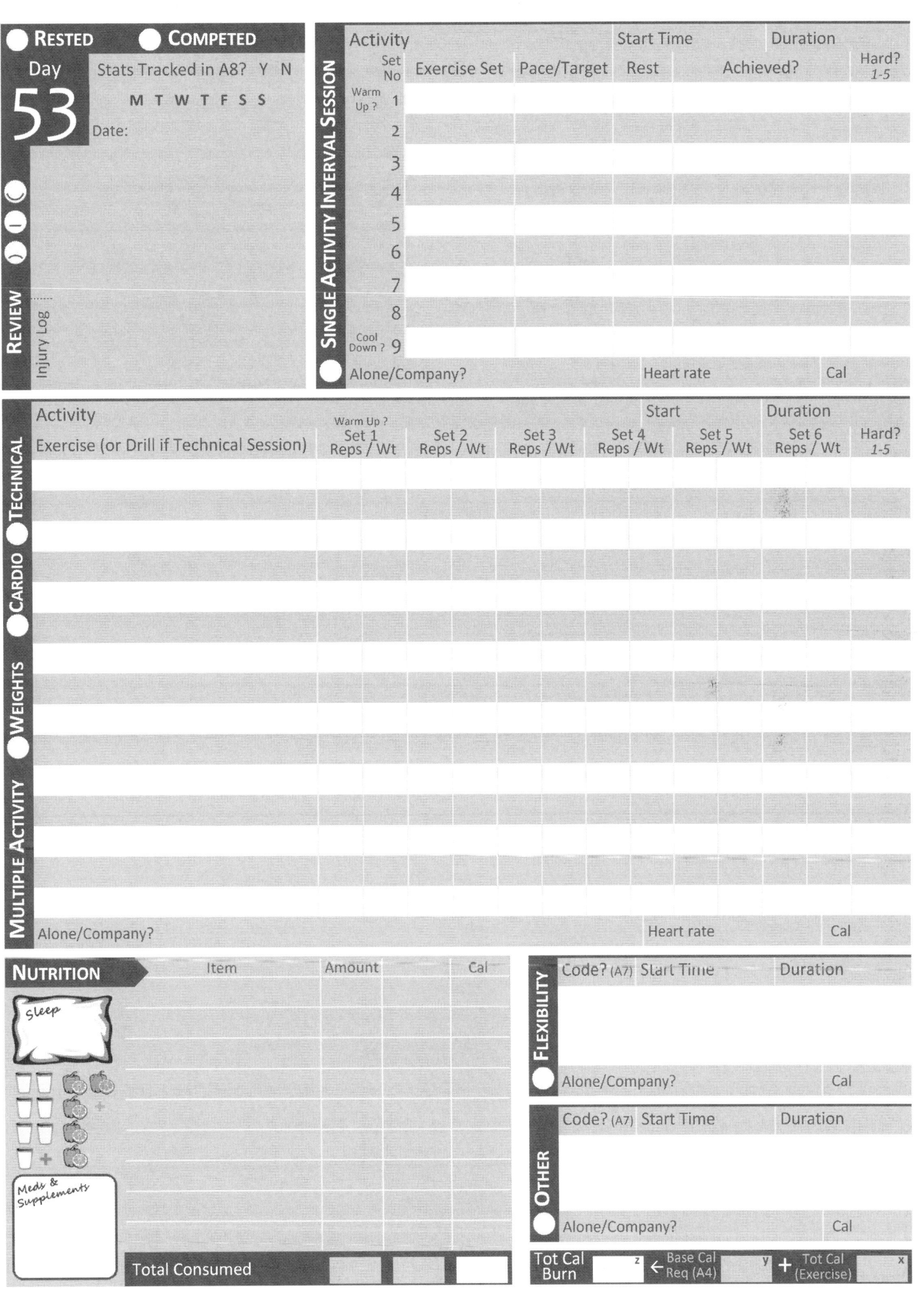

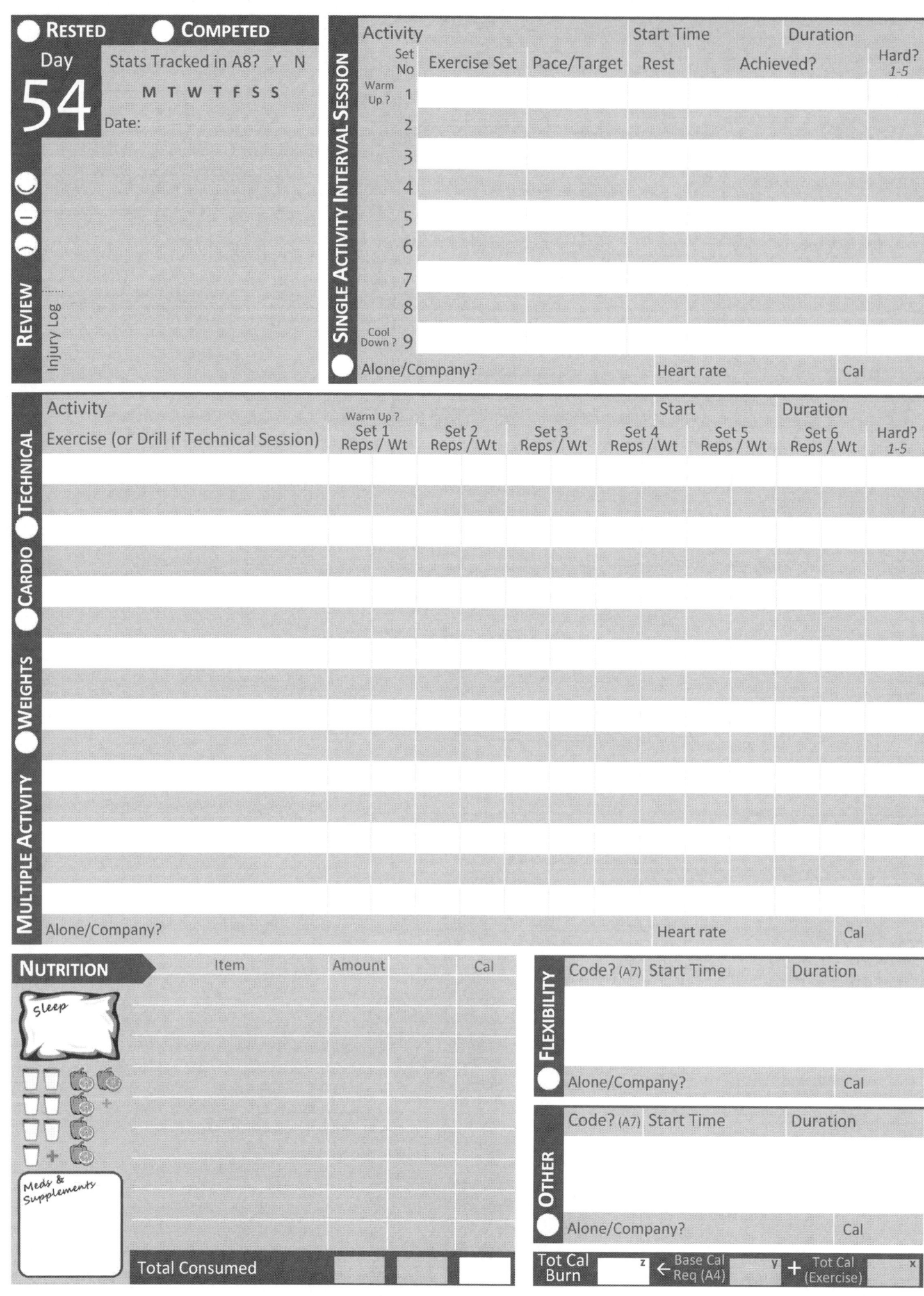

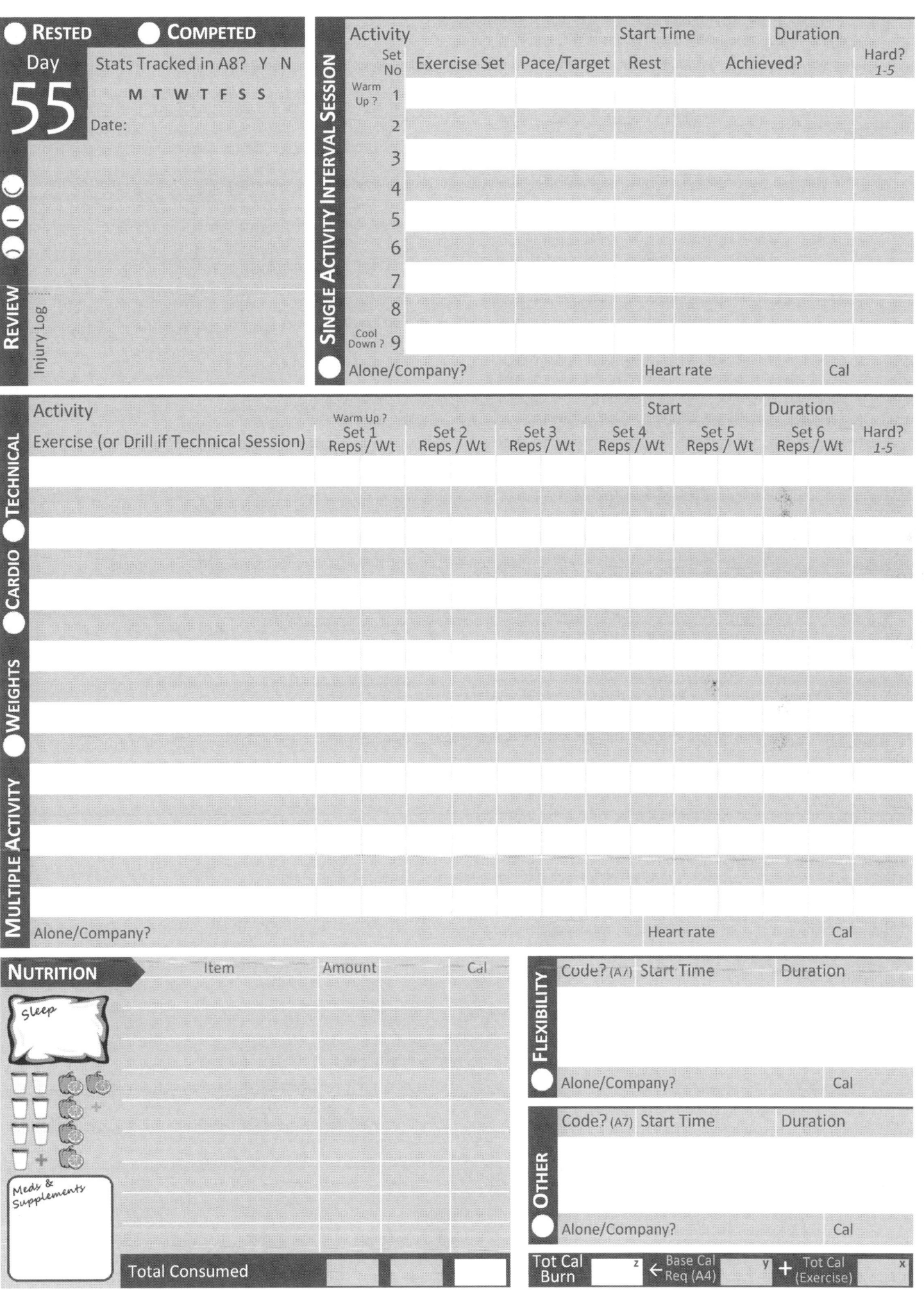

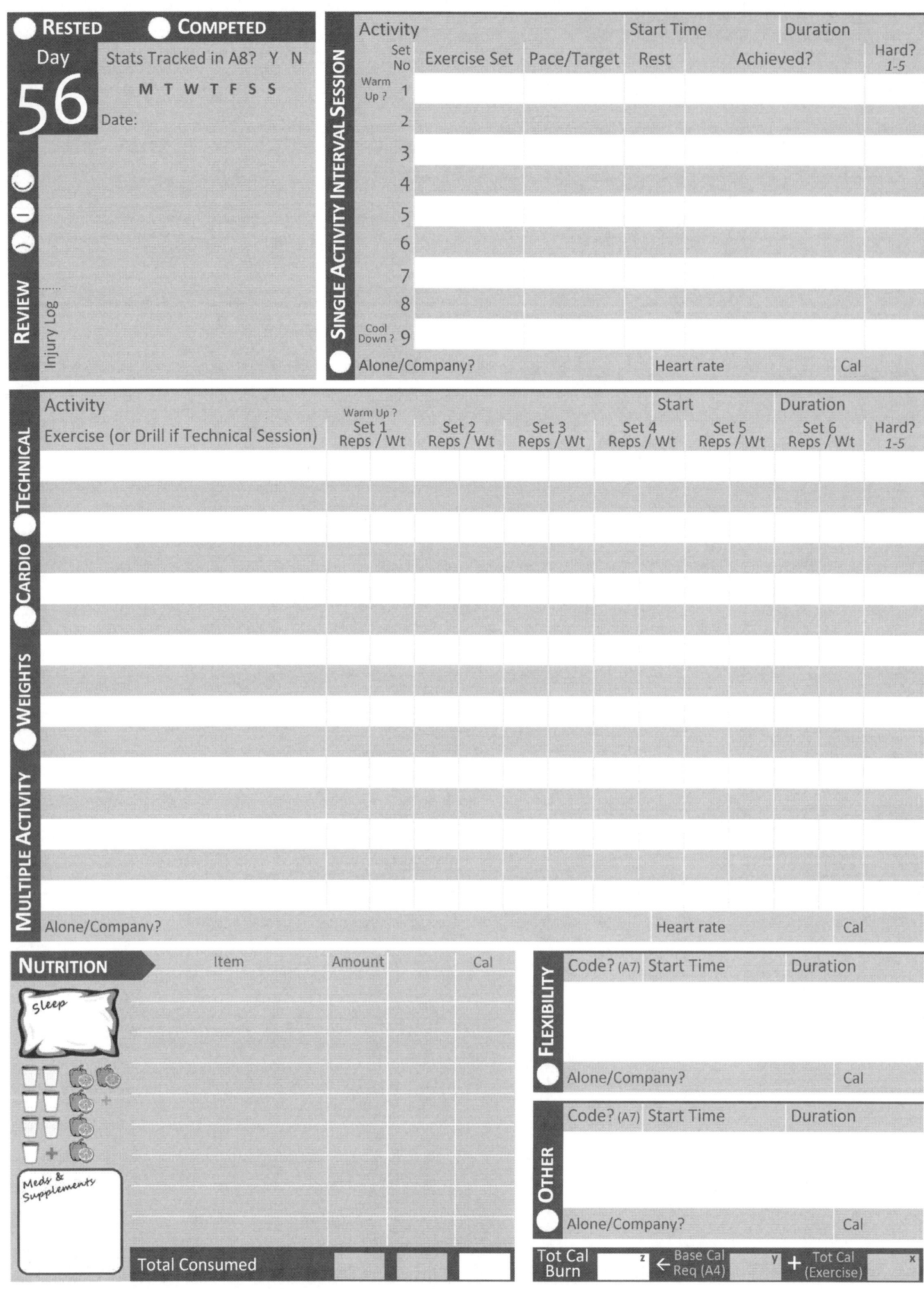

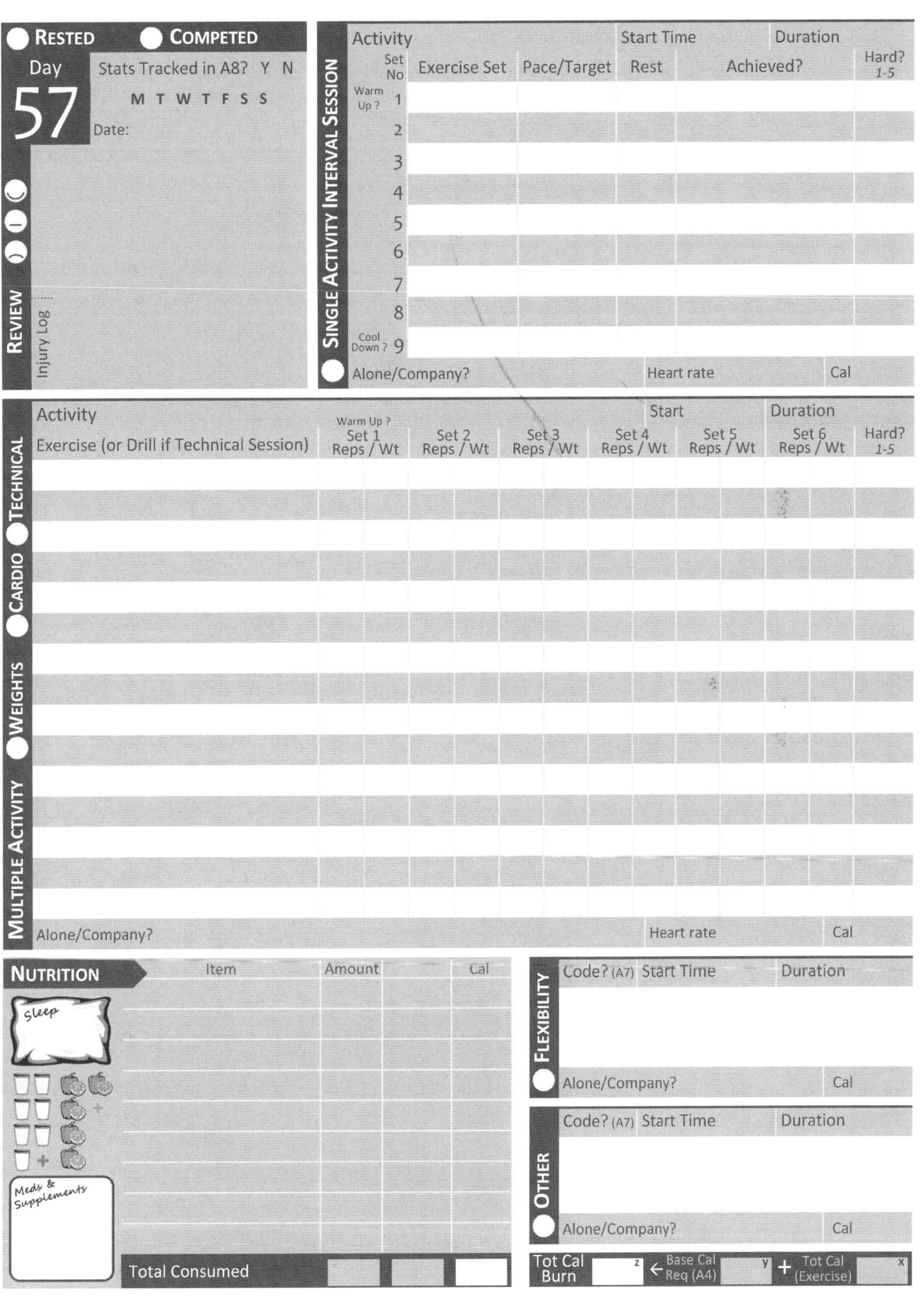

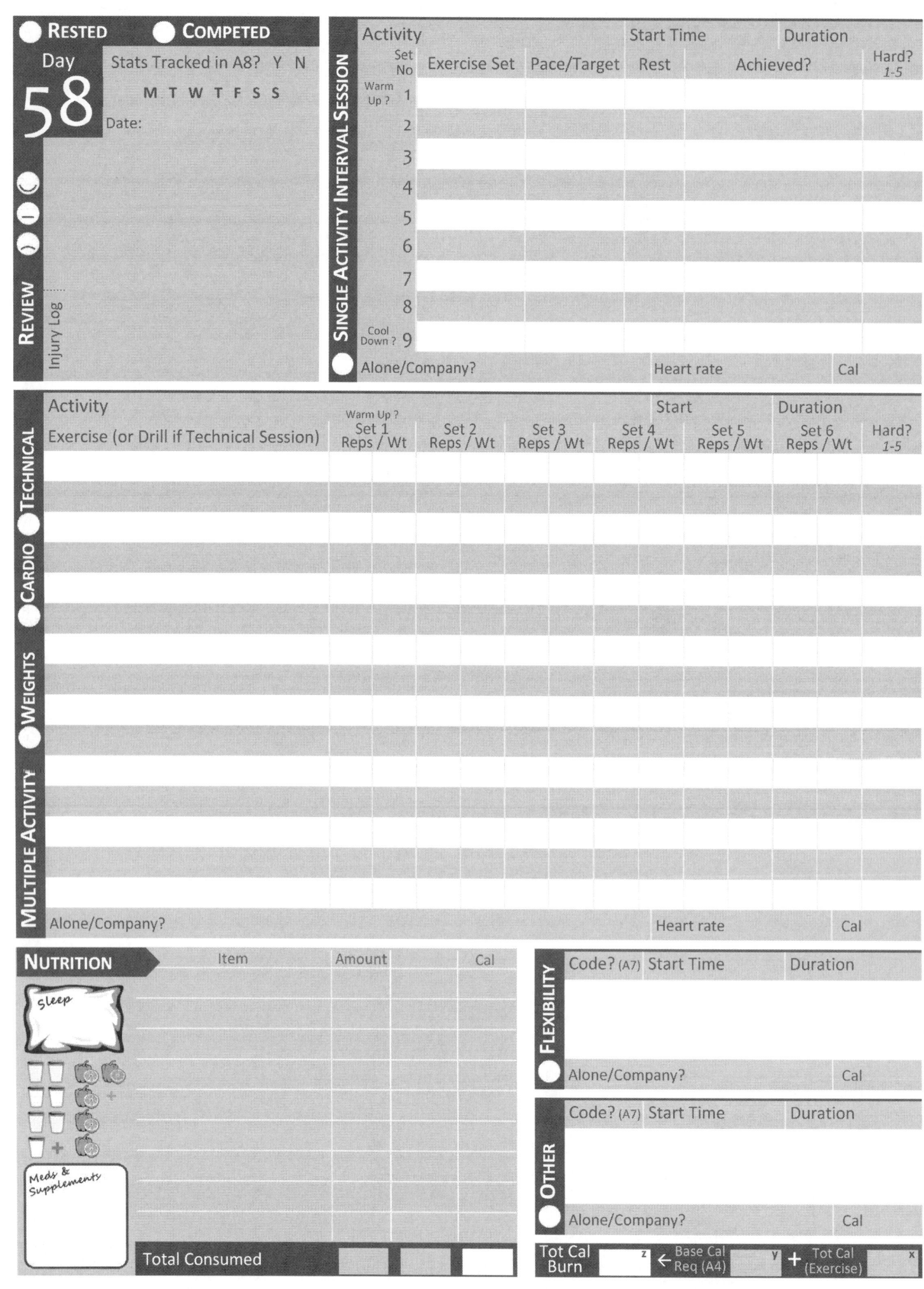

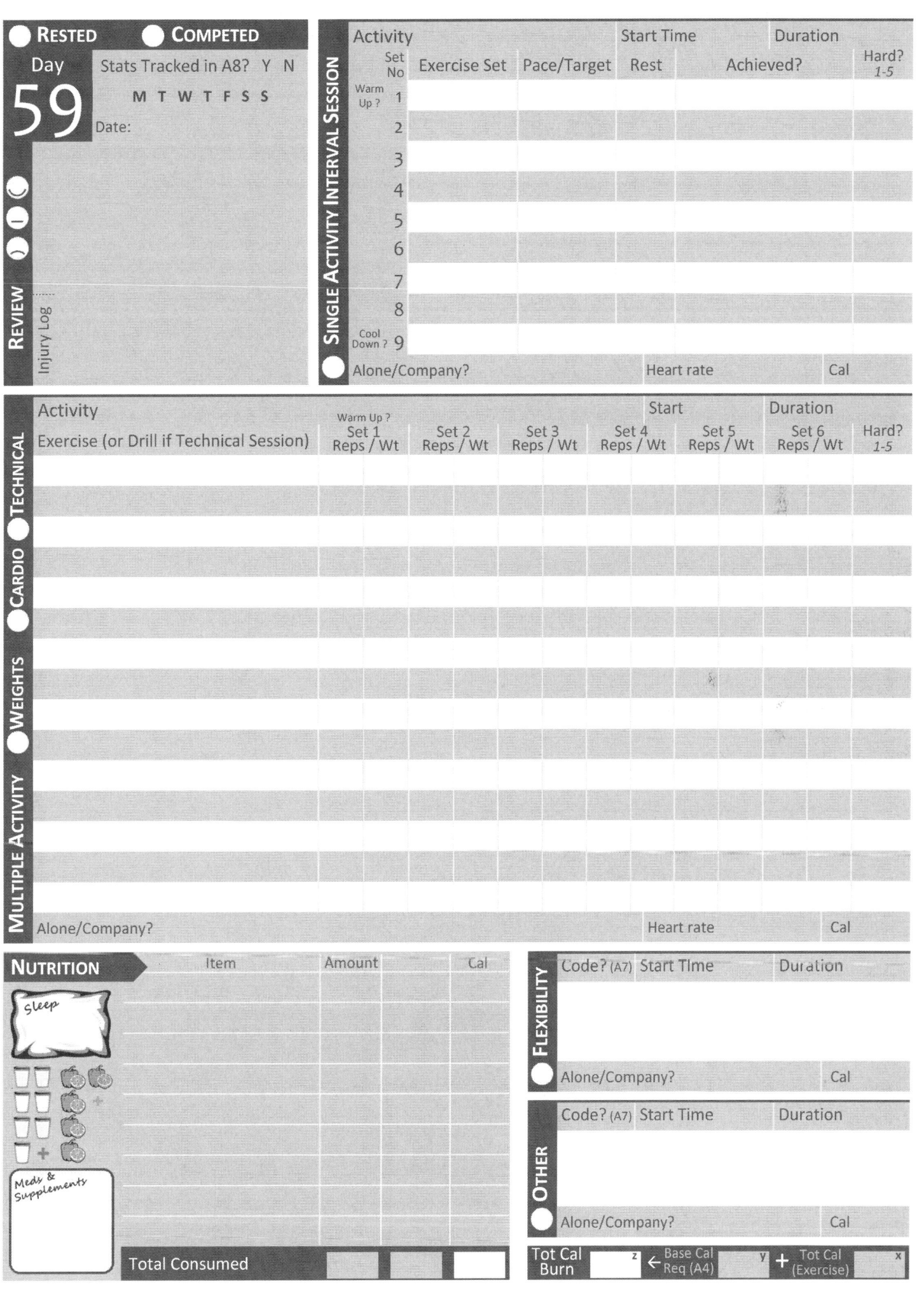

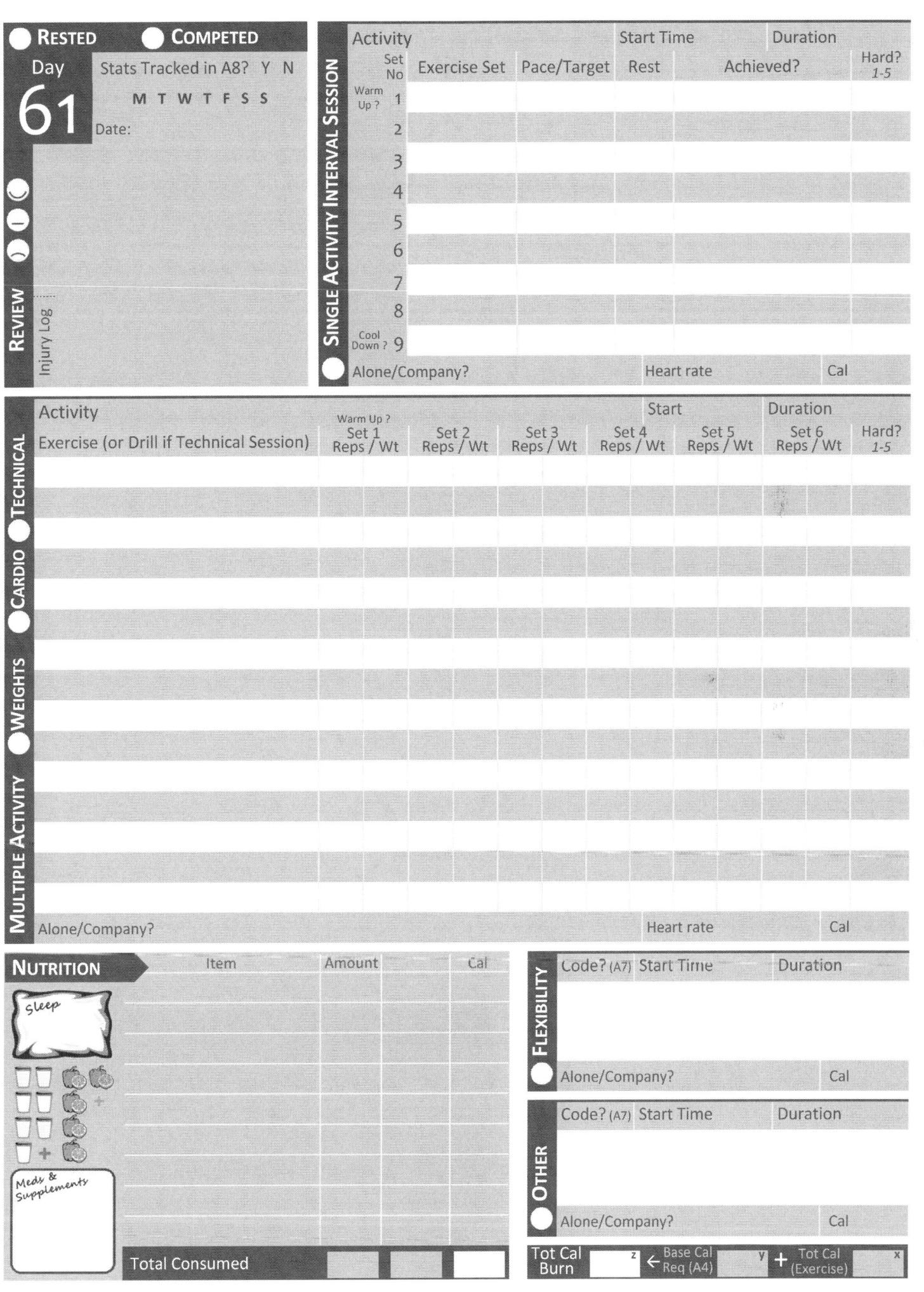

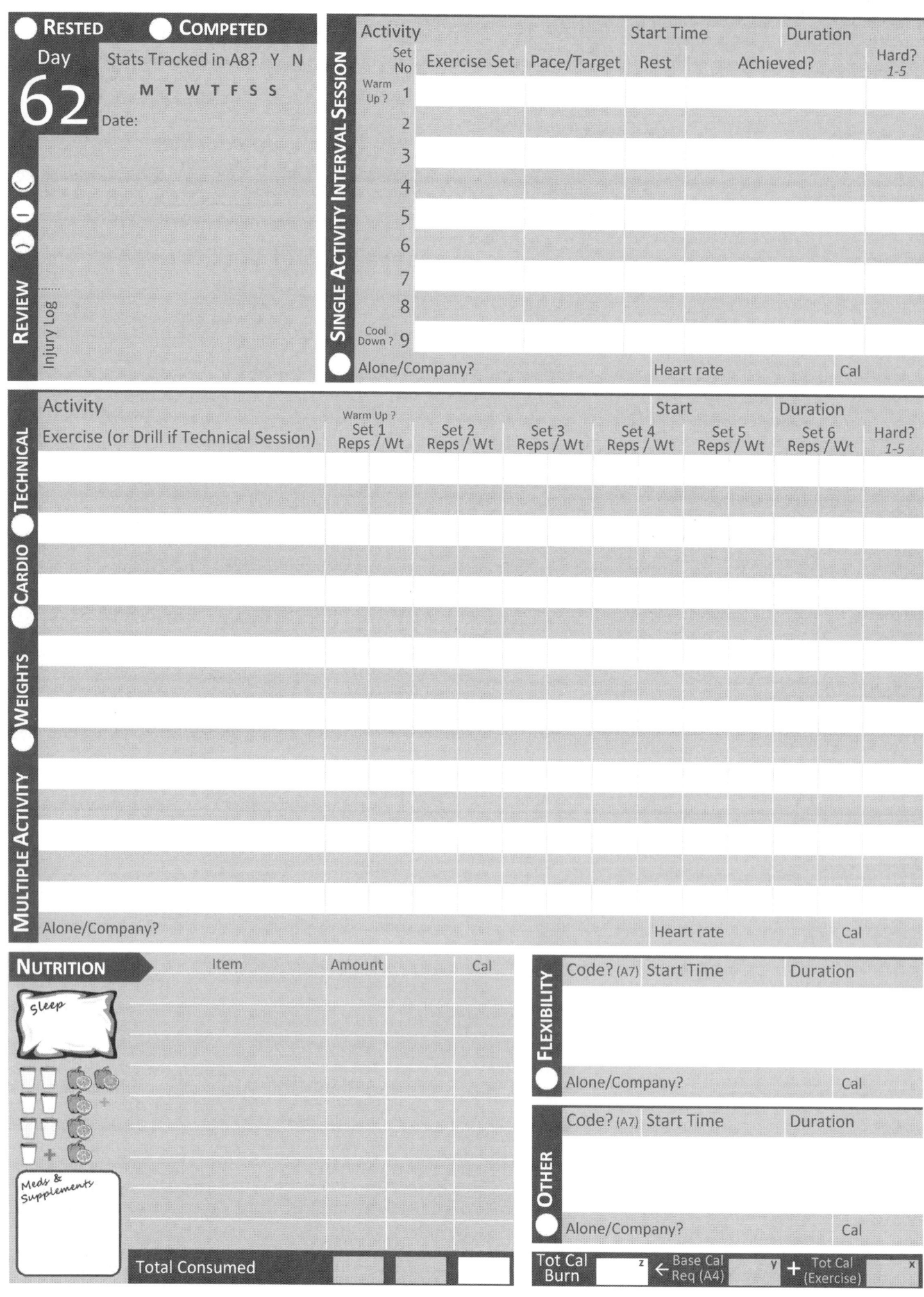

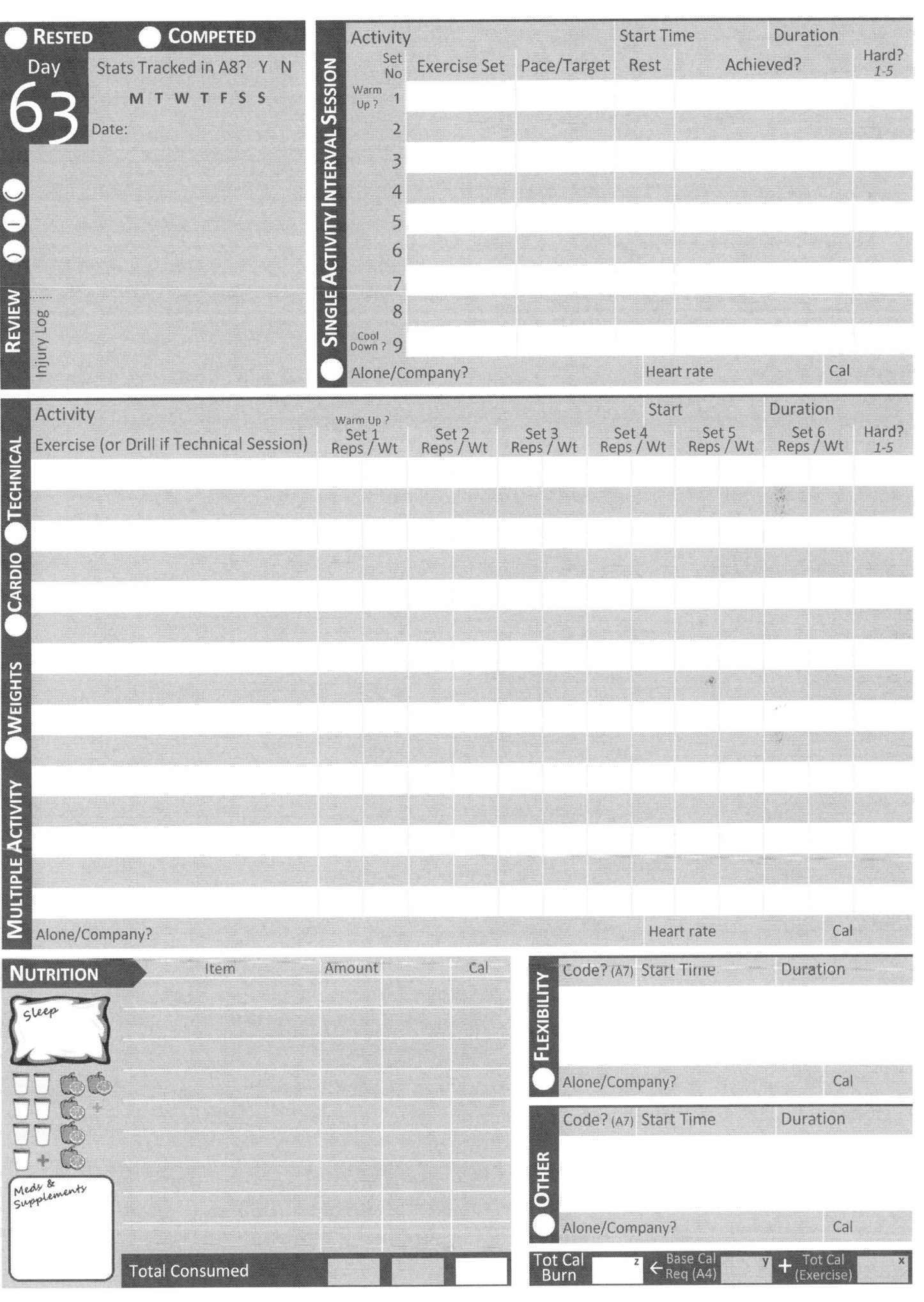

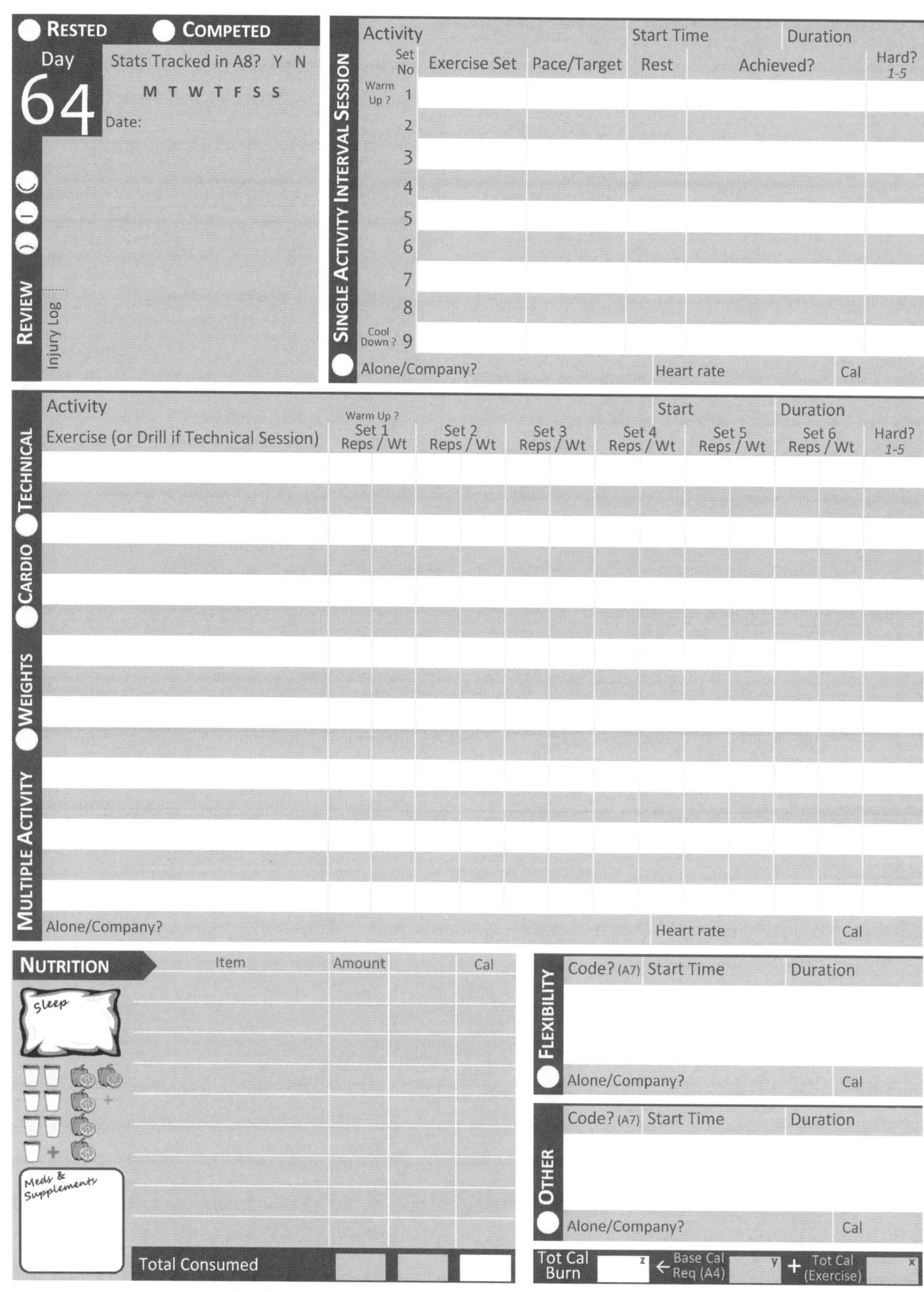

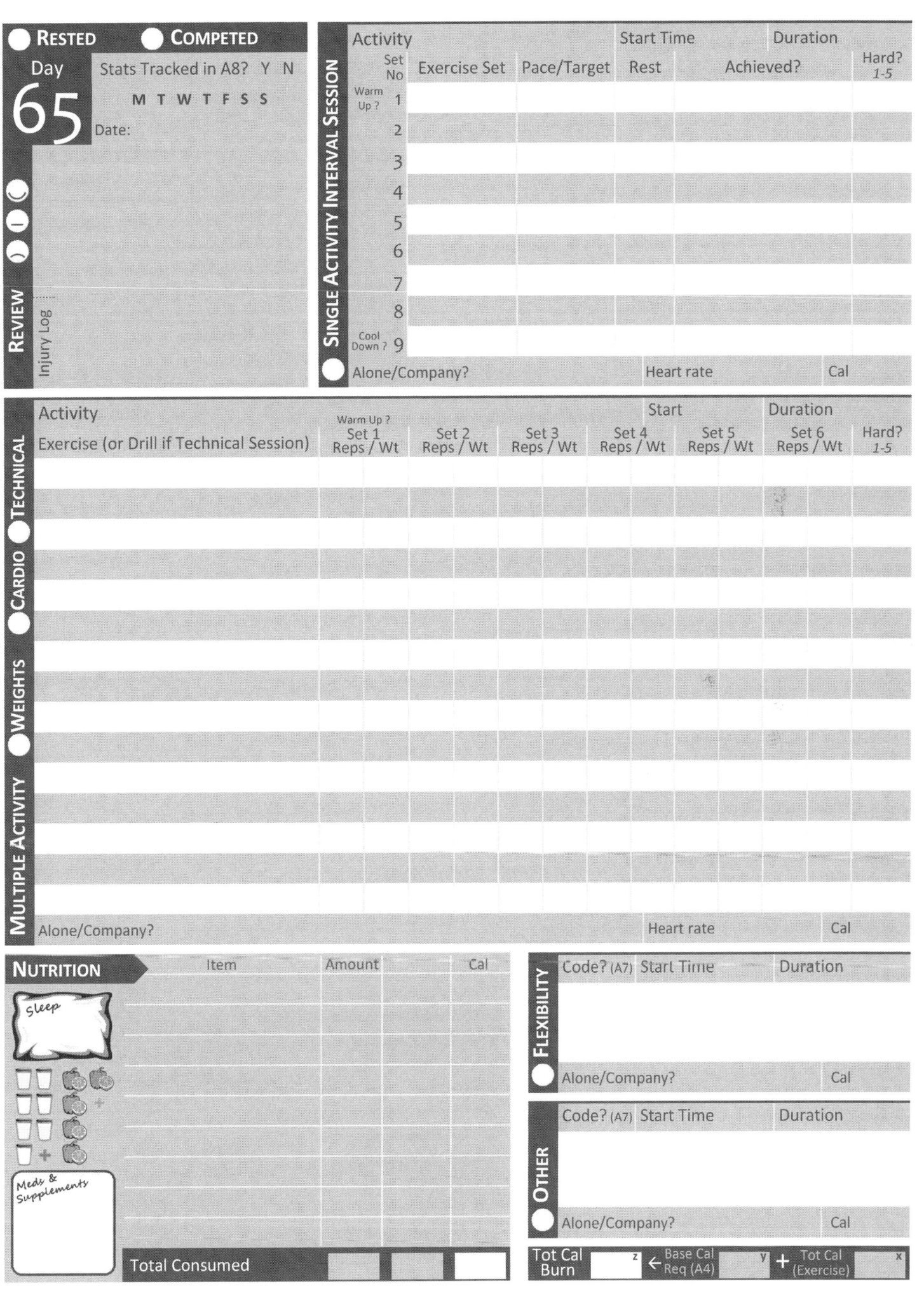

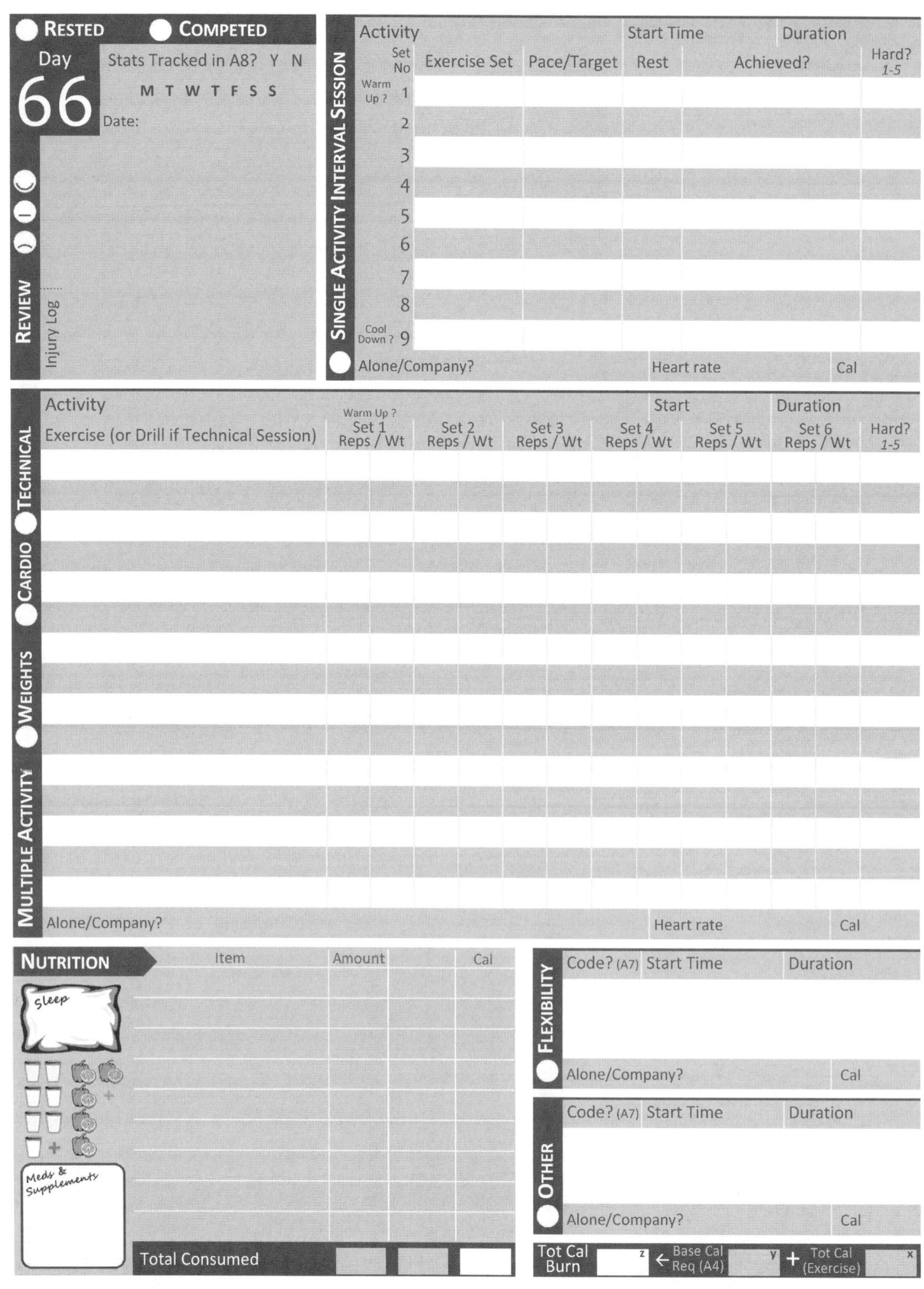

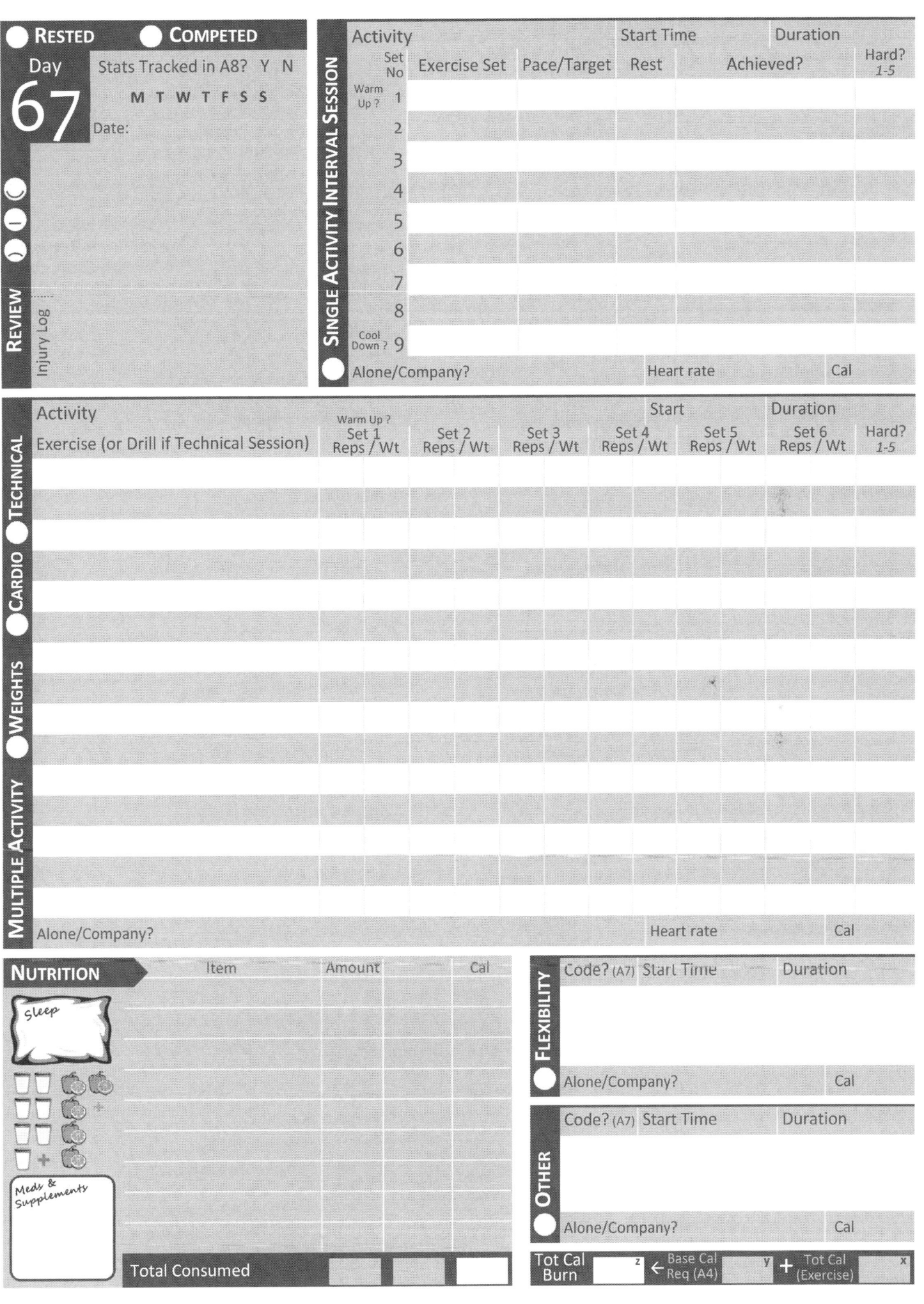

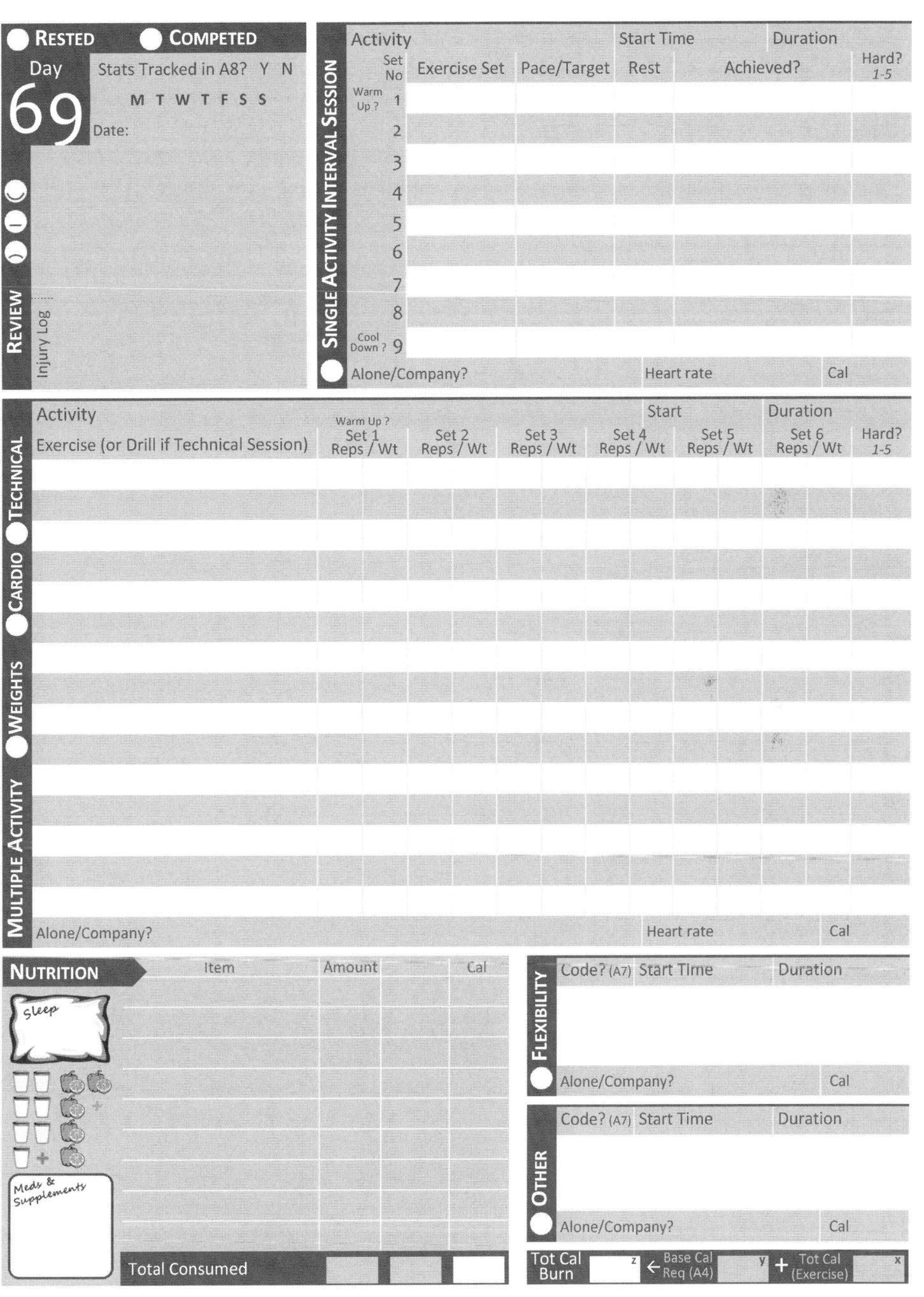

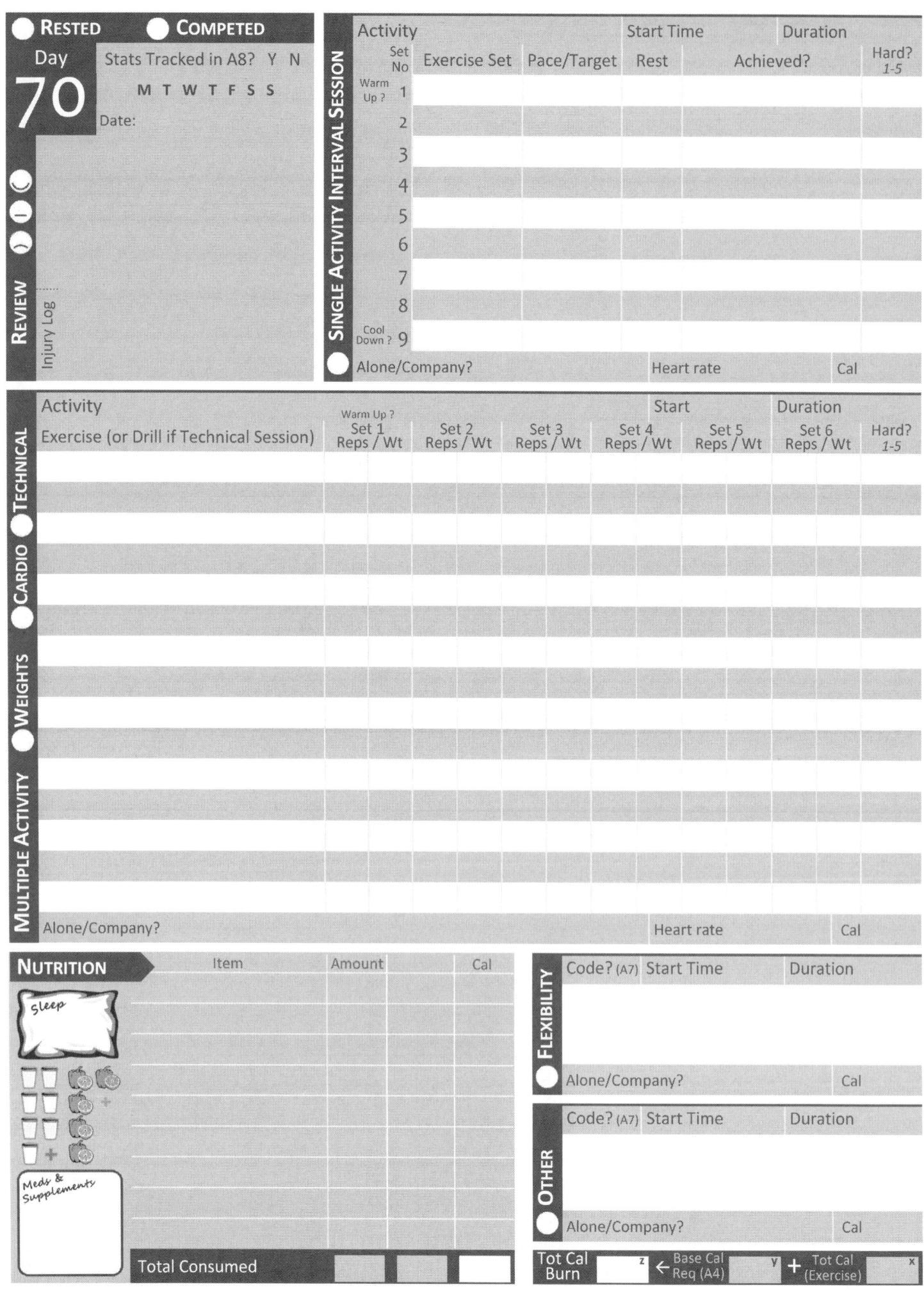

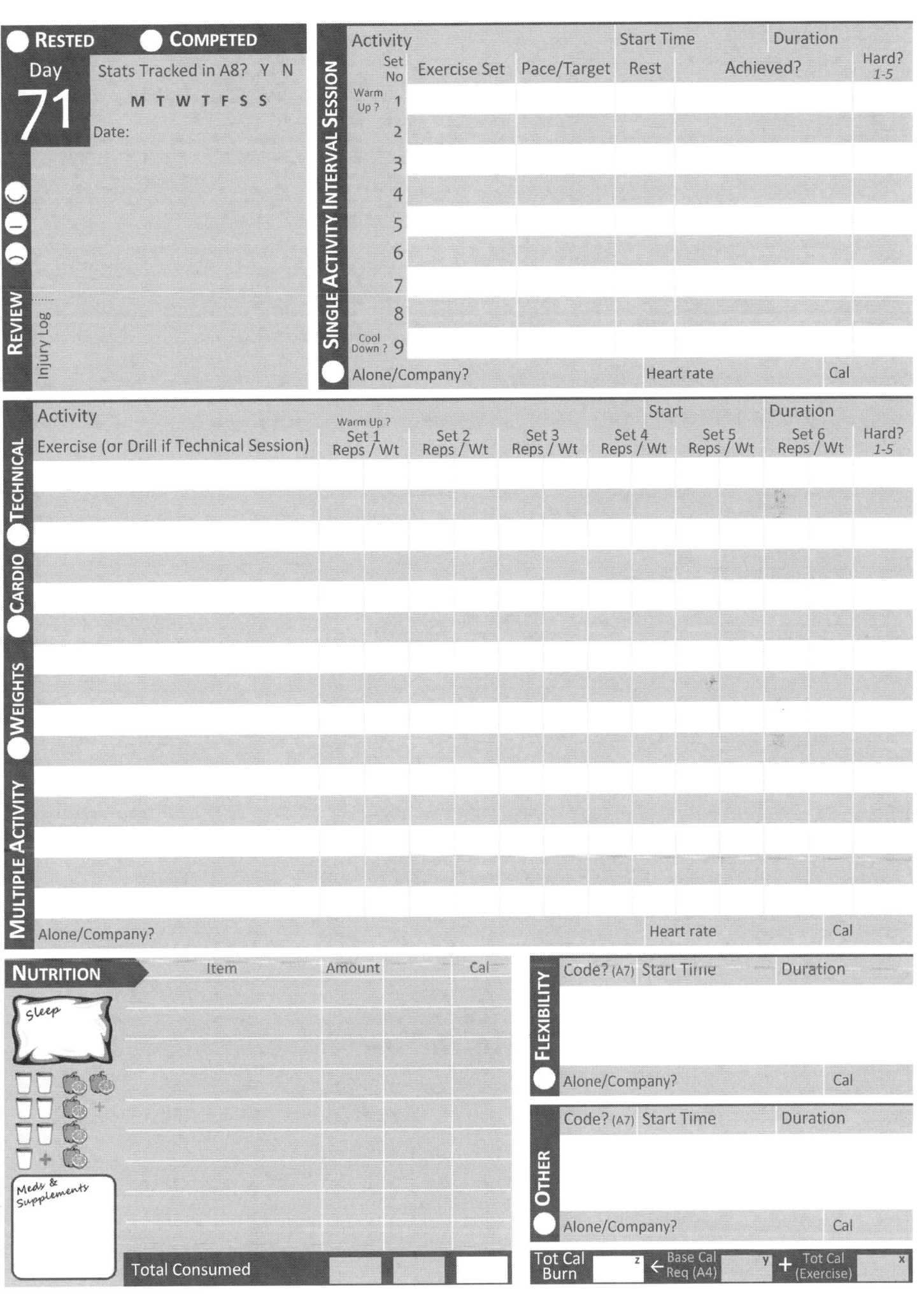

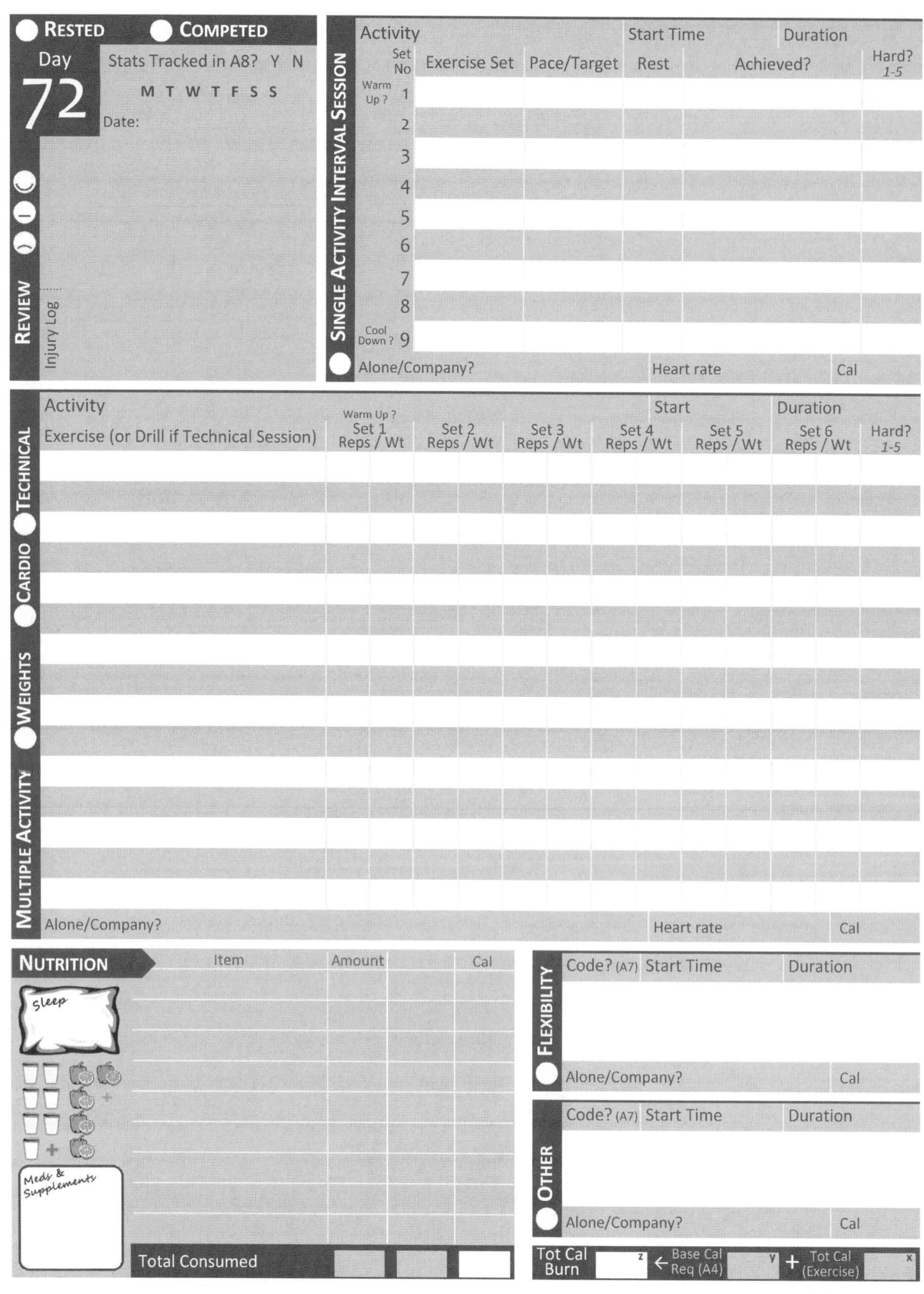

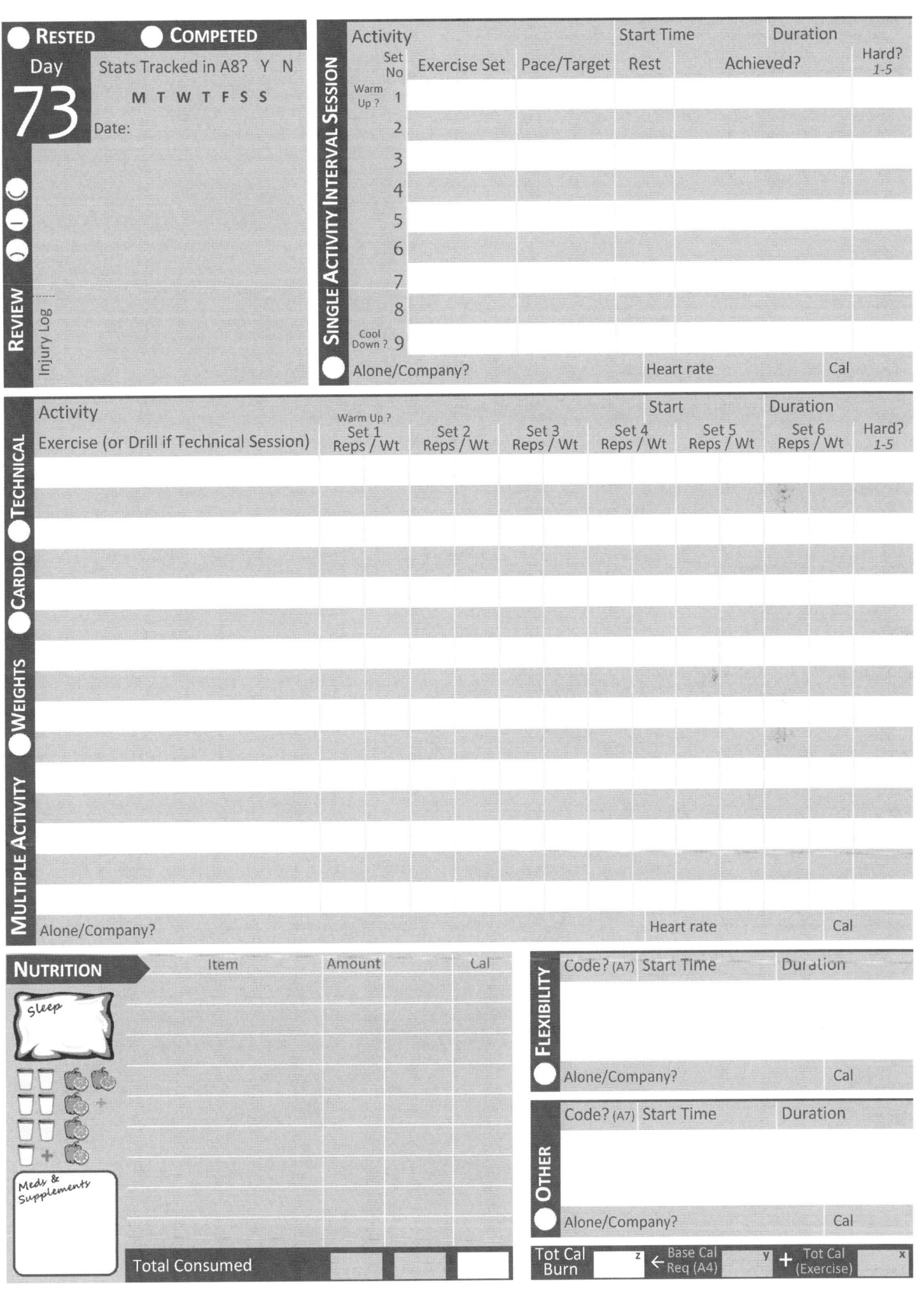

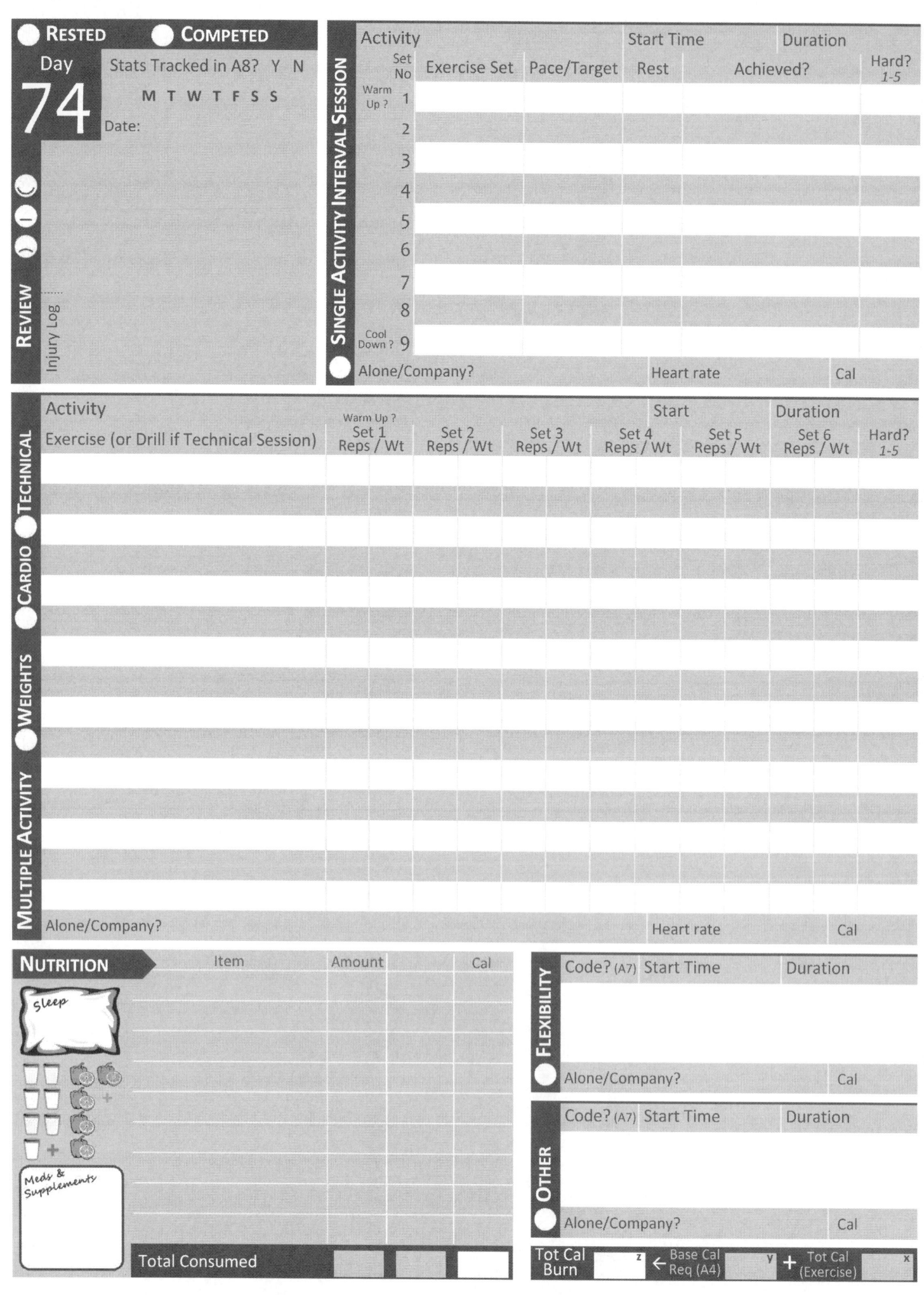

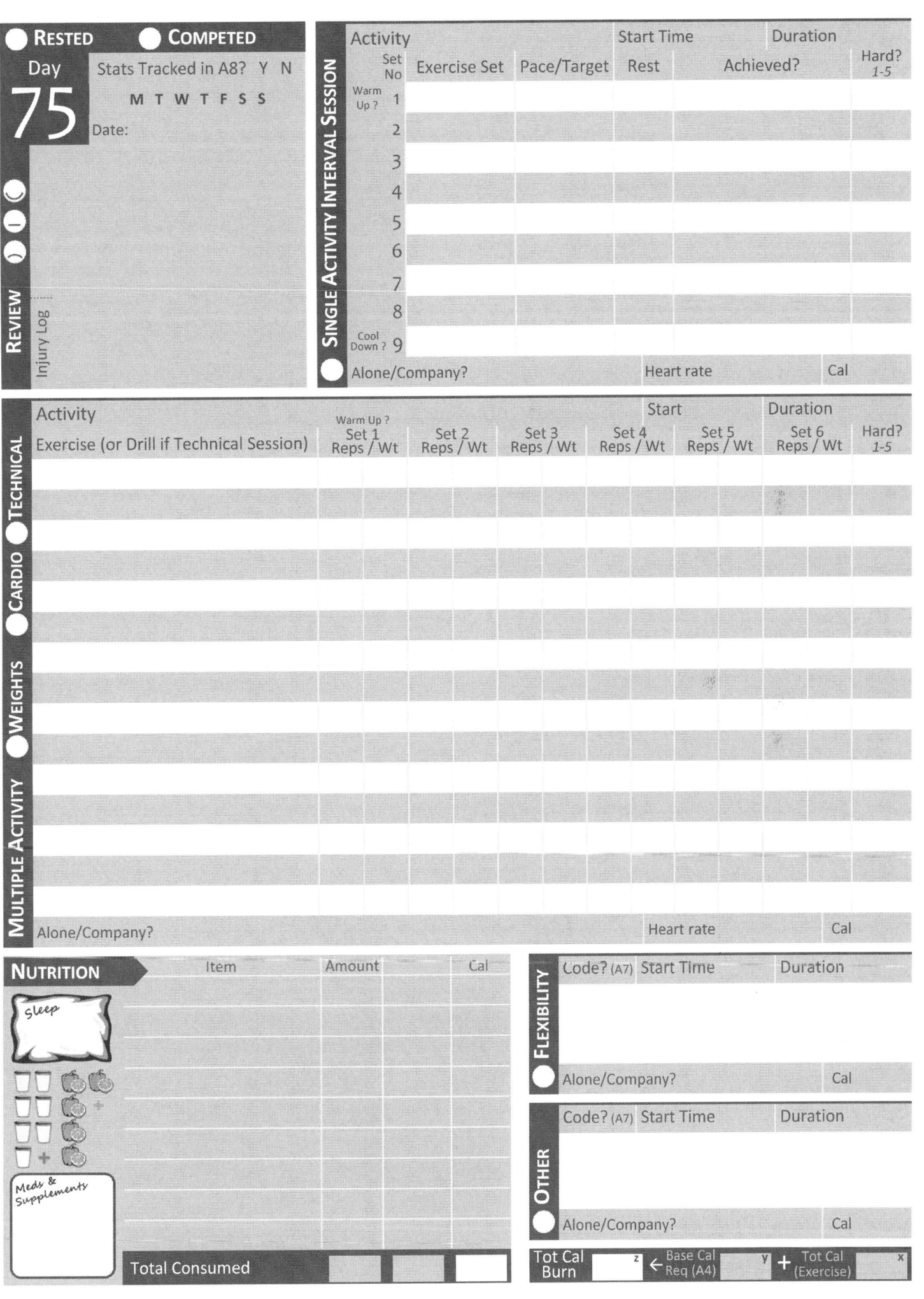

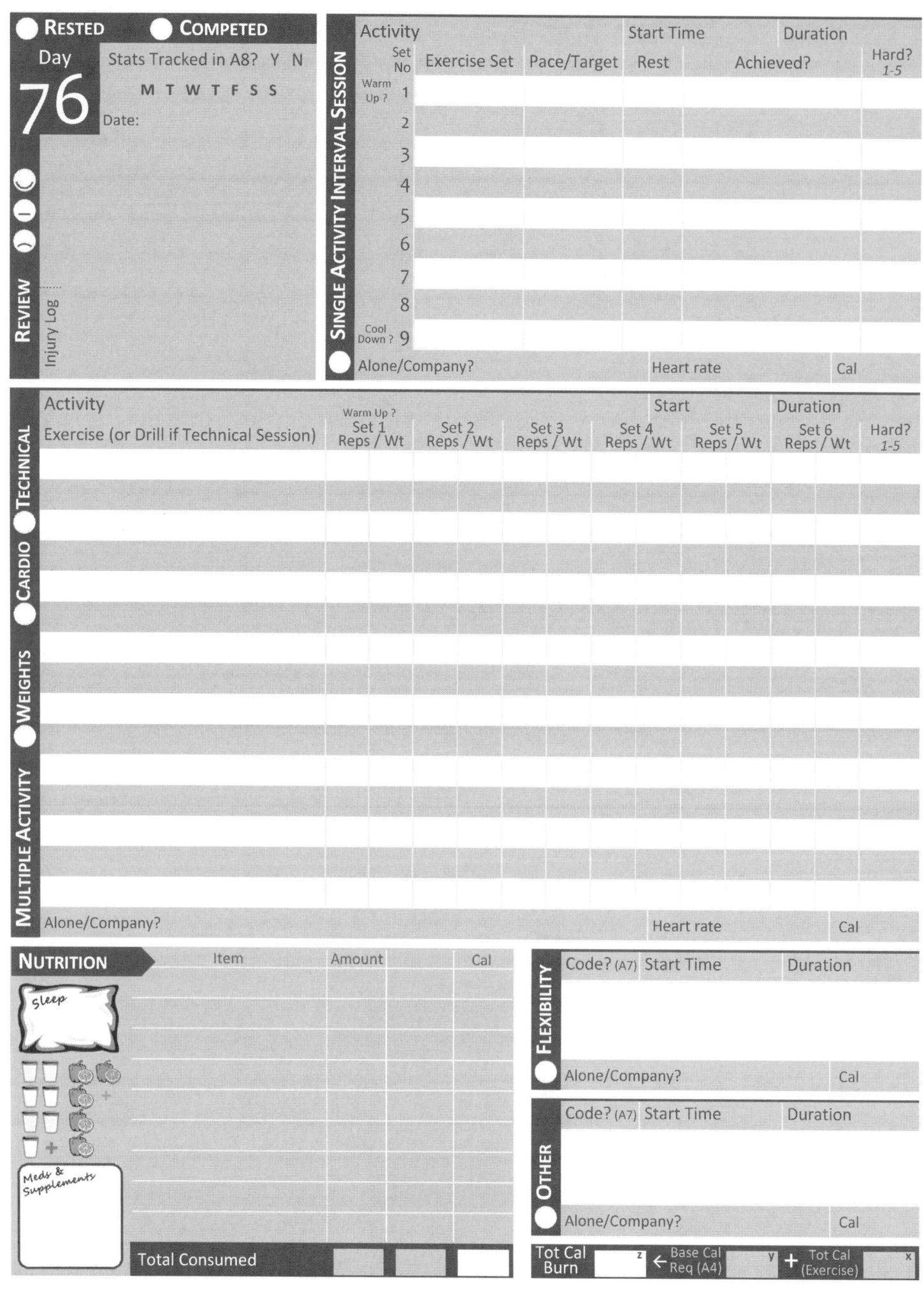

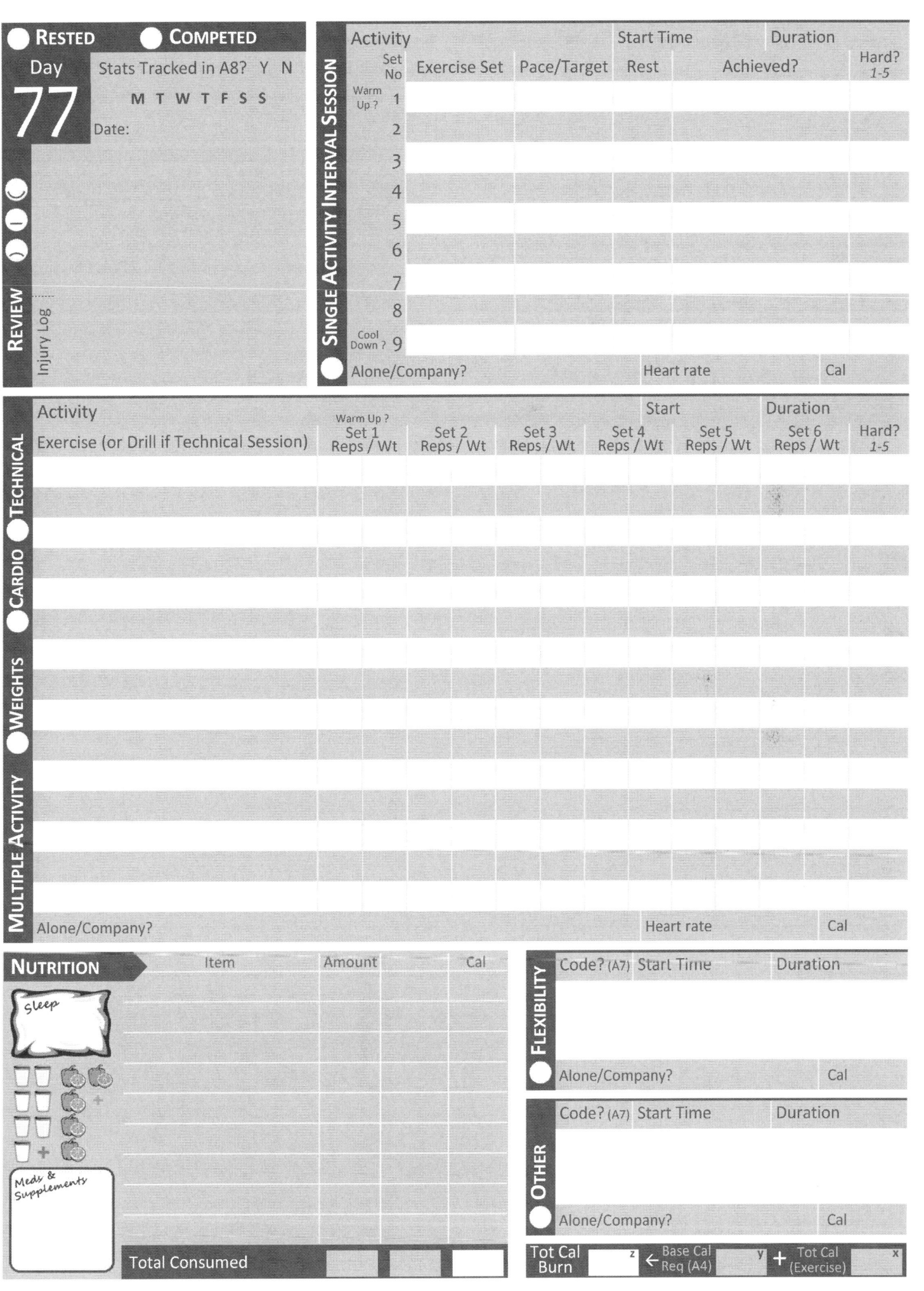

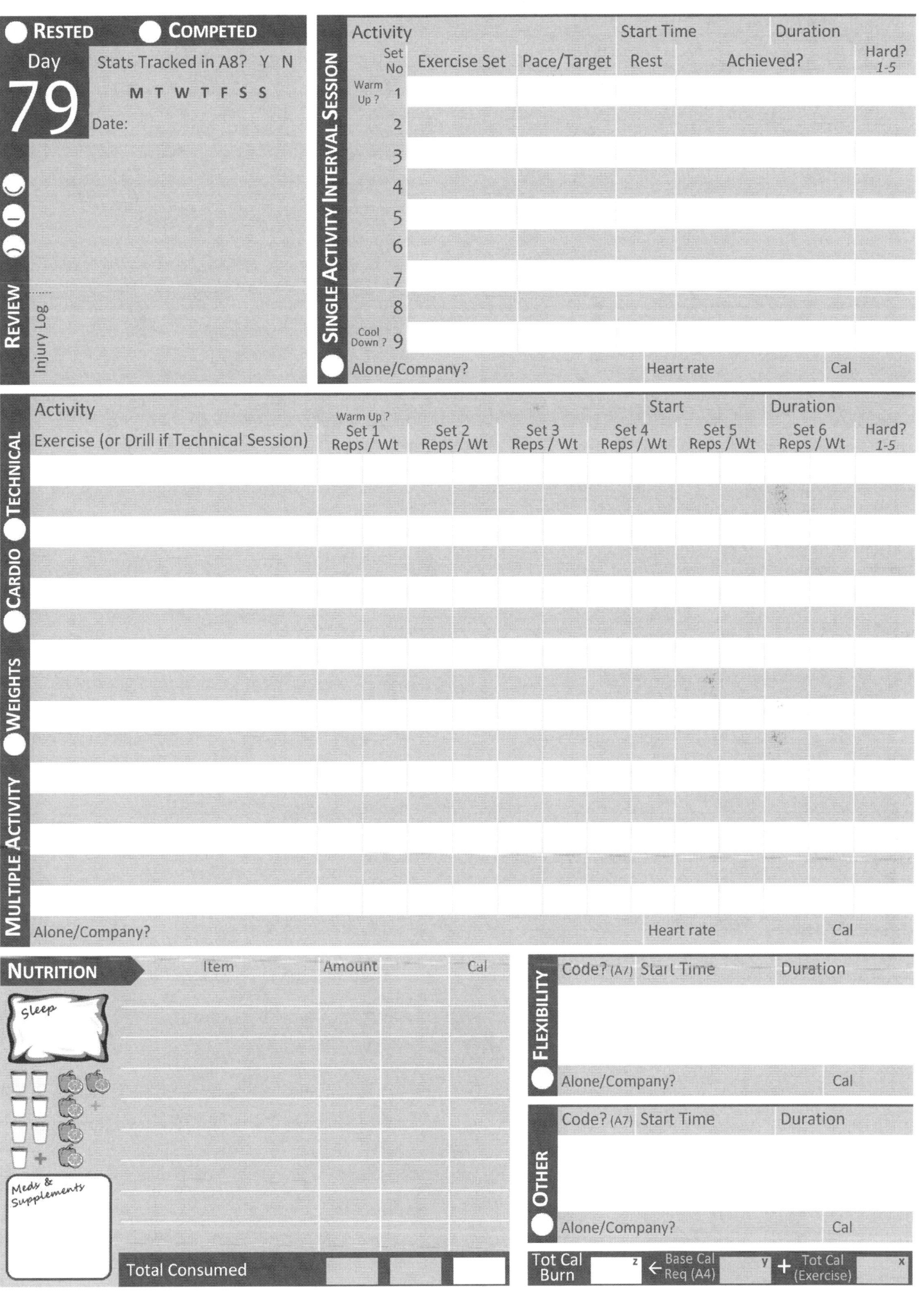

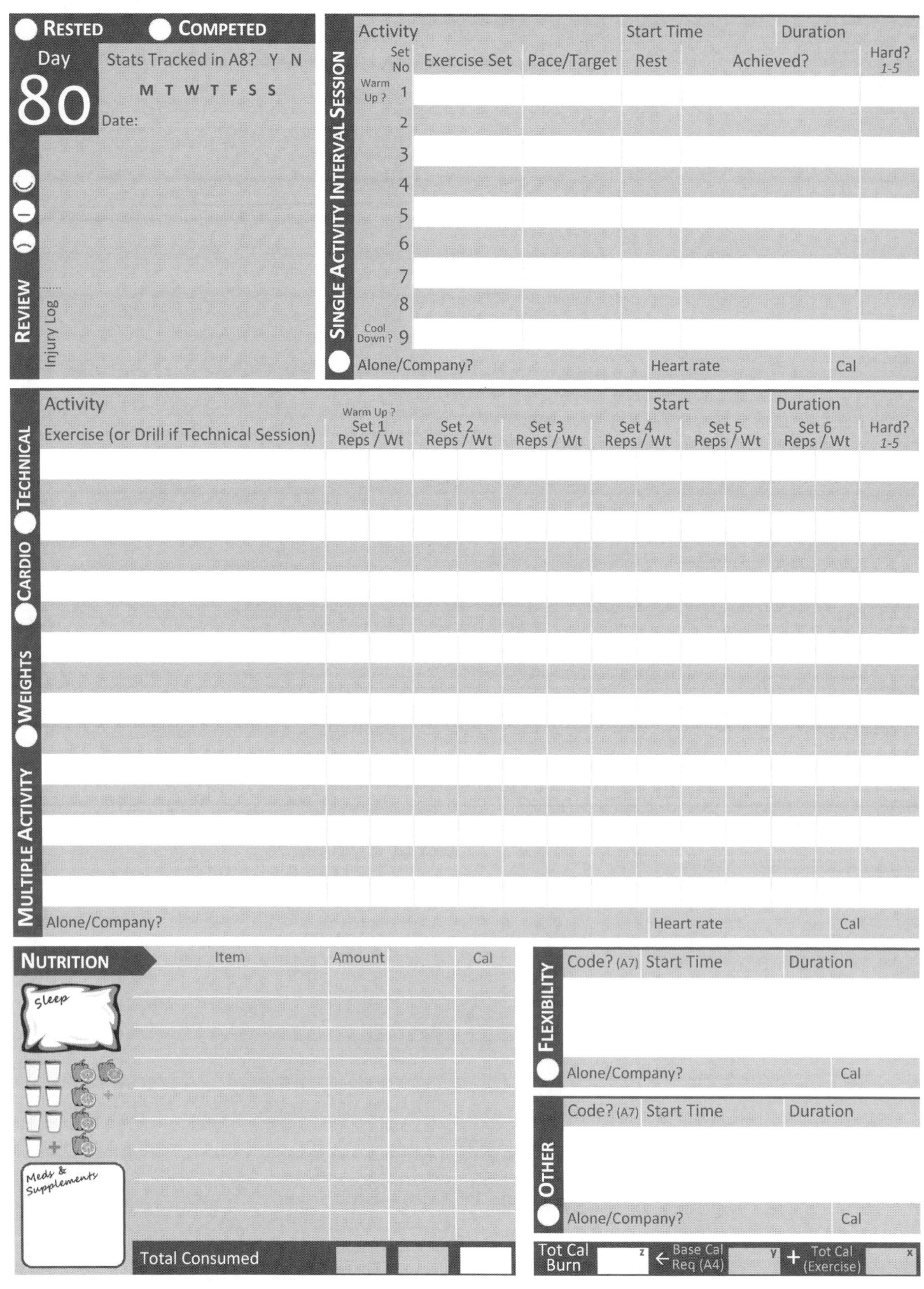

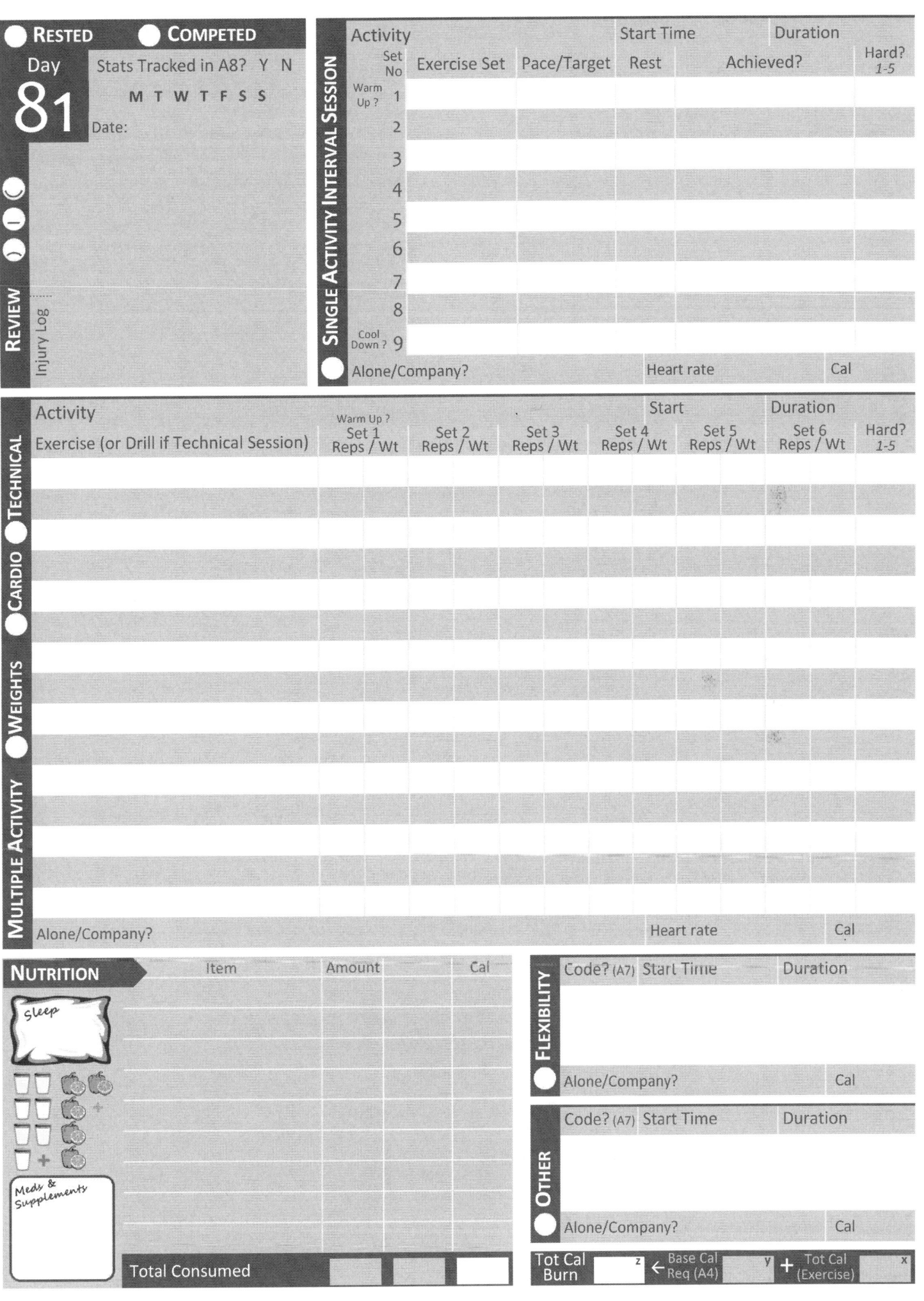

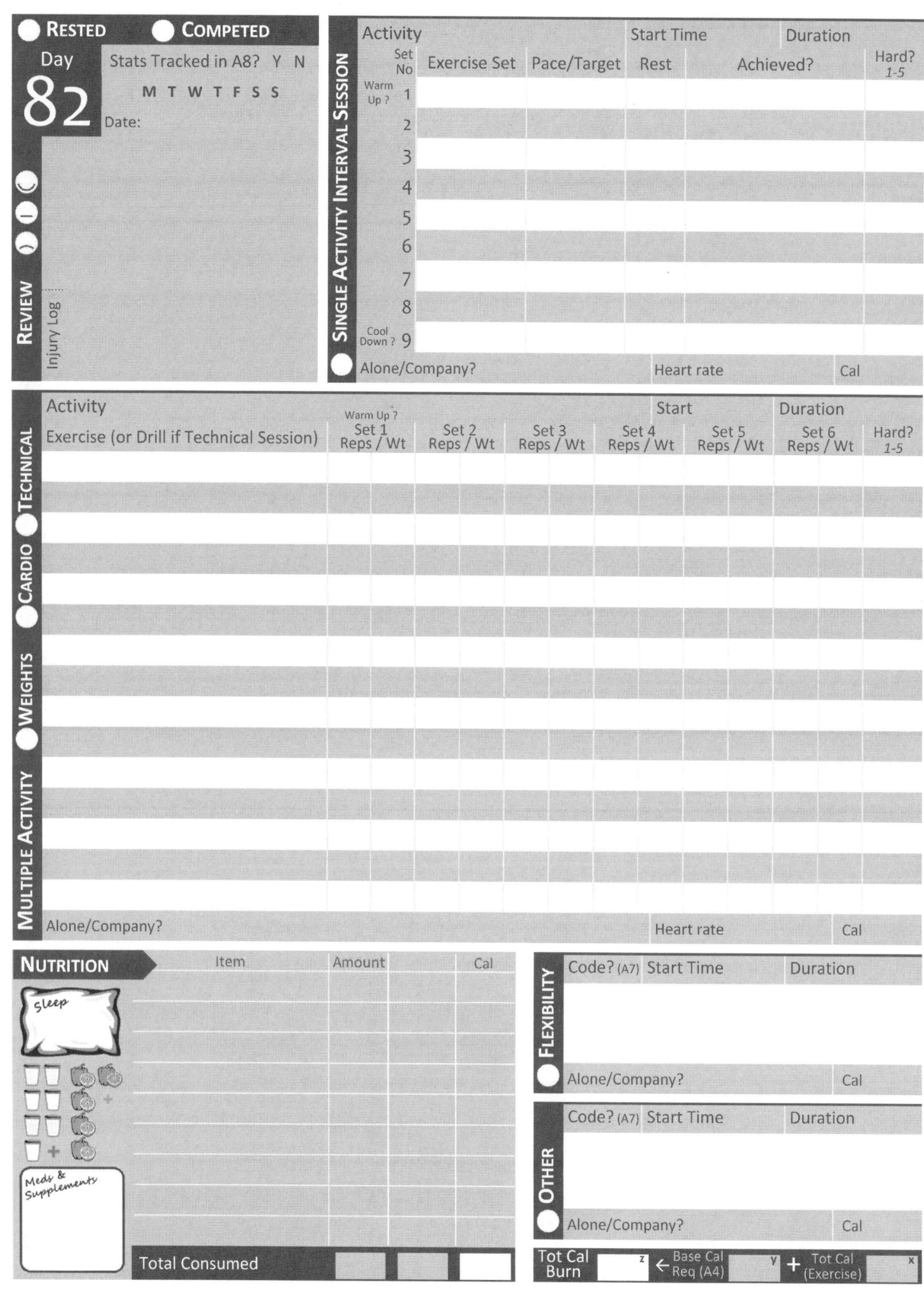

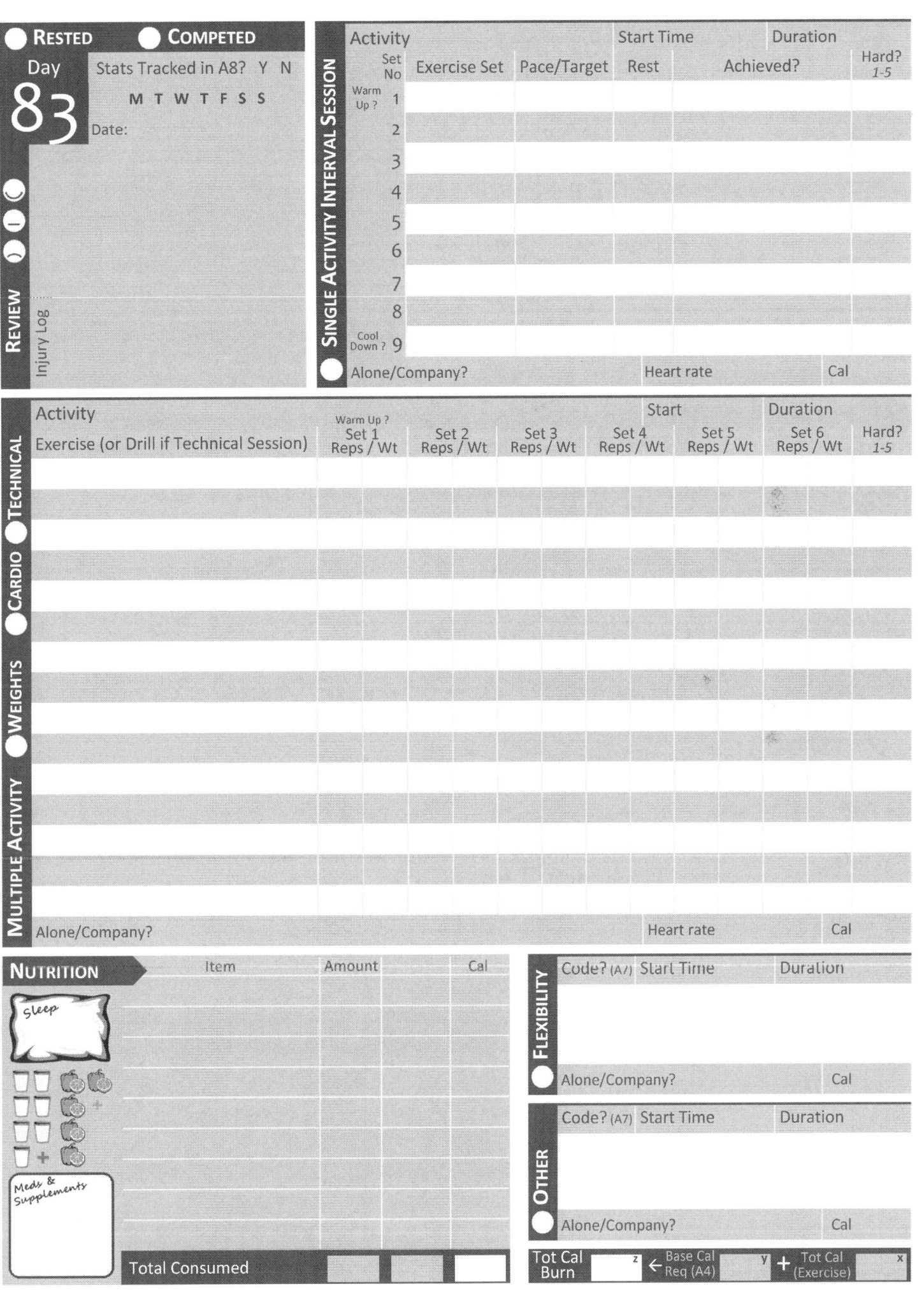

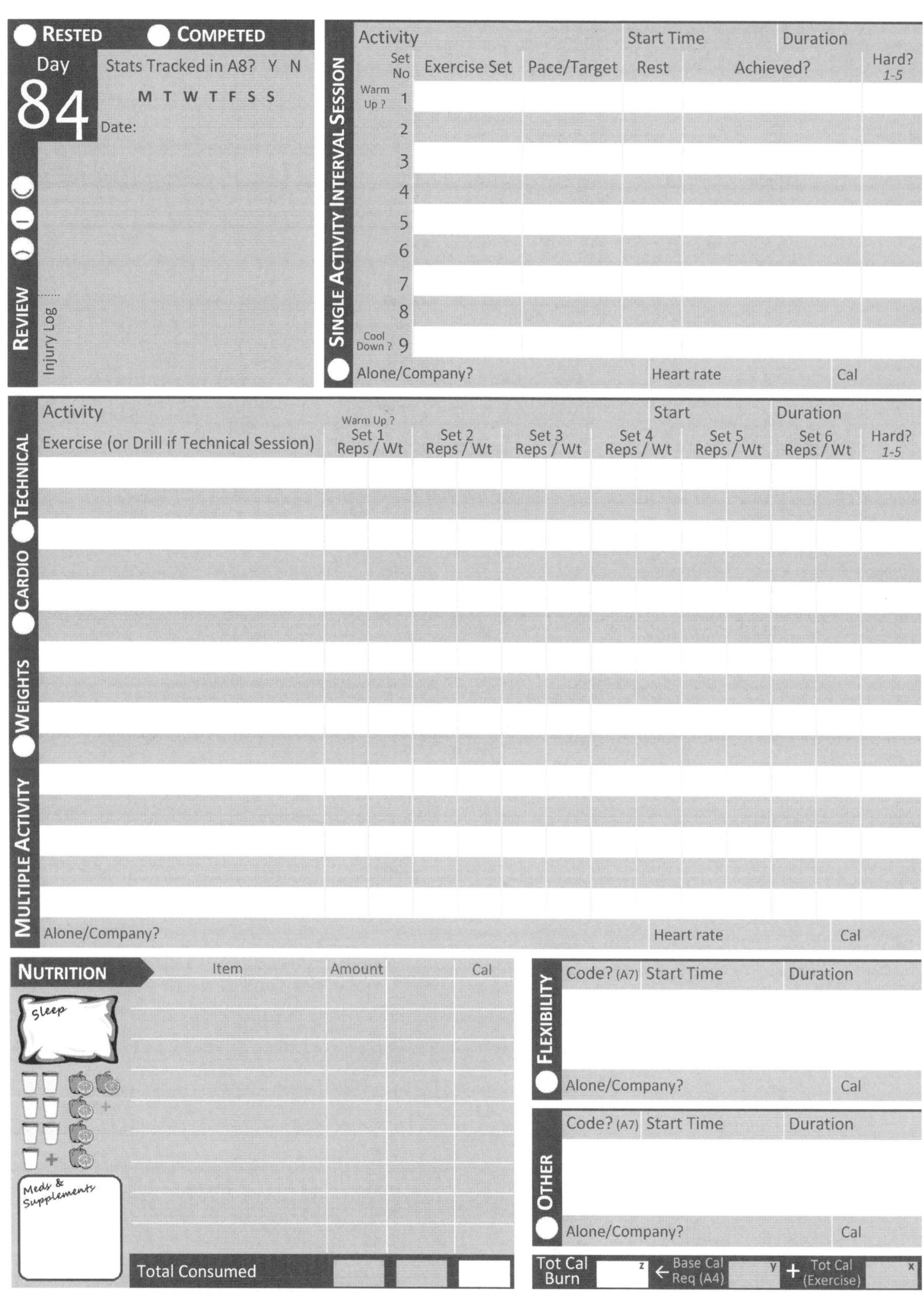

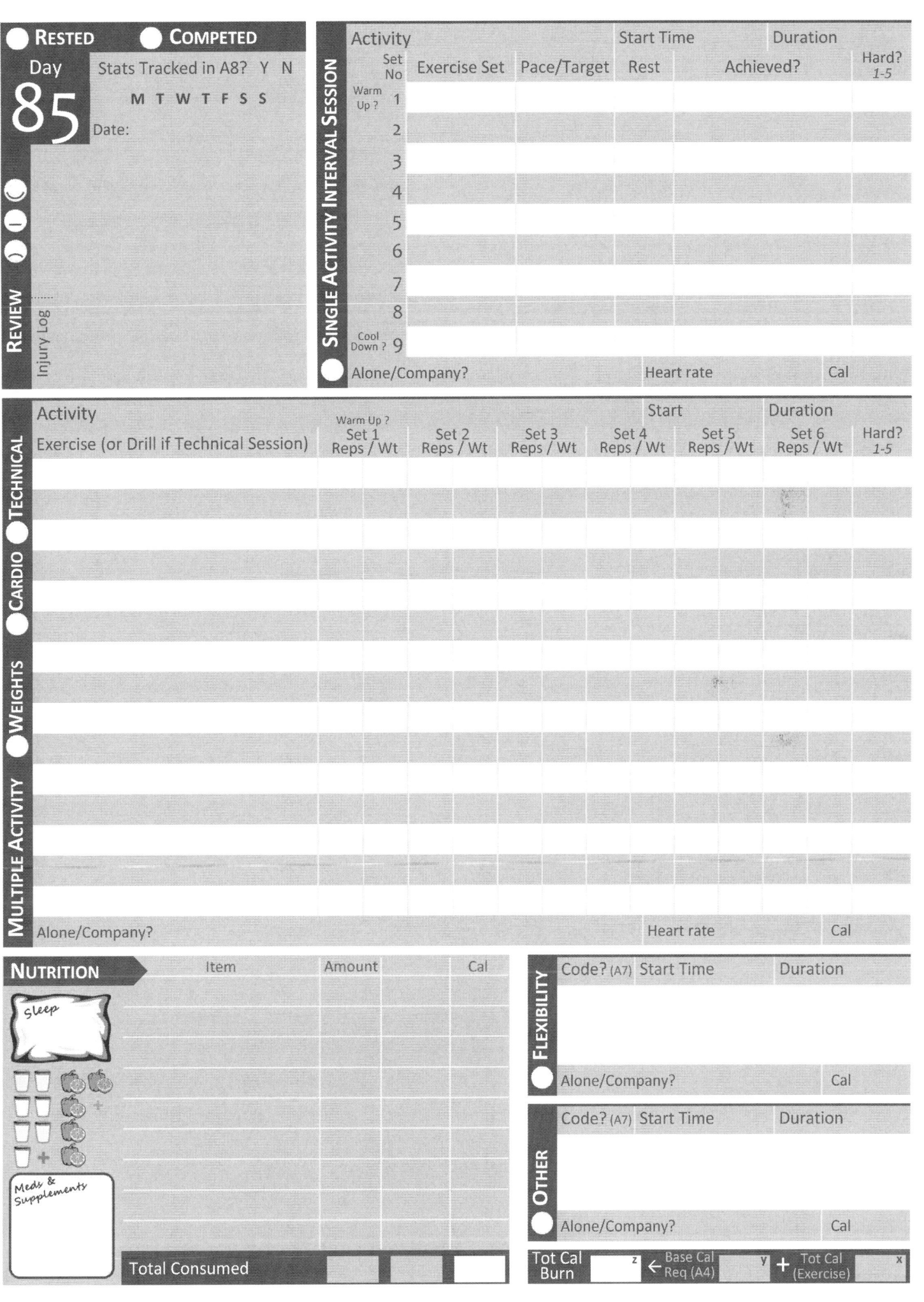

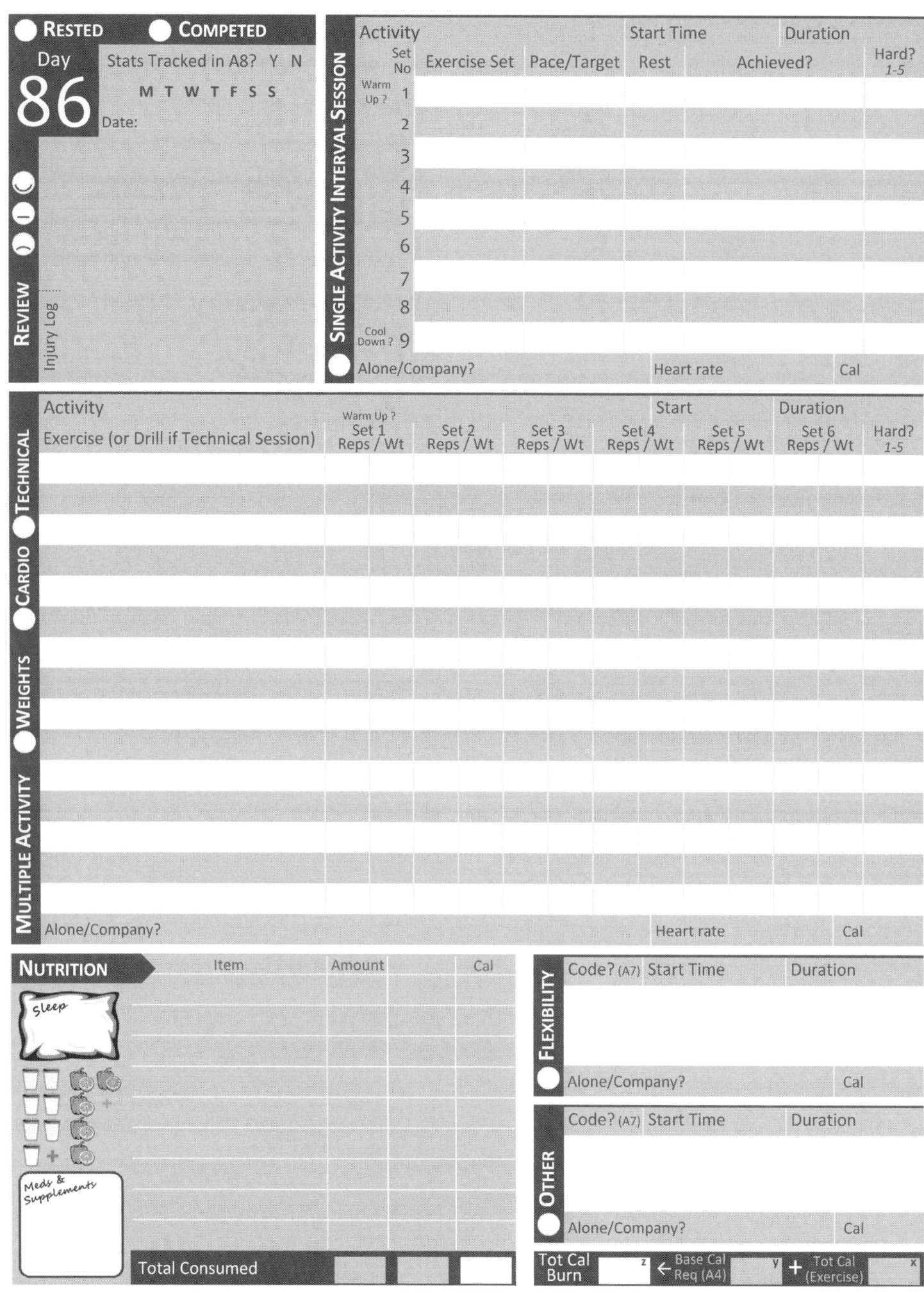

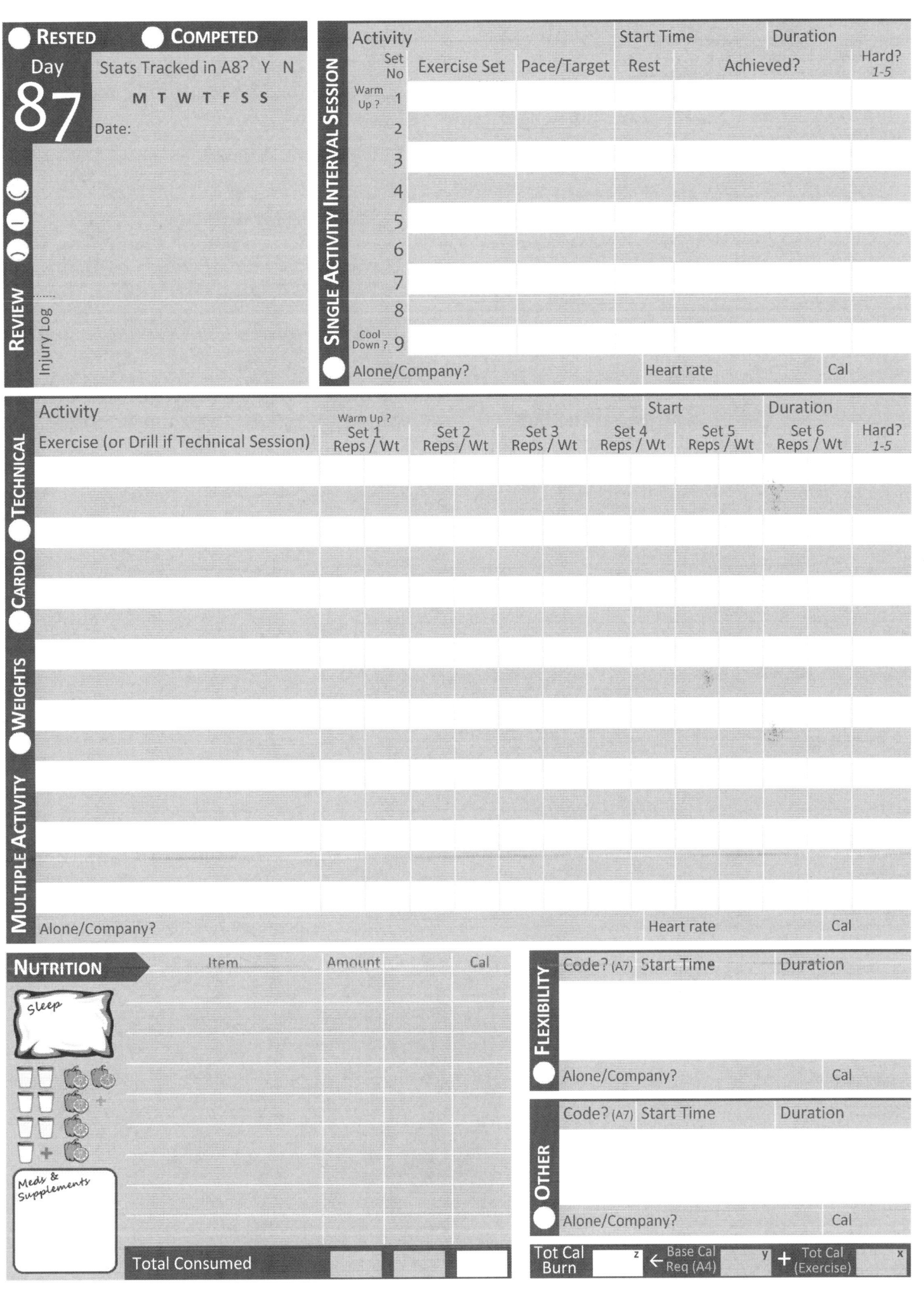

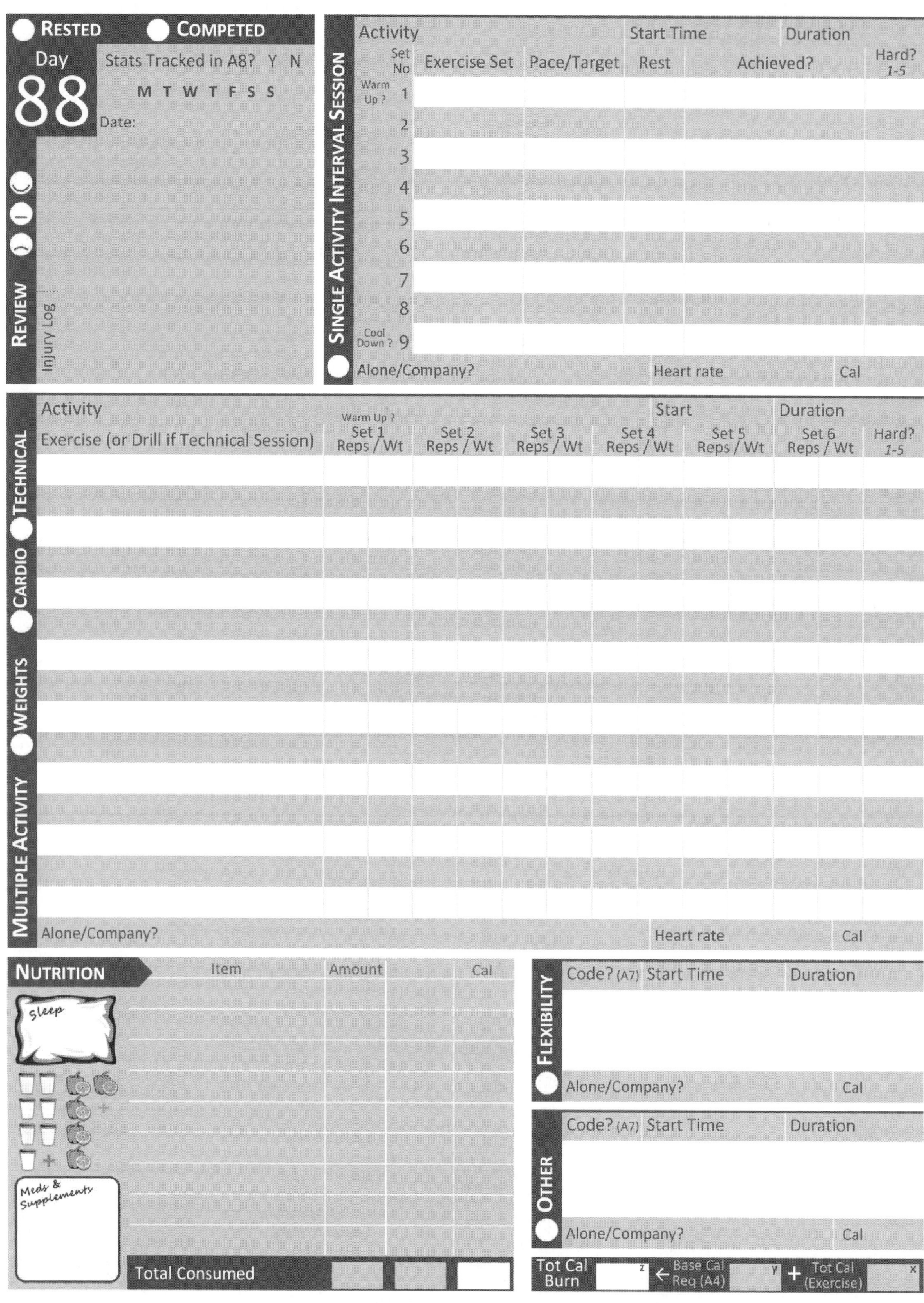

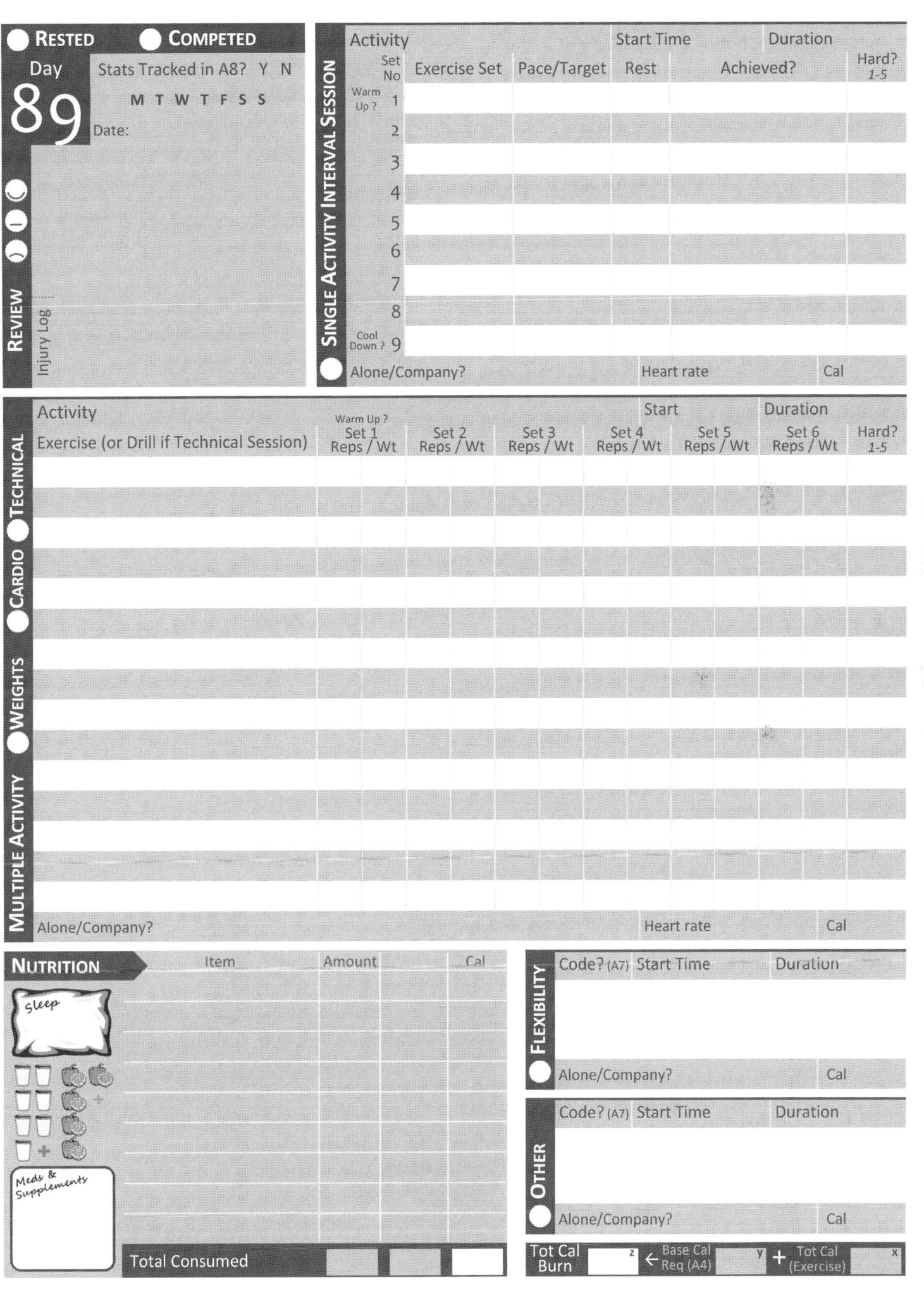

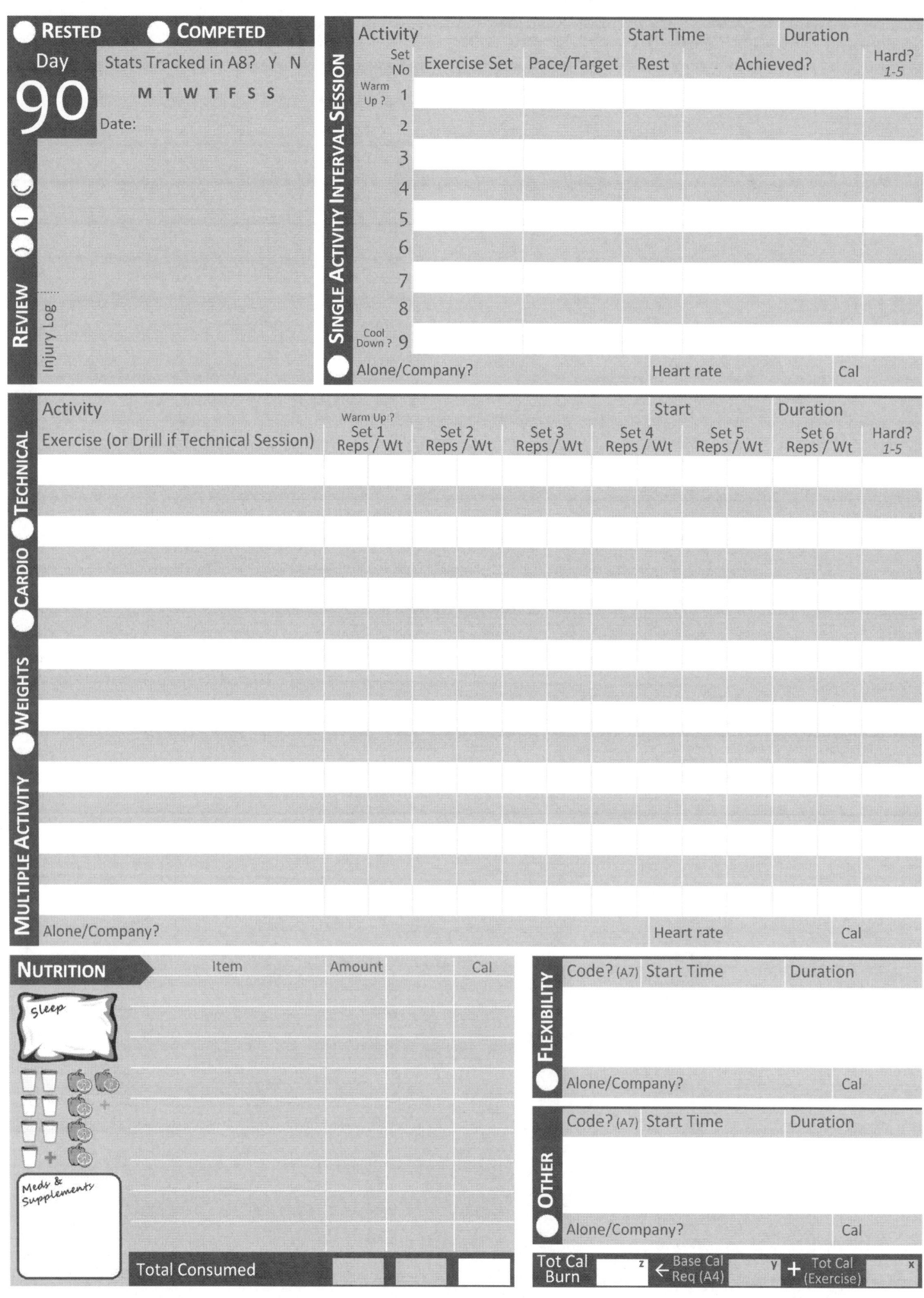

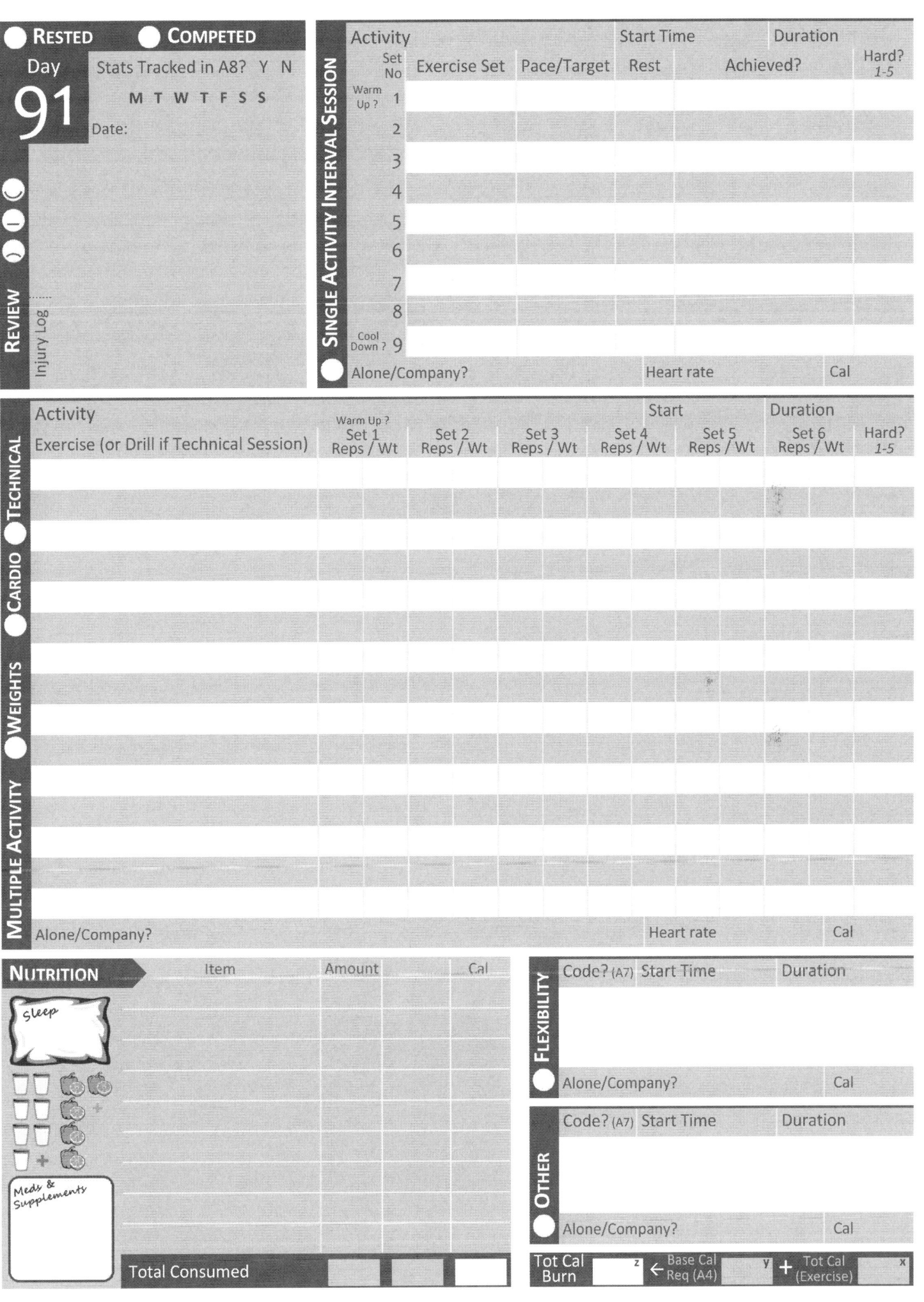

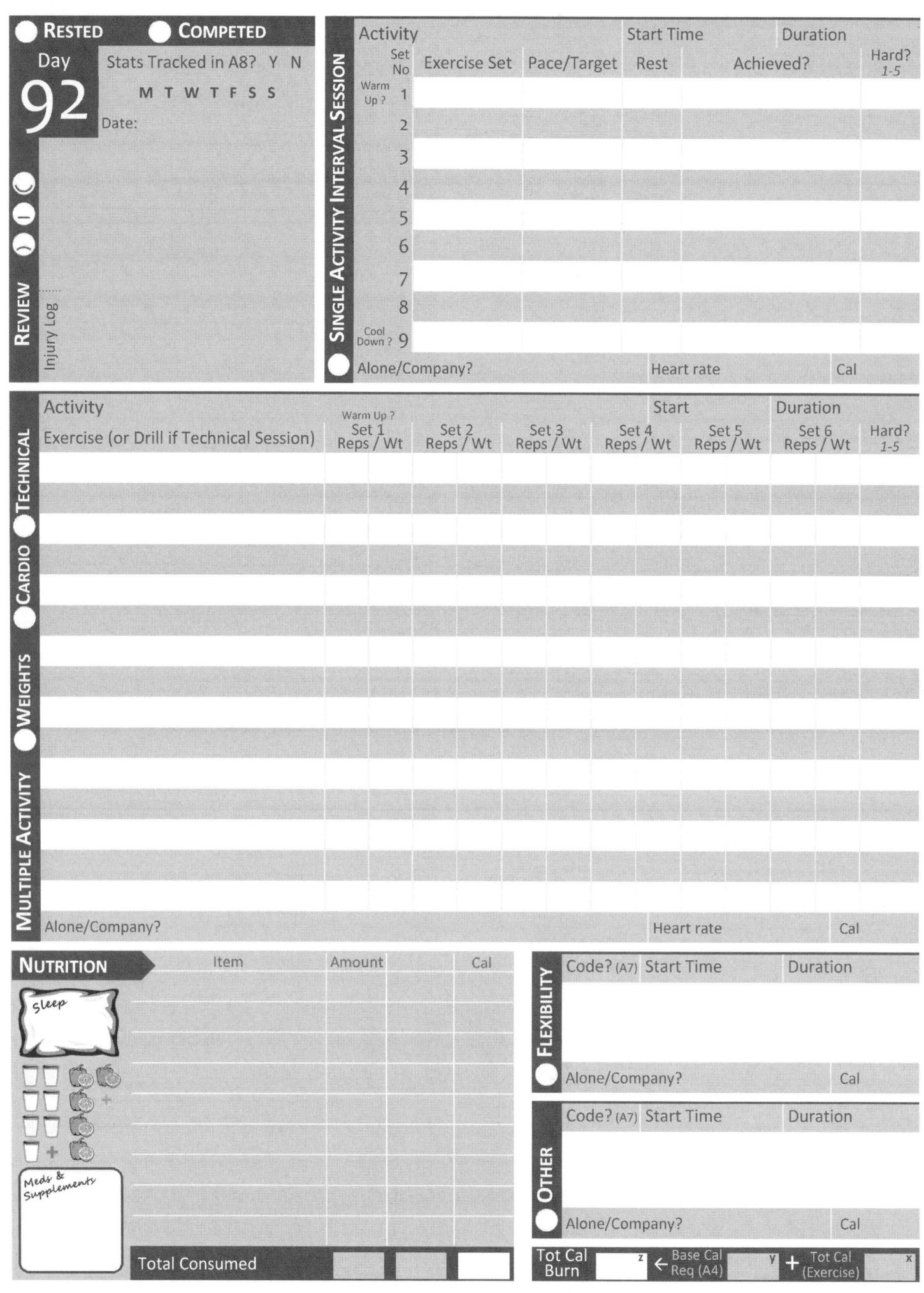

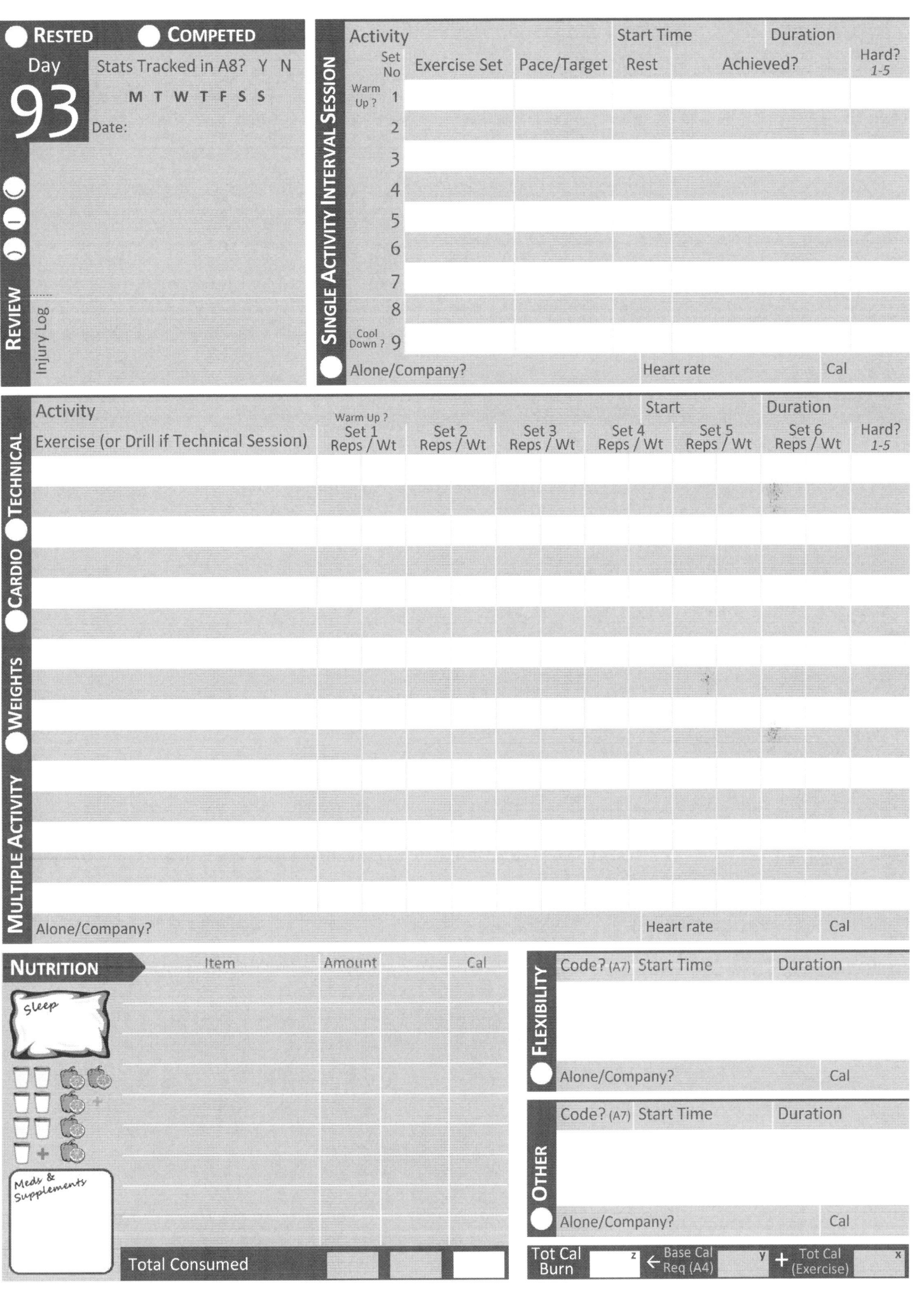

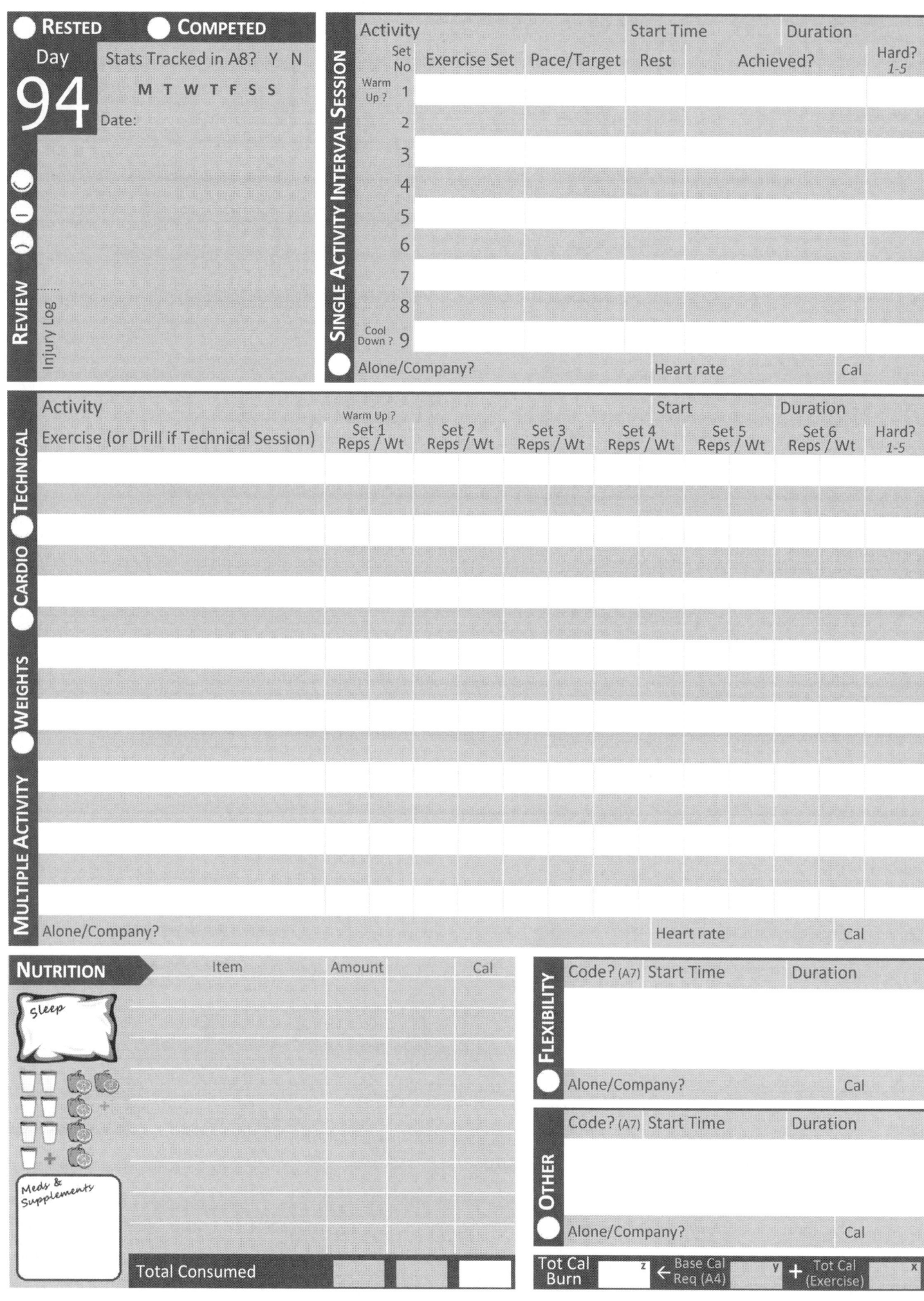

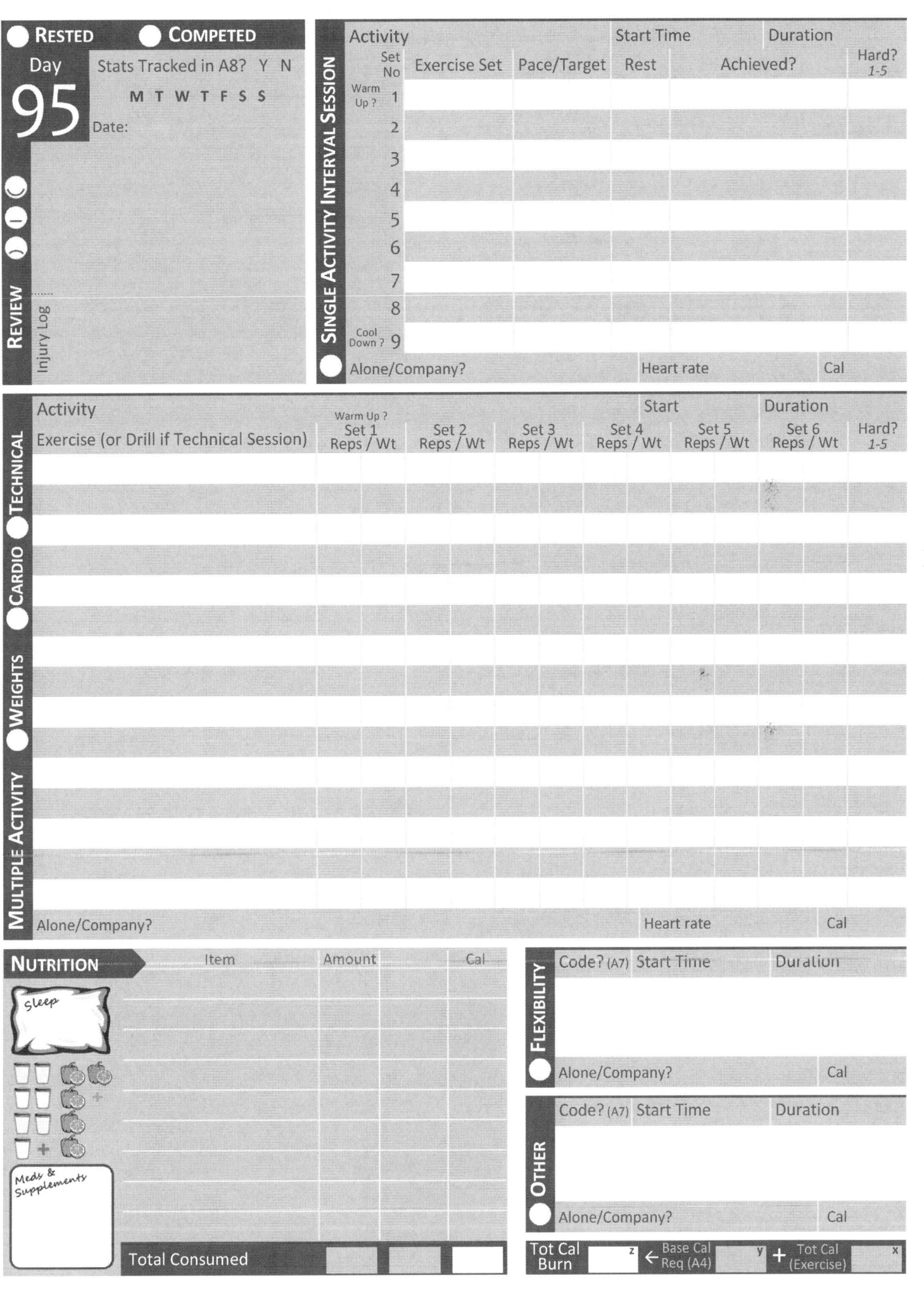

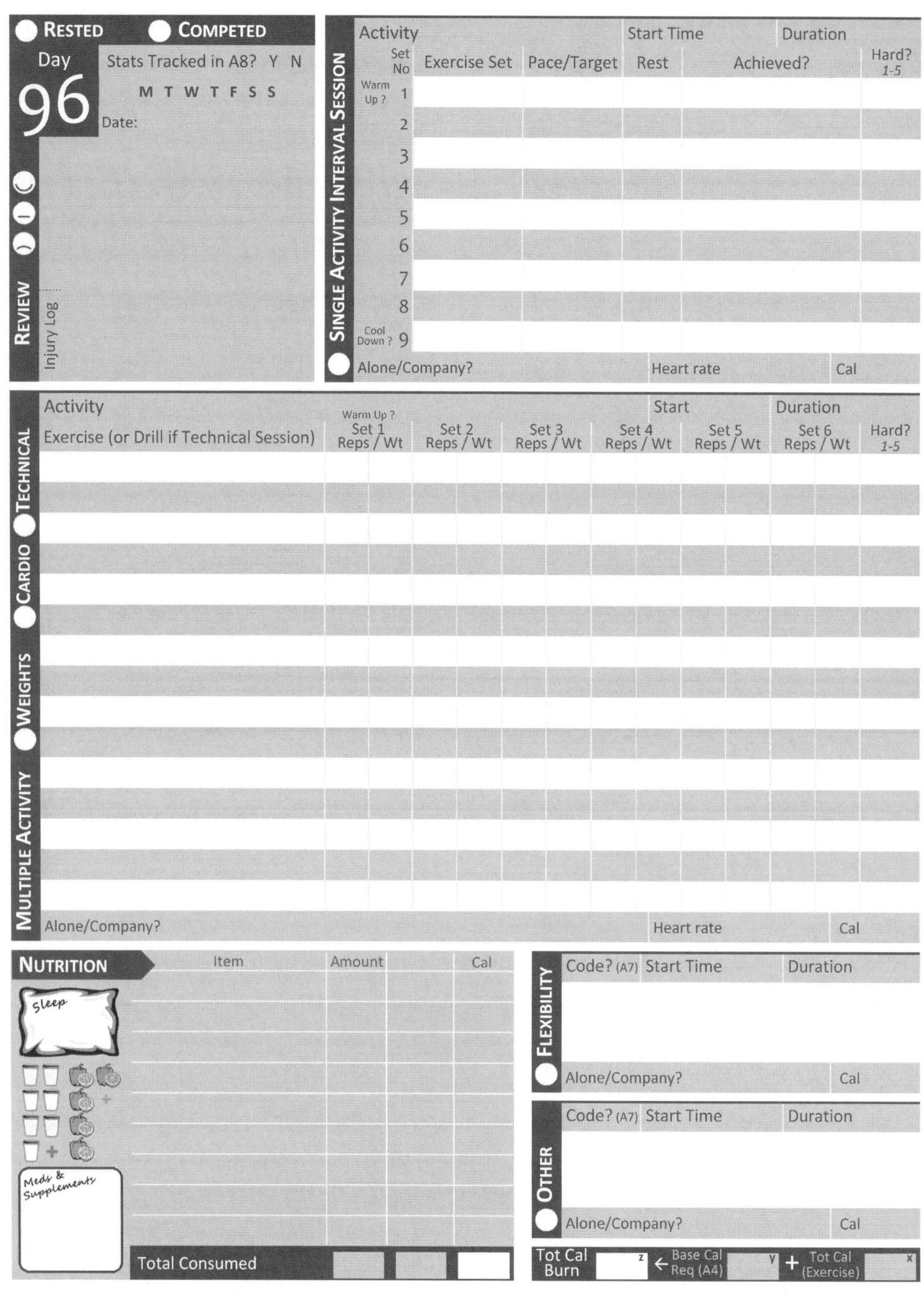

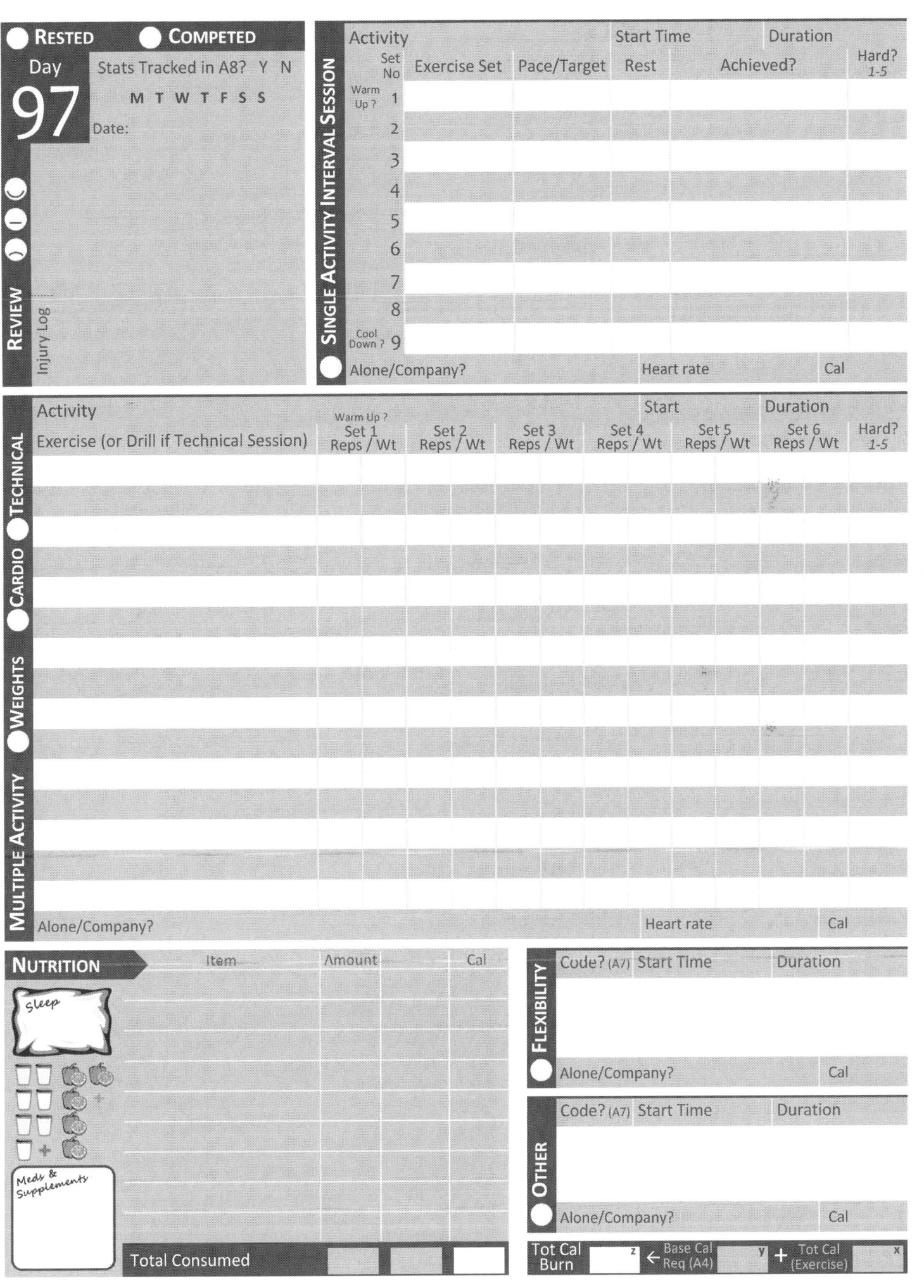

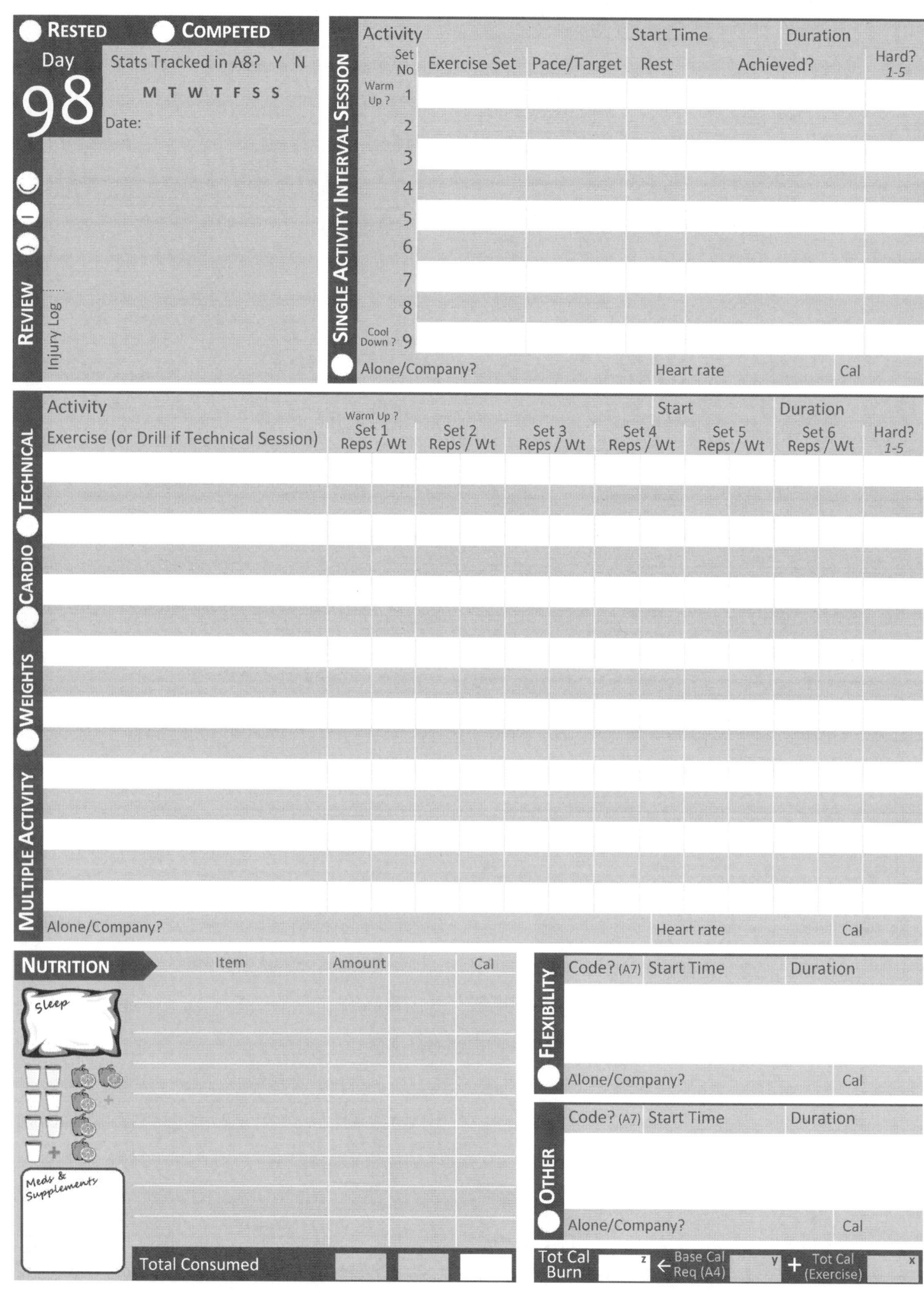

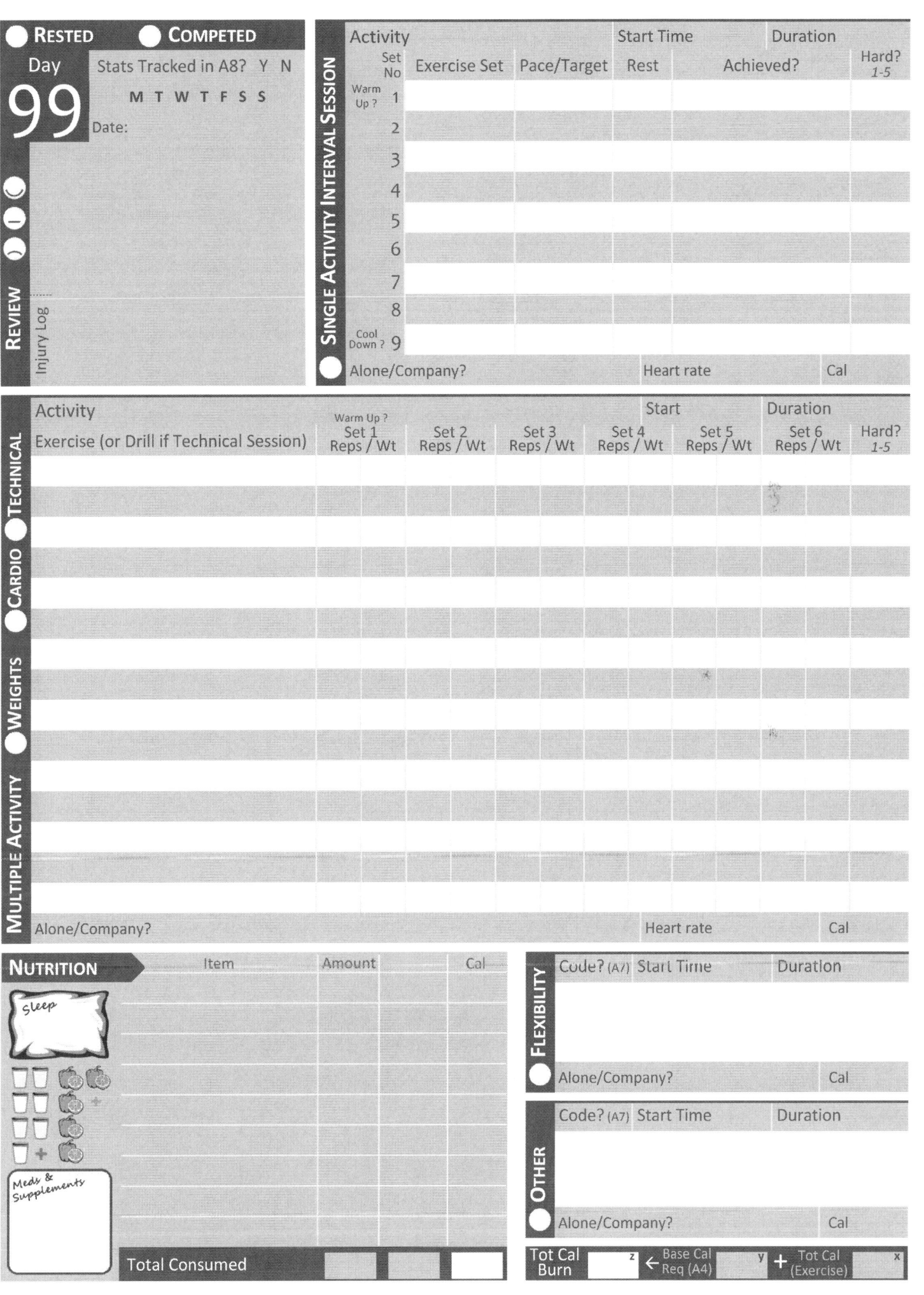

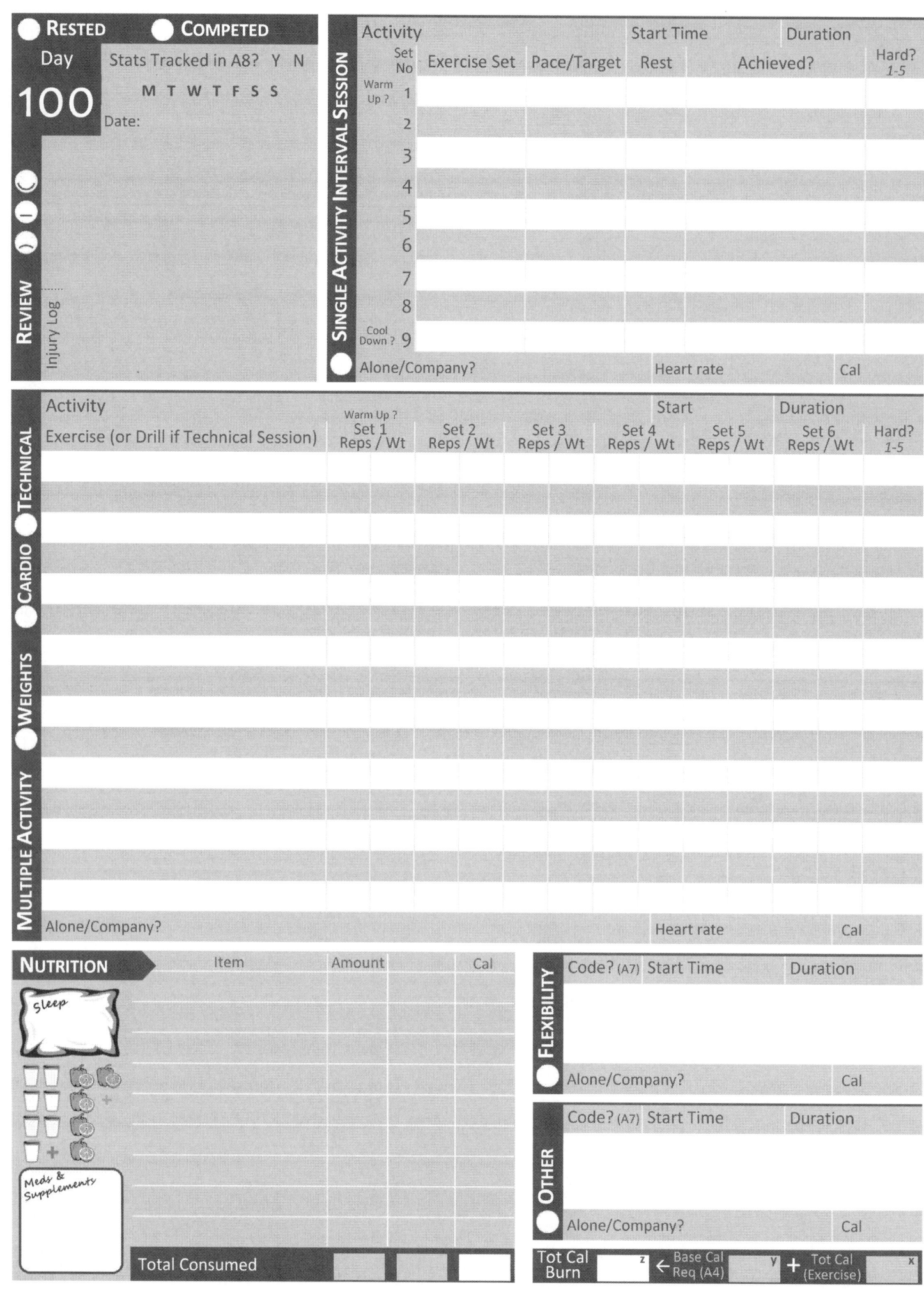

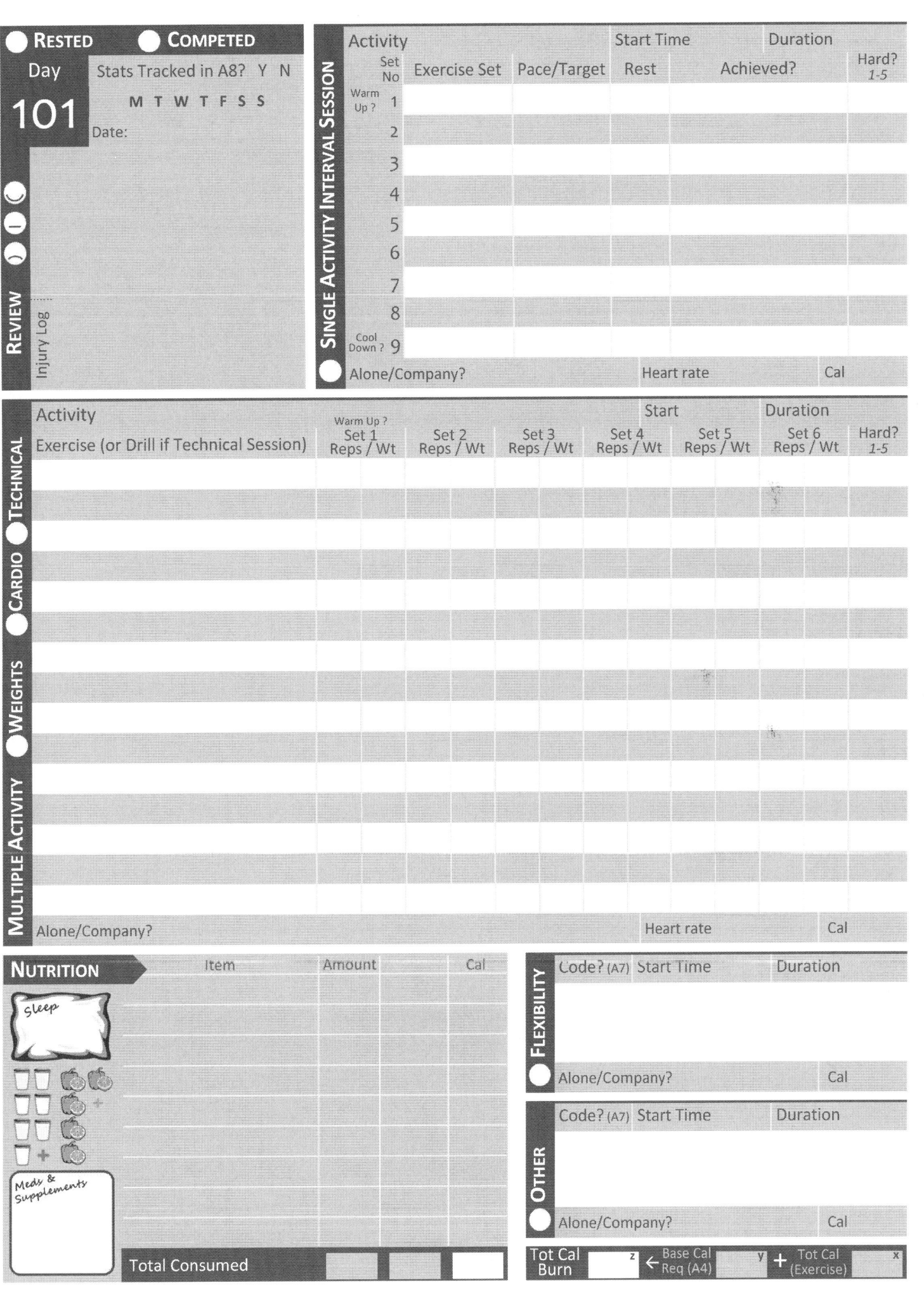

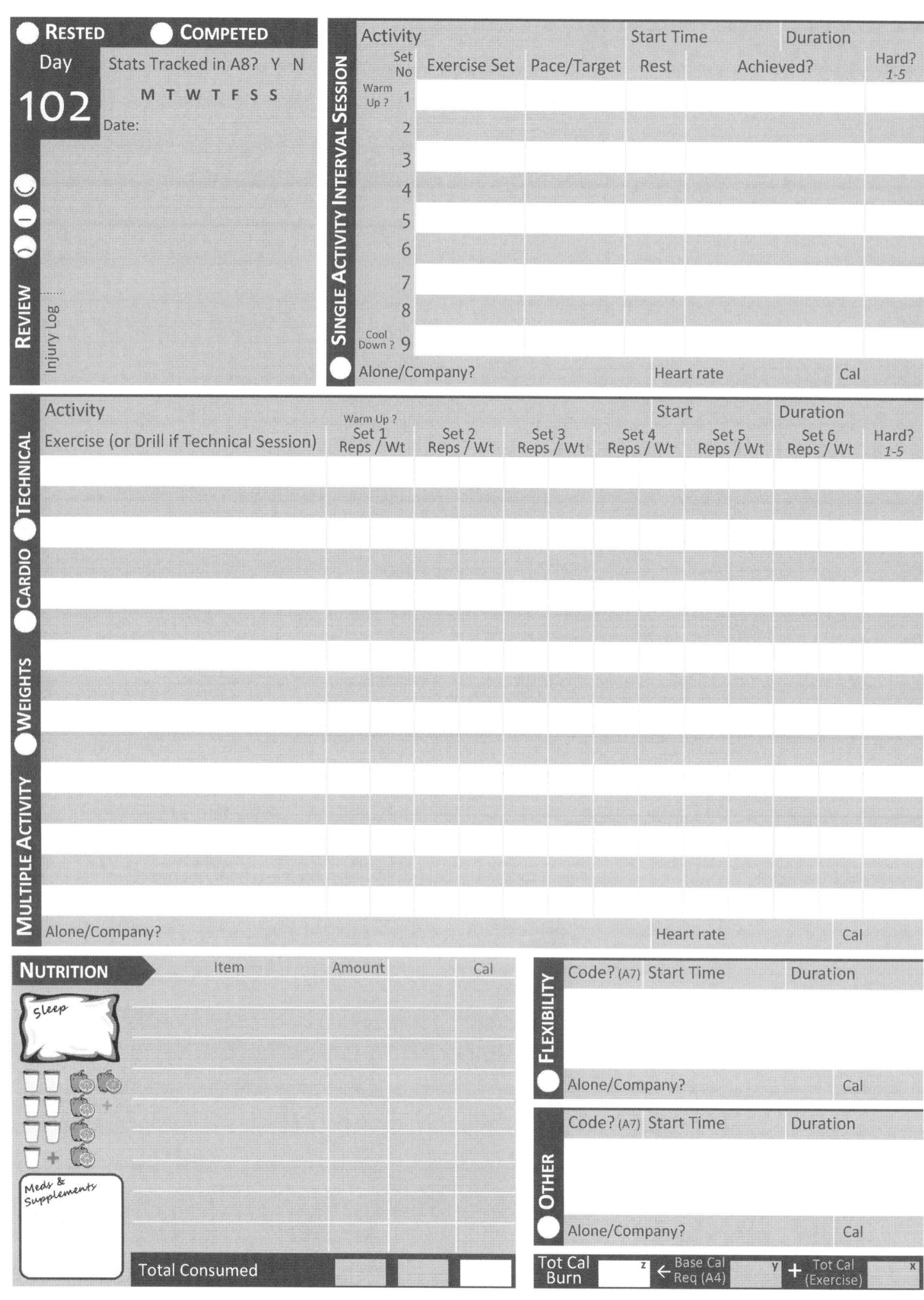

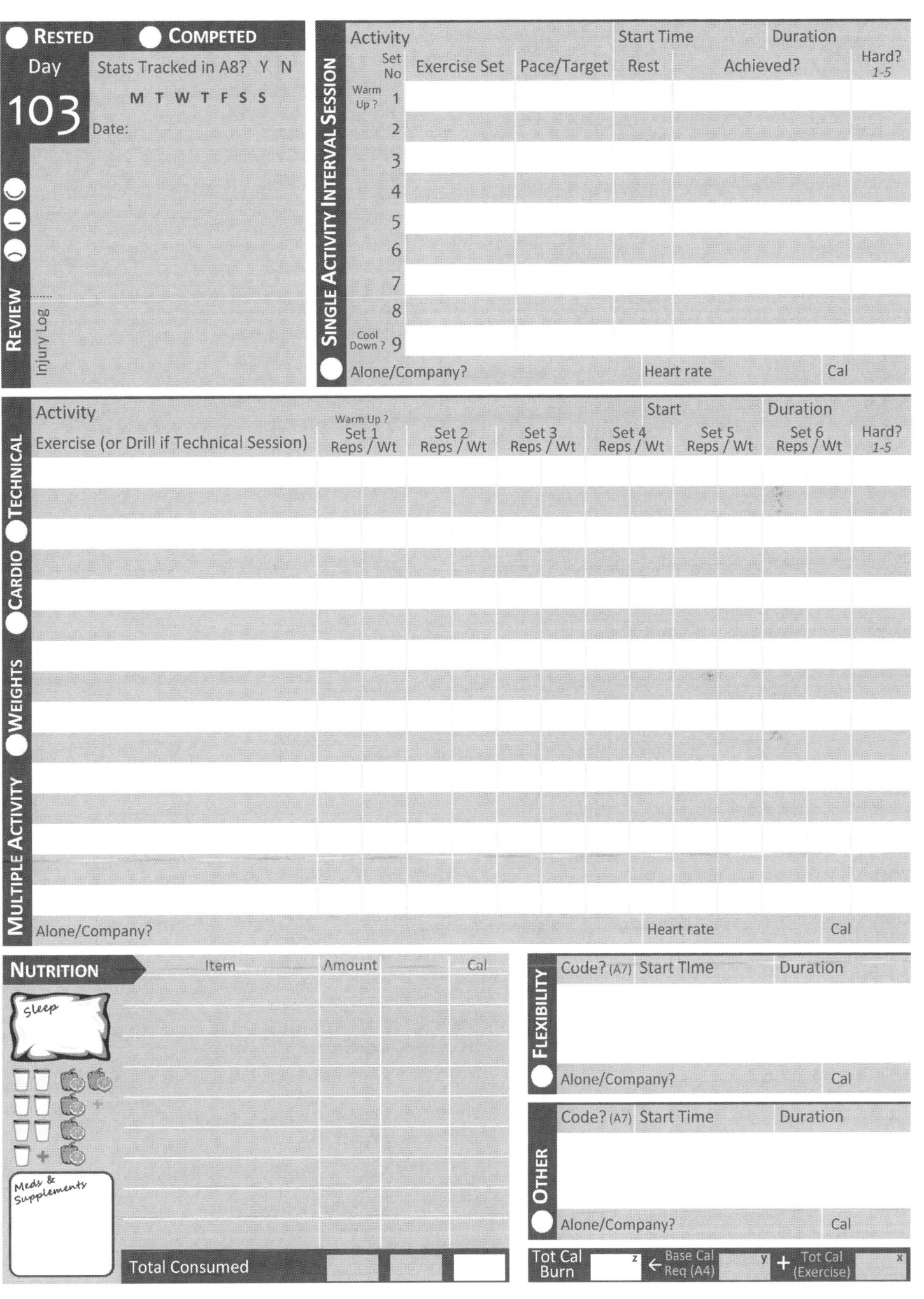

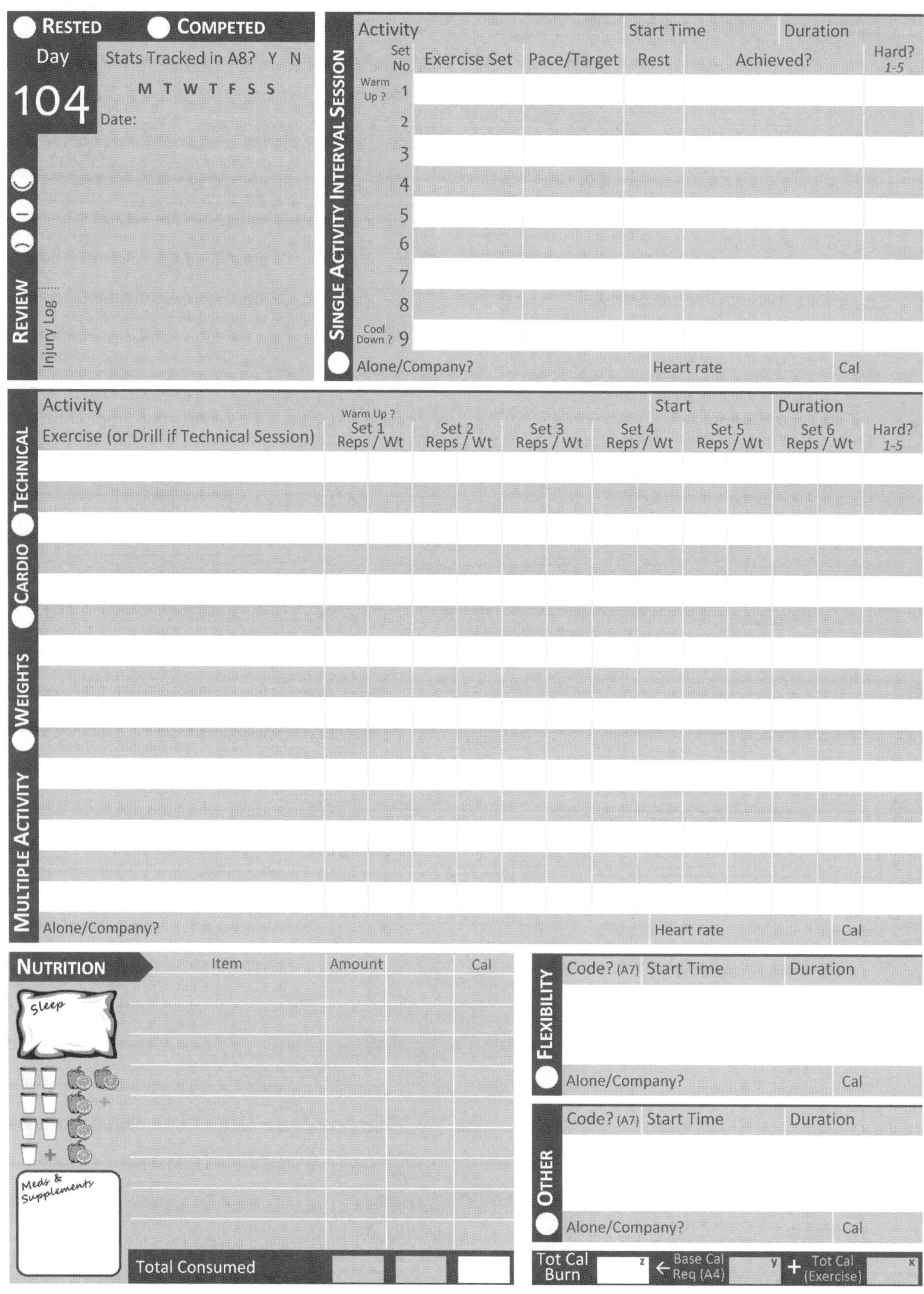

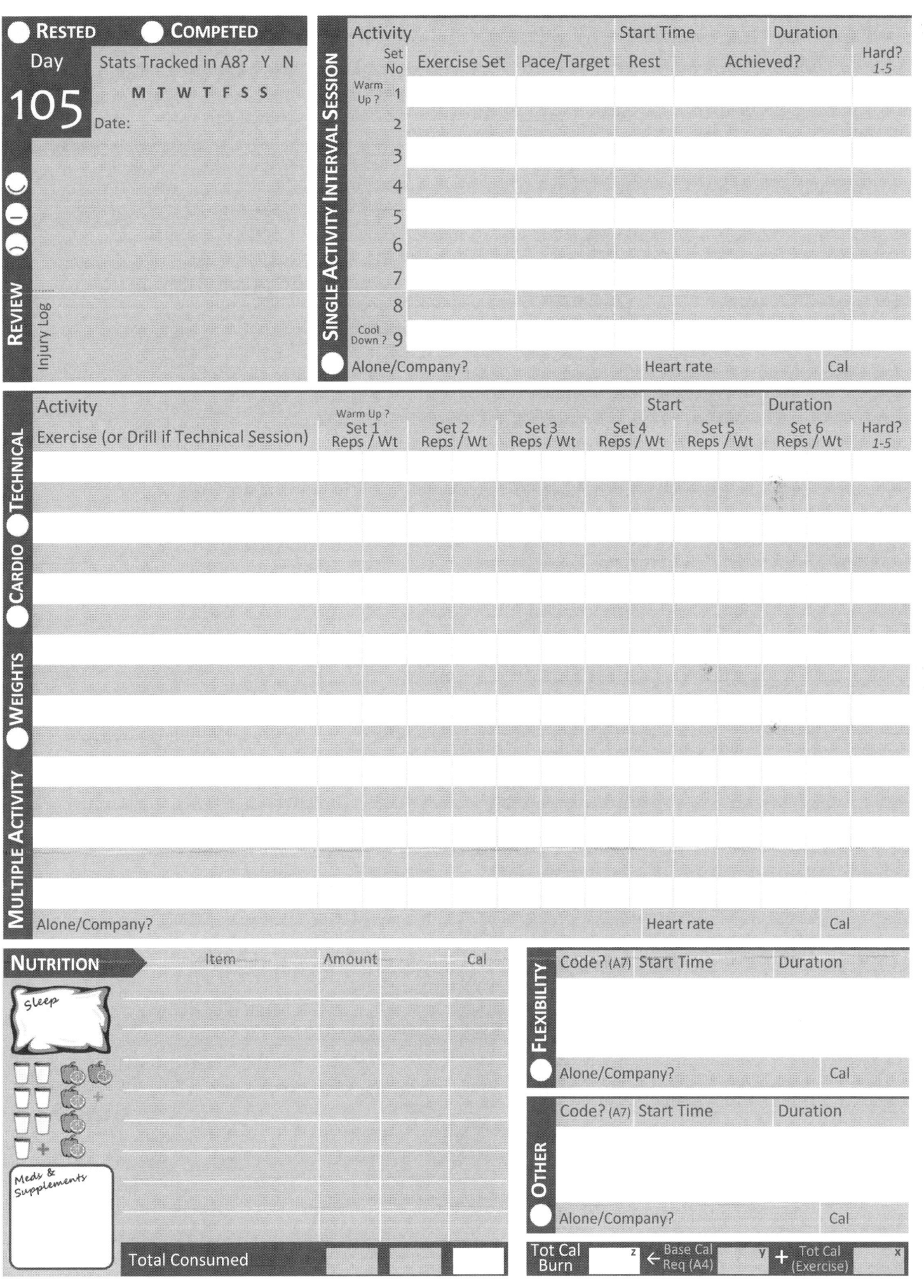

AI: Skeletal Muscle Map

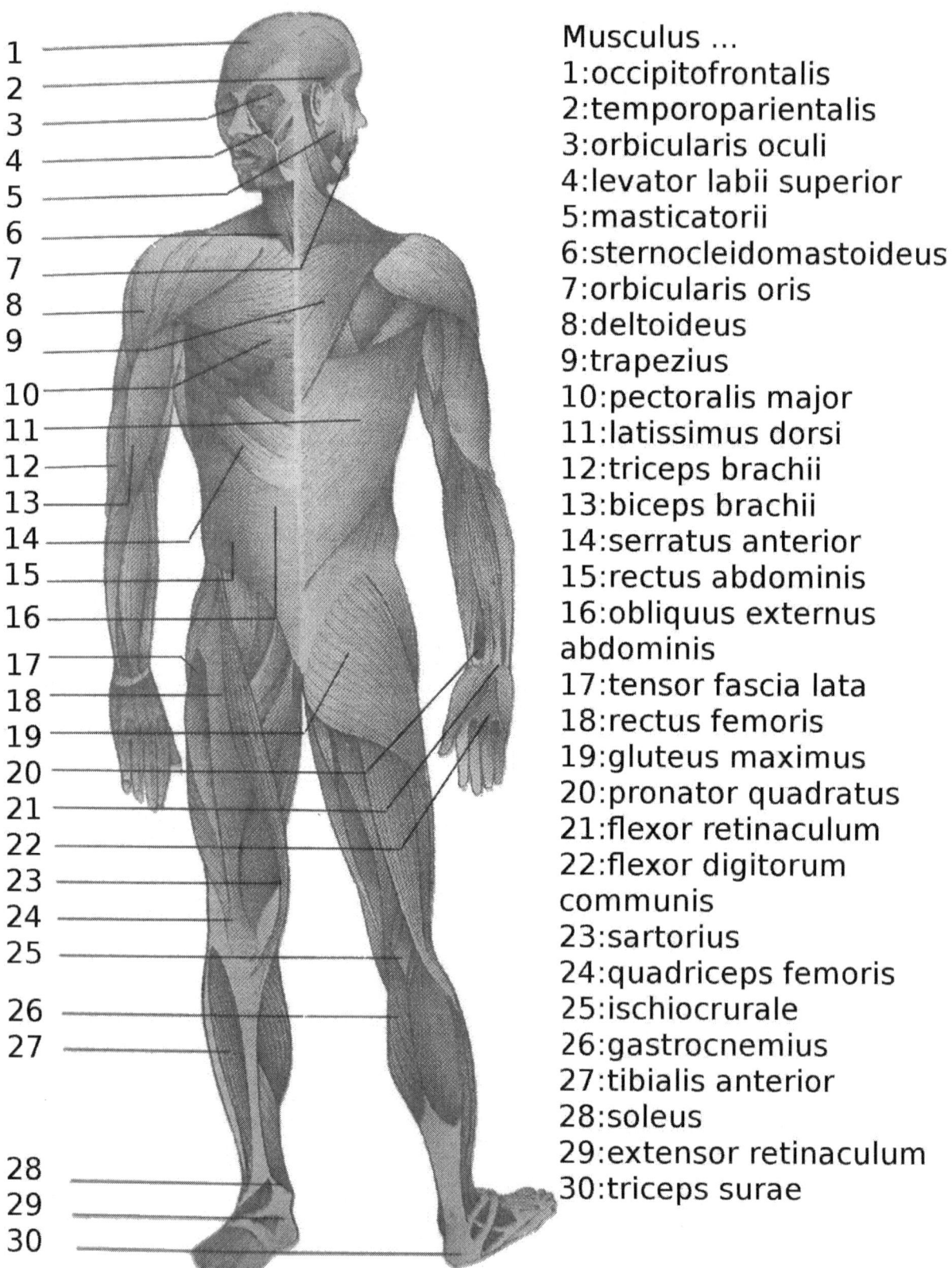

Musculus ...
1: occipitofrontalis
2: temporoparientalis
3: orbicularis oculi
4: levator labii superior
5: masticatorii
6: sternocleidomastoideus
7: orbicularis oris
8: deltoideus
9: trapezius
10: pectoralis major
11: latissimus dorsi
12: triceps brachii
13: biceps brachii
14: serratus anterior
15: rectus abdominis
16: obliquus externus abdominis
17: tensor fascia lata
18: rectus femoris
19: gluteus maximus
20: pronator quadratus
21: flexor retinaculum
22: flexor digitorum communis
23: sartorius
24: quadriceps femoris
25: ischiocrurale
26: gastrocnemius
27: tibialis anterior
28: soleus
29: extensor retinaculum
30: triceps surae

Image kindly provided by the Wikimedia Commons Database

A2: Contact Details for Suppliers and Sports Clubs

Name:		Date:
Postal Address:	URL:	
	User/Login:	
E-mail:	Password:	
☎	Notes	
☎		

Name:		Date:
Postal Address:	URL:	
	User/Login:	
E-mail:	Password:	
☎	Notes	
☎		

Name:		Date:
Postal Address:	URL:	
	User/Login:	
E-mail:	Password:	
☎	Notes	
☎		

Name:		Date:
Postal Address:	URL:	
	User/Login:	
E-mail:	Password:	
☎	Notes	
☎		

Name:		Date:
Postal Address:	URL:	
	User/Login:	
E-mail:	Password:	
☎	Notes	
☎		

A3: Fitness Expenses Log

Date	Item	Cost

A4: Base Calorie Requirement when Sedentary

Age	Men	Women
16-18	2400	1800
19-20	2600	2000
21-25	2400	2000
26-40	2400	1800
41-50	2200	1800
51-60	2200	1600
61+	2000	1600

If you want to track calories, use the data above to estimate your base calorie requirement, i.e. the amount you'd burn if you had a non-active day. Enter the appropriate value for you into the box labelled 'Base Cal Req' on your daily record page (the box has a small 'y' in the top right hand corner). You can then add this to the total calories you burned through exercise that day (x) to give your total daily calorie burn (z).

A5: Calorie Expenditure by Activity (per minute)

Activity	Body weight			
	56kg / 124lb	62kg / 137lb	68kg / 150lb	74kg / 163lb
Aerobics – medium	5.8	6.4	7.0	7.6
Aerobics – intense	7.5	8.3	9.2	10.0
Badminton	5.4	6.0	6.6	7.2
Basketball	7.7	8.6	9.4	10.2
Boxing – in the ring	7.7	8.6	9.4	10.2
Boxing – sparring	12.4	13.8	15.1	16.4
Canoeing – leisurely	2.5	2.7	3.0	3.3
Climbing	6.8	7.5	8.2	9.0
Circuits / Aerobics – medium	5.8	6.4	7.0	7.6
Circuits / Aerobics – intense	7.5	8.3	9.2	10.0
Cycling – leisure	5.6	6.2	6.8	7.4
Cycling – racing	9.5	10.5	11.5	12.5
Hockey	7.5	8.3	9.2	10.0
Golf	4.8	5.3	5.8	6.3
Gymnastics	3.7	4.1	4.5	4.9
Judo	10.9	12.1	13.3	14.4
Running – 11.5 min/mile	7.6	8.4	9.2	10.0
Running – 8 min/mile	11.9	13.1	14.2	15.4
Skiing – cross country	6.7	7.4	8.1	8.8
Skiing – down hill	5.7	6.5	7.1	7.7
Soccer	7.4	8.2	9.0	9.8
Standing up	2.1	2.3	2.4	2.7
Squash	11.9	13.1	14.4	15.7
Swimming – breast stroke	9.1	10.0	11.0	12.0
Swimming – fast crawl	8.7	9.7	10.6	11.5
Swimming – slow crawl	7.2	7.9	8.7	9.5
Tennis – doubles	6.1	6.8	7.4	8.1
Walking at medium pace	4.6	5.1	5.3	6.0

A6: Personal Nutrition Charts
(Use these tables to store data on meals that you regularly eat, for quick reference)

Item	Amount	Protein	Fat	Carbs	Calories

Item	Amount	Protein	Fat	Carbs	Calories

Item	Amount	Protein	Fat	Carbs	Calories

Item	Amount	Protein	Fat	Carbs	Calories

Item	Amount	Protein	Fat	Carbs	Calories

Item	Amount	Protein	Fat	Carbs	Calories

A7: Session Store

A8: Statistics Tracker

Day No. or Date	Body Weight	Waist	Cholesterol	Blood Pressure	Resting Heart Rate	Body Fat		

Use blank cells to track stats of your choice, e.g. BMI or personal best performances e.g. weights lifted

Notes

Manufactured by Amazon.ca
Bolton, ON